MW01196376

ISBN-10: 1448620023
ISBN-13: 978-1448620029

Captain of My Soul
A Memoir
Whitney Gracia Williams

The events in this book are true and are written as I remember them. The names of the people and their definitive characteristics, the names of the Greek lettered organizations (as well as their respective colors and insignias), and the name of the university in this memoir have been changed, combined, and/or omitted.

My personal and group emails that are printed in this account have been printed as they were sent and/or received with the exception of the email addresses/names that appear. In regards to the other emails that are printed, while the content remains analogous to the original emails, they have been edited for legal purposes.

The text messages that are included in this account are printed in Courier font.

This book contains the poem *Invictus* by William Ernest Henley.

For my loving and supportive mother, LaFrancine Maria Bond-Edwards. Thank you for being understanding and listening to me when no one else would. You're my greatest encourager, my biggest motivator, my number one supporter, and I love you.
I finally finished something, Mommy...

Acknowledgments

First and foremost, I would like to thank you, God, for everything you have ever done for me. I love you so much and I am thankful that you blessed me with the ability to write.

I would like to thank my friends and family for reading bits and pieces, putting up with my late night calls, and answering my random texts about certain sentences and paragraphs. I love you all and I really appreciate your support: Sharifa Callender, Allyson Conley, Tiffany Downs, Chace Edwards, William R. Edwards, William Ray Edwards II, Shaina Emmanuel, Tanisha Hill, Jazmin Hunt, Alonna Grigsby, Barry "B-Dot" Johnson, Courtney Johnson, Tamisha Joiner, Eric Jones, Eugene Jones IV, Fred Jones, Jamillia Kamara, Latrenda Leonard, Courtney Martin (special thanks to you for the first cover), Anthony McClain, Antoine Neal, Enyinna Nwachuku, Leon Paramore III, Lepold Phiapalath, Christina Royster, Sherbrina Shephard, Aster Teclay, Barrett Warden, Ashley Warren, Raina Warren, Cheryl Walton, Ciara Walton, Christian Walton, Gregory Walton, Jennifer Cie Williams, Jay Williams, Nadira Williams, Arienne Wrigley, and "The Seven"—it took countless reminiscing sessions with you all to get this done.

Thanks to all the English teachers I have ever had, especially Leslie Rubinkowski, Lisa Crosthwait, Jennifer Alejo, Scott Harrison, and Bruce Dobler. I am forever grateful for all you have taught me.

Author's Note:

Before you begin to read this book, especially if you're not familiar with black fraternities and sororities, there are a few things that you should know. In the realm of black undergraduate Greek life, nothing is more important than *how* you got into the organization. If you didn't illegally pledge, weren't "on line" being hazed for weeks, and simply turned in your transcript, monetary dues, and letter of interest to become a member in a matter of days, you are considered "paper" and *you don't matter.* It makes no difference how much money you've raised for a charity, how well organized your campus programs are, or how much community service you've achieved. You will receive no respect from other black Greeks on campus, and you can bet that every time you speak to a group of black Greeks, the word "paper" will etch itself across their minds.

But, if you choose to go against your organization's rules and illegally pledge, not only will you be respected, but you will feel as though you worked hard for your letters and be considered "thorough," "made," or "real." Although not all chapters abide by these ideals, if you wanted to pledge the Epsilon chapter of the sorority that will be mentioned in this book, this is what you would need to do to make it: 1.) Do your research. Know the platforms of the sorority inside and out, know the founders and their ideals, and know the chapter's charter history. 2.) Go to all of the sorority's events and sign the attendance book. Always mingle with the members afterwards, and although they will be mean to you, try to get as much "face-time" as possible. 3.) Find a way to get each sorority member's phone number. You will have to stalk them, find out where their classes are, and wait outside their apartment buildings until you have them all. 4.) Call and get to know them. Don't be put off by their attitudes when you introduce yourself. Attempt to have a normal conversation *without* mentioning pledging. (They will ask you questions regarding pledging later in the process) 5.) Invite them out to lunch, but know that you might have to pay for it. Try to eat lunch with each member at least twice this semester. 6.) Be consistent. After months of calling them (NEVER stop calling them, you should be calling each member at least twice a week—at LEAST), taking them out to lunch, and attending events, you will be selected for an "interview" if you are deemed a worthy candidate. 7.) Pre-pledge. Report to late night study sessions for a couple of weeks, run errands for the sorority members, and always answer your phone when they call. 8.) Pledge. You will pledge for 6 to 8 weeks, meaning that you are "on line." You will be on social probation. You are forbidden from going to any parties, campus events, or social gatherings. You, and every girl that is on line with you (your "line sisters" or "LSs"), will be given a blank book (a "mind") in which you will write down everything you learn, along with what happens to you as you pledge. Almost every night you will be verbally abused, beaten, slapped, kicked, punched, and thrown. You will have eggs thrown at you, you will have mud thrown at you, and you will have to consume concoctions so gross and disgusting that they dare not be discussed. You will buy food, gifts, and anything else that the sorority members demand in short amounts of time. You will clean their houses, make early morning wake-up calls, and master the difficult art of "discretion." You will recite page after page of sorority history, poems, and songs at the risk of being beaten—all while pretending that none of these things are happening to you when you go to your classes in the morning. 9.) Tell NO ONE (not even your parents). 10.) Become brainwashed. 11.) Forget what life is like outside of the dark, dank basement you report to every night. 12.) Finish. After six to eight weeks, you will finally be done with pledging. The women that were abusing and mistreating you (your "prophytes") will lovingly extend their arms to you as you become a new member ("neo") of their sorority. 13.) Show off. You will have a "probate," a show that signifies you "crossing" into the world of black Greek life, for all the members of the black college community (and even your family who will fly up for the celebration) to see. You are now in the organization and it is up to you and your line sisters to handle most of the chapter's business.

When you put on your first program there will be lots of new girls ("interests") who wish they were in your shoes. Now it's your turn to do to them what was done to you.

Introduction:

The rules said it took three days to become a member. The rules said that I wouldn't be degraded, that I wouldn't be hazed, and that I would gain a dynamic sisterhood and a newfound love for community service. The rules said that all I had to do to qualify was have a good GPA, be an active student on campus, and if I was chosen, it would take *three days*. I wasn't naïve enough to believe that those were the only requirements necessary to become a member, but I had no idea that a year of my life would be dedicated to joining an organization that I never became a part of.

I remember seeing the white sororities on campus, expecting them to be my sole interaction with Greek life since the school was predominantly white, but I soon discovered that there were black sororities: four of them. I saw the sorority that I'd wanted to become a part of since I was a little girl: Theta Eta Theta. There were only a few members, and I only saw them when they were at social functions sporting their violet and emerald letter jackets or fundraising in the student union's lobby.

In retrospect, I probably didn't see them much because I was only vaguely interested in Greek life for most of freshman year. I had seen the probates for other black fraternities and sororities, and each time I would say to myself, "That'll be me one day," but I was more focused on maintaining my scholarship.

When sophomore year rolled around I knew I wanted to pledge, but I didn't know *everything* that pledging entailed. (My mother's stories about her pledge process were Disney tales compared to the Epsilon chapter's process.) As soon as I became an interest my world was no longer mine. Almost every thought was about Theta Eta Theta and being chosen to become a member. Yet, once I was chosen, once I was selected to pre-pledge, a part of me died each day.

It's all so clear now—the social probation, the intimidation, the financial woes, the fear, the incessant worrying, the verbal abuse, and the heartbreak were all for nothing.

Every time I see the words "Theta Eta Theta" etched onto a license plate or sewn onto a woman's lanyard I wonder: "What did she go through to be able to wear that? How much did she have to do to get in? Was she *paper*?" Although I'll never be able to ask every woman of Theta Eta Theta that question, I can live with myself for making the decision I made.

I want to make it clear that I'm no sell out, no bitter bitch who secretly wants to see a certain chapter burned to the ground; no ex sorority prospect turned religious; no victim vilifying my past experiences in hopes of garnering sympathy; nor am I a starving author in search of a paycheck. I'm a writer. That's it. I chose to write this book as an act of closure, a way to express my feelings, and a way to say goodbye to the person I used to be.

Farewell.

Out of the night that covers me,
Black as the pit from pole to pole,
I thank whatever gods may be,
For my unconquerable soul...

I. Embark

"Last night was hell. I HATE being on line. We all knew our information; they just wanted to beat us up. My ass is in so much pain from taking wood...Big Sister [Ominous Arachnid] punched me in the stomach and pushed me to the floor. I was too weak to get up by myself. Number 7 had to pull me up, and when she did Big Sister [F.F.] slapped me eight times...I've eaten at least ten onions this week and I can hardly taste anything. I'm so TIRED! But I can't sleep...I've got to make wake up calls in the next hour and take Big Sister [Ominous Arachnid] her breakfast at 7...I'm going to seven eleven to get a drink. Write later."

I flipped through the rest of her mind's pages and skimmed as much as I could. I found similar terrifying anecdotes on every sheet, but none of them made me falter in my desire to join the sorority by going through the same process in the fall. I was in my second month of pre-pledging, cleaning a sorority member's bedroom, and I was determined to stick it out until the end.

I copied a few lines from her mind and returned it to the bottom of the chest that stood in the corner of the room. I made sure that her black comforter quilt was laid evenly onto her bed frame, vacuumed her light beige carpet, and organized her closet. I cleaned her bathroom, her living room, and her kitchen. I made sure that no appliances were left on, and as I walked out of her house I carried two trash bags to the dumpster. I had half an hour to get back to campus to pay for another sorority member to eat dinner.

While heading towards campus, I reminisced about how my life used to be—a life where I could wear any color I wanted, a life where I would never wake up at 5 am to ride with someone I didn't know to the airport, a life where "sisterhood" was a two way street and never left me financially weak and weary. I wanted to go back to that life, but I was too far in to give up. All I had to do was pay for a few more meals, go to a few more study sessions, get degraded a little bit more, and pre-pledging would be over. I could enjoy my free time in the summer, and in the fall I would take wood strokes, dish out whatever money was needed when necessary, and go through hell for eight weeks. That's all I had to do, that's all I had to think about.

When I approached the dining hall I saw the sorority member standing outside the entrance amongst a group of people. Her name was Ivyana. I stepped close enough so that I would be in her sight. She looked at me and turned away. On cue, I walked behind her, made sure no one was watching, and placed my meal plan card in her purse. Once she felt that the transaction had been made, she looked at her watch and walked into the dining hall.

I traveled two blocks and felt my phone vibrate. It was Ivyana. A text:

```
When I say 7:08, I MEAN 7:08!!!! Not 7:09!
Go across the street from the cathedral and
wait for me at the bus stop. Hurry up!
```

I ran towards the cathedral, not caring if anyone I knew might see me. I forced myself to think that I was full of energy, that I wasn't sick and drowsy, and made it to the bus stop. Ivyana shook her head and said, "If you continue to be late like this you'll *never* make it on line."

"I'm sorry. I mean I apologi—"

"Yes, you *are* sorry. But I already knew that," she pulled out a set of keys. "I need you to go get my gray notebook that's on my kitchen counter. Bring it with you to study session. Don't be late."

She handed me my meal plan card and walked down the street. I sat inside the bus stop shelter fiddling with her keychain.

I looked out from behind the glass and saw a couple of girls across the street laughing. They were trudging the sidewalk slowly so they wouldn't fall. They were holding onto each other, hoping to make it home without a bruise. They were blissful despite the miserable weather, and I was starting to wonder if I remembered how it felt to be like that, how it felt to be happy.

I couldn't. It was too long ago.

I started to reminisce about my past world again, but this time it was more than a list of logical thoughts and intangible realizations. This time I could remember specific places, times, and people. This time I remembered exactly how I ended up sitting on a bus bench waiting to get a gray notebook for a TET.

II. Outward Bound

A year and a half earlier...

Pittsburgh's yellow iron bridges extended their arms across a dark river as the sky sparkled bright blue. The glossy gray buildings of the skyline gazed down at me and dull colored city buses followed each other in the lane to my right. The Steelers' heralded golden stadium, Heinz Field, stood proudly from afar as downtown welcomed the family car.

The streets were lined with theatres, open-air restaurants, high end fashion stores, and buildings that were tall enough to kiss the sky. The buildings gradually became shorter and downtown waved goodbye from the rearview mirror. The college neighborhood of Oakland embraced the car as it began to coast down Forbes Avenue.

I glanced at three giant towers that had been made into dorms, at the businesses that were interlocked between campus buildings, and at the diners and shops that lined each side of the street. I took a quick look at the students walking on the patio of the student union, and turned away from the bright wooden benches and flowers that were nestled within Schenley Park. My eyes became fixated on The Cathedral of Learning, the building that was imprinted on every packet the university had ever sent to me.

Its tall, sandy brown body sat against the sky and its broad rectangular shoulders climaxed high into the clouds, taking the shape of a rook chess piece. The thousands of windows that were pressed into its build glistened in the sunlight. The fountain that sat at its base spouted streams of water amidst red and yellow blossoms.

I had once envisioned that Pittsburgh was this wonderful place where the sun always shined and where the people welcomed strangers with open arms. I had hoped that it would be more exciting than my days of high school in Memphis, and prayed that I would continue to do well in my studies. I even made a dream list in my journal about how my college experience would go: *"8/8/2006...Dear Journal, I'm about to start college, and if I have things my way, I'll dive head first into Pre-med Courses and excel in them, I'll be a social butterfly and join multiple organizations, I'll become a TET like my mother, I'll study abroad after my sophomore year, get two or three essays published by my junior year, fall in love somewhere in between, study hard for the MCATS, get into a great med school on scholarship and graduate summa cum laude."*

I arrived at the university student center, picked up my room keys, and began helping my family set up my room. Since I made it my personal mission to give the worst answers possible on the roommate compatibility test, I was living in a dorm full of single rooms. Each room came with wooden bedroom furniture, a desk, a large window, a mirror, and a small closet. There were fourteen floors. Each floor had its own lounge, two large communal bathrooms and a resident assistant on duty. Despite those amenities, the dorm didn't have air conditioning, it was located far from my classes, and it sat at the top of a steep hill. Nonetheless, I was excited. I couldn't believe that I was finally in college.

"We should all take a tour of the city before we have to leave," my mother said as she handed me a box.

"Do we have to?" I sighed.

"Well, we're leaving tomorrow Whit. You're going to be up here all year and you'll be able to tour the city whenever you want. All of us aren't going to have that chance."

"Ma..."

My younger sister rolled her eyes. My stepdad looked out of the window, and my younger brothers averted their gazes towards the floor. My mother ignored their lack of enthusiasm and pressed on, "The school has a tour around six. They gave us the paper in the parent meeting today. It's up to you though."

Anytime my mother said, "It's up to you though," it usually meant, "You better do what I say or I'll never stop reminding you that you didn't."

I smiled and said, "Sounds like a good idea. I'm down," and within an hour we were on a school sponsored bus tour.

At sunset, the bus weaved through the university's campus, which was more like a city with university buildings artfully placed wherever there wasn't a hospital, café, museum, or business. It snaked past the massive athletic complex, the lecture halls, the research buildings, the upper campus dorms, the lower campus dorms, the historical buildings, and eventually off campus past the aesthetic sections of downtown.

The tour guide rambled off historical facts as the bus continued to move towards Station Square, an area across the river that was illuminated by the bright lights of restaurants, clubs, and shops.

"That," the tour guide said as she pointed to two parallel lines of lights that were meshed into a hill, "is the Monongahela incline. Before we venture into Station Square, we're going to go to the top of the hill, also known as Mount Washington, and ride the incline in small groups. It'll take you right down to Station Square, and then you're free to explore until ten o' clock."

The view from the incline was mesmerizing. The city was more beautiful than before. As the carriage made its way down, I watched the Pittsburgh city skyline reflect itself onto the river.

My mother and stepfather said their "We're so proud," and "We love you" goodbyes as they walked out of my dorm. I stood inside and watched from the windows as they got inside our gray Trailblazer and drove away. When I turned around and walked towards the elevators, I saw a cute guy dressed in a white muscle shirt and shorts. He introduced himself as Damien and insisted that I join him, a girl named Crystal, and a guy named T.R. on the lounge's couch.

"So Whitney, where are you from?" Crystal asked.

"I'm from Tennessee, you?"

"I'm from *Jersey* all day!"

"What made you come all the way up here?" T.R. asked.

"I wanted to get far away from home," I admitted. "Where are you from, T.R.?"

"I'm from Philly. It's like six hours away from here."

"And you, Damien?" I asked.

He smiled. "I'm from Georgia."

"He's been braggin' about that for the past fifteen minutes!" Crystal laughed. "Everybody knows that *Jersey* is where it's at!"

We talked about our hometowns and high school days for hours, exchanged numbers, and eventually went to our rooms to get sleep before orientation.

Every aspect of the next day's orientation process annoyed me. Thousands of us students had to listen to speech after speech about how it was our chance to show the world who we were, how the next four years would be the greatest years of our lives, and how we were the future of America. The endless paperwork, long lines of registration, and the fact that the campus was so large that I had to ask for directions everywhere I went didn't make the day go by any smoother.

When I returned to my dorm later that night, Damien was standing outside. He suggested that we ride the elevator to the fifth floor to hang with other freshmen. We sat inside the lounge with a group of ten other people and flirted with each other.

Over the next few days, Damien and I started to talk more. He became the third guy I'd ever kissed, and a friend. We spent countless hours joking and making fun of each other's mannerisms: His voice was unusually high pitched and he had an odd way of saying "Yea, man" at the beginning and end of every conversation. I never once thought that we would be in a relationship together, but I started to have feelings for him.

I spent nights in his room, and he spent nights in mine. I told him that I hadn't heard from my biological father in nine years, and that the last time I checked he was serving time in an Oregon prison. He told me that he and his father chose when they wanted to be close, and that he preferred to be a loner. I told him that for years I couldn't bear to look at myself in the mirror. He told me that he never had that problem and couldn't understand why I would either. He asked me to explain.

I wanted to tell him everything. I wanted to spill my soul onto the floor and have him mop it up with understanding, but I didn't. I shrugged and lied, saying that it was so long ago that I couldn't remember why. I steered the conversation away from personal matters and continued to ask simple questions.

He told me he had never really studied a day in his life and that he had written his college admissions essay in minutes, the day it was due. Although he was never the star athlete in high school, he was more interested in becoming a football player at the university than being a scholar. He seemed impressed that the university had given me a full scholarship, but when I told him that I wanted to be a writer after college he said, "A writer? Damn, you must be really good at it. Hope you don't end up teaching bad kids and driving a Volvo for the rest of your life though."

I agreed to accompany him to Wal-Mart one afternoon, under the condition that he knew which bus route to take. He assured me that he had it all "figured out" and that there was "no need to worry."

We got lost.

Per his suggestion, we got off five stops too early and had to walk across the expressway for half an hour. When we finally reached the correct bus stop, we saw the top of the blue Wal-Mart sign in the distance and decided to continue walking.

Once, while we were watching a movie he asked, "How many people have you slept with?"

"None," I responded.

"None? You're a virgin?"

"Isn't that what *none* means?"

"I've never done it with a virgin before."

"Well, when you find a virgin that's willing to sleep with you let me know how it goes."

He laughed. He started to bring up sex more often in the continuing days of our friendship, and each time I would make a sarcastic remark or plainly say, "I'll never sleep with you."

When he got tired of *asking*, he attempted to use the persuasive strategy. He would talk about his female friends that he had slept with and say, "We're still friends. If it didn't change anything between me and them, it won't change anything between me and you," "It's not that big of a deal," or "You should sleep with me, I've spent most of my Pitt-life with you."

A few weeks and several movies later, we were eating pizza in the student union and he asked me if I was saving my virginity for marriage. I didn't answer. I slurped on my sweet tea and stared out of the window that stood behind him. He picked at his pizza and sighed, "I need sex. I haven't had any in awhile. You're not the only girl here. I'll eventually get it from someone else."

I didn't have a problem with that. I was actually relieved at the possibility that someone else would sleep with him so he would stop asking me about sex. Eventually he did, and he used the time that he would normally make sex inquiries to make me feel bad about myself.

"Why don't you like going out to parties like everyone else?" "Don't you think that you should dress up more like the other girls here? That's probably why I'm the only guy that has approached you here because I don't care how you dress." "We're not boyfriend and girlfriend. People keep asking me that. You're making me look bad." "College is about having fun, you're boring me." "You're a pretty girl, you're just not a *dime*." "You're pretty, but you're just *regular* pretty."

Soon, he stopped hanging around me as often. He stopped calling and when he saw me around campus he wouldn't speak unless he was around other people. I didn't want to let it show, but when I would see him laughing amongst a group of other girls, I would get angry.

One night during a university event that was supposed to be a capstone experience for the black student association, he brushed past me without saying a word. I texted him, asking, "What's your problem?" He responded, "You're the one who seems to have the problem."

I left the event, missed an amazing speech by Cousin Jeff, and went down to Damien's floor later to ask why he was acting so differently.

After minutes of silence, he put his earrings in his ears and said, "I told you before I didn't want a girlfriend—you nagged me all the time! I needed a break! Damn! You never went out and you expected me to stay in with you all the time! I'm trying to be nice to you, but you won't accept it! We don't have to be friends if you're gonna be like that! I never liked you like that anyway!"

I was speechless. I wanted to yell and curse him out, but I forced myself not to. I went to my room while he went out to a party.

I branched out and met new people. I met a girl named Tiara from Atlanta, a guy named Reeve, and a girl that I wasn't too fond of, Alexis. I didn't like Alexis because I thought she was stuck up and I only hung with her when Tiara was around. But, as luck would have it, since Tiara was busy, Alexis and I were studying in a lounge together one night with Reeve.

"He's acting like an asshole. I just don't get it." she said to Reeve.

"Well, it *is* college, can you blame him?" he asked.

"No, but what's the point of him comparing me to other girls and stuff? What's the point of us spending a lot of time together and him telling me that he likes me, if he's just going to talk about other girls?"

"I don't know Alexis. I can't really relate because I'm a guy, but it does sound like he's being a jerk."

"Sounds like a jerk to me too," I offered, attempting to be nice.

"It's complicated though. It's hard for me to explain," she sighed. "Like, at first, he was extra nice and I liked spending time with him, but then he started doing stupid stuff and asking me about sex. We just got here. I'm not trying to sleep with anybody and I don't trust him like that. And my ex is still acting crazy towards me so I'm not trying to get in a relationship. I just need to find a way to cut him off. We can still be friends."

"You would still want to be friends with someone like that though?" I asked.

"No, not really. Friends is better than nothing though....Oh, Damien."

"Damien? The Damien that's from Georgia?" I asked.

"Yea, why?"

"No reason, just wow."

"Wow?" she laughed. "What do you mean, wow?"

"I can't say. He'll probably continue to act like a jerk towards you though."

"How do you know?"

"Um, I used to talk to him."

"When?"

"Like, we started hanging out the first week I got here, but I stopped speaking to him like two weeks ago."

"Really? I've been talking to him for like the past *four* weeks."

"That explains a lot…"

"Ah man," Reeve sighed.

"Wait," Alexis leaned back. "He compared you to other girls too?"

"Yea, he was doing all the same stuff you said earlier actually."

"That's crazy! I should have known last week that he wasn't serious about liking me. He took a nap in my room and when he got ready to leave I was about to sign him out but he was like 'No, that's okay,' and left. But the security guard at my dorm is really strict, so I decided to sign him out anyway. When I left my room, I saw him go upstairs to another floor instead of getting on the elevator to leave. And I know it wasn't to hang out with a guy because he would've invited me."

Reeve shook his head. "This is sad, pure sloppiness. I gotta tell him to tighten up his game."

"No, tell him to kill himself and tell him I said it," I laughed.

"So, that time that you and I were in his room because he had that allergic reaction, you and him were still cool?" Alexis asked.

"Yep."

"See, I thought he called you because you were close by and had Benadryl. I had no idea about the other stuff."

"No, your friend Raya called me from his phone and told me that he needed me to help him because he was food poisoned. When I got there he was acting like he was *delusional*, not food poisoned. Then, when you knocked on the door he was like, 'Oh no, don't let Alexis come in! She's a *dime*! She can't see me like this!' I was pretty fed up with the comparisons to other females so when he fell asleep, I bounced."

"Oh, that makes sense. I thought you were evil the way you got up and left like that—me and Raya thought that you hated us."

"Just a tad bit," I laughed.

For the rest of the night, Alexis and I compared our experiences with Damien and realized that he wasn't really serious about anything. She and I eventually became good friends, and for the rest of the semester Damien told everyone how I was a "hater," and how I ruined his chances with Alexis because I was jealous. It initially hurt my feelings to hear what he was saying about me, but after a while I stopped caring.

Somewhere amid the seventh and eighth week of classes, the sun stopped shining in Pittsburgh. Raindrops signaled the mornings, gray skies hovered over the city for weeks at a time. Every now and then the sun would make a guest appearance, but her appearances were few and far between.

As for my dream list, I dove head first into Pre-Med courses and drowned. Despite going to my Biology teacher's office hours twice a week for help, I pulled off a consistent D+ on every exam. I hadn't joined a single organization, and although I enjoyed having new outgoing friends, I became unmotivated and slipped into a state of despair.

I don't know how it happened or what triggered it, but after waking up crying countless mornings and being apathetic for weeks, I diagnosed myself as depressed. I took it upon myself to go to the counseling center as an emergency patient to see if a professional agreed with my diagnosis.

He didn't.

He asked, "So *Whitney*, where are you from?" "Do you think you're homesick?" "What's going on at home?" "Are you involved on campus?" "You're a writer and you're not involved in any publications?" "What makes you think you're depressed?" "Don't you think you'll feel better if you just get involved and make more friends?" "Can I read some of your writing?"

He prescribed F.A. and H.T. (Fresh Air and Happy Thoughts) and continued to ask questions to fill the sixty minute time slot.

In the last seconds of the session, I handed him an essay I had written in Seminar in Composition. He glanced over the words, scanned over the paragraphs, and skipped several pages before saying, "Okay, good." He assured me that I wasn't depressed, that I was "perfectly fine," and that everything would be better if I started thinking positively about life. I thanked him for seeing me and left the counseling center feeling worse than I had before.

I never went back to see him again.

Thanks to my lack of motivation, my GPA at the end of the first semester was a 2.875, below the 3.0 requirement I needed to keep my scholarship.

For the second semester of college, I headed back to school determined to get better grades. I'd spent Christmas break relishing in the things I used to love about Memphis—the warmer weather, the predictability, and the sense of belonging—but it was time to return to the irregularity that was Pittsburgh.

I stood outside the Pittsburgh International Airport watching my breath suspend in the air. The snow was falling down so heavily that I couldn't make out anything farther than ten feet away. I kicked at my luggage and looked off into the distance, becoming increasingly frustrated that the headlights of a city bus had yet to appear. Just as I was about to head towards the taxi platform, one of my freshman mentors, Taylor, approached me.

"Hey, Whitney! How was your break?" she asked.

"It was good. I got a lot of sleep and saw a bunch of movies. How was yours?"

"It was okay. How'd your grades turn out?"

"They were okay. I'm going to try and do better this semester though. I wasted a lot of time last semester."

"Yea, that's what I did freshman year. I kind of lost focus and partied all the time. And I…"

Her voice trailed off and I could tell that she had triggered some unpleasant memory. Her eyes became fixated on the blue bus stop sign that stood ahead of us and she looked like she was in a trance. She didn't speak for a few minutes, but after she noticed me staring she said, "Are you really hype for this semester? Basketball season is usually fun."

"I'm not really into basketball, but I'm kinda excited about this semester."

"Are you going to the step show?"

"When is it?"

"It's in February. All the black people will be there," she laughed. "It's usually good."

"Are you in it?"

"Me?" she laughed harder. "No, I'm not down with that sorority stuff. No purple and green girls and no blue and cream girls for me. I'm too independent for that."

"Oh. Who won the step show last year?"

"Ummm, I think it was—I forgot. Do you think you'll join a sorority?"

"Maybe. I just, I don't know, I—"

"Well," she interrupted. "If you do ever decide to join one, be very discreet about it. No one except the sorority members should know that you're interested."

"Why?"

"Don't ask me, that's just how it works. My friend pledged last year and she told me that those are the rules."

"But how do I let them—I mean, if I ever got interested, how do I let the sorority know?"

"Well, from what I've heard every sorority is different and it depends on which one you want to join. You should probably start by going to all of their events and introducing yourself. I wouldn't know what else to tell you about that though."

"Oh okay. Thanks."

A year later I would learn that Taylor became interested in joining Theta Eta Theta's rival sorority, Mu Beta Xi, or as she might've once described them, "the burgundy and ivory girls." She had attended all of their events, shared small talk with most of the members, and even befriended two of them. However, when new member intake came around she wasn't invited.

The first few weeks of the new semester proved to be easy. I turned in my assignments on time, spoke to each of my professors during their office hours, and did extra credit when I could. I was starting to feel renewed, like God had given me a second chance.

One evening after returning from a night class, I saw my floor mate Renee sitting in the lounge by herself. I let myself in and shut the door behind me.

"Renee, are you okay?" I asked.

She turned away from me. "Yes, I'm fine."

Renee was a year ahead of me. She had always been there when I needed a shoulder to cry on or someone to listen to me. She was from Texas and her accent pervaded her every syllable. ("girl" was always "gurl" and "square" was always "squarah") She was in seven different organizations and always looking for a way to change the world.

"I don't believe you. Tell me what's wrong, I won't tell anyone," I prodded.

She turned to face me and cleared her throat. "Well, I've wanted to be a TET since I was a little girl. My mom was one and I always wanted to be able to share that with her, but...They already picked the line."

In that moment I realized that Renee had never expressed her desire to join Theta Eta Theta with me. Despite all the early morning breakfasts, the late night talks, and the never ending phone conversations between us, she had managed to keep TET business to herself.

"What do you mean?"

"They picked the line last semester and the girls they picked are about to go on line."

"Is there any way you could talk to somebody about it? If not, you could always try next year with me."

"You want to be a TET too? Wow, I never would have guessed. You don't understand though. I'm going to be a junior next year and they prefer sophomores. I wanted to do it this year because I might not have time next year."

"Um, it only takes three days right? At least that's what my aunt told me. You don't think you'll have time to set aside three days?"

She wiped her face with her sleeve. "Three days? It takes weeks."

"What? Are you serious? Why?"

She stood up and walked over to the door. She opened it and poked her head out to see if there were any listeners in the hallway. She shut the door and sat back down.

"Whitney, they pledge people here. They're not *paper*."

"Okay... I don't understand."

She sighed. "You're lucky you're getting to know this now before you become a *serious* interest. Paper means that you just pay your money to nationals, go through the three day process, and then you become a TET. For TET here, you pledge for weeks, go through the three day process, and then you become a member."

"Oh, like back in the day. Can't they get in trouble for that though?"

"Yeah, but it's the only way that makes people feel a real bond between each other. Three days is nothing and doesn't make people feel like actual sisters. I can't believe I'm not going to be able to do it."

"How do you know they already picked people?"

"My friend made the line and she told me yesterday."

"What friend?"

"I can't tell you that."

"Well, at least you know she'll pick you for next year's line."

"I don't know man, people change when they cross. I'm not saying she will, and I hope she doesn't. I've seen plenty of people get dissed by their own friends when it comes to things like this though."

"Did you go to all of their events?"

"Most of them, but I stopped at the end of October. I should've kept going."

"Don't beat yourself up about it. Everything happens—"

"I've wanted it for so long! Do you know how powerful it is to be a TET? There's so much networking after college, there's this bond between you and your line sisters like no other, and you're in it for the rest of your life."

I simply nodded my head and suppressed the urge to roll my eyes. All I could do for the rest of the night was assure Renee that everything was going to be okay and promise that next year I would become a more serious interest so we could both make it.

I left the lounge after talking to her. I went on the TET website and familiarized myself with some of the basics: Founded in 1908 at Haven University by twenty women, official colors violet and emerald green, programs geared towards the black family and community service, and lifelong bonds with successful women from all over the world. I went on other sites, read the biographies of the founders, and became captivated by their motivation to form a sorority, their goals at taking part in community service, and their commitment to the betterment of society. I spent hours sifting through the historical aspects of Theta Eta Theta and reading about the other three black sororities. There was Mu Beta Xi—colors burgundy and ivory, Beta Phi Chi—colors sky blue and cream, and Pi Upsilon Tau—colors indigo and bronze.

A week later I saw a flyer hanging in the student union advertising the step show: Three girls wore blue and cream shirts, three girls wore variations of violet and green, one girl wore a burgundy jacket, and one girl wore an indigo jacket. Each of the colors represented a black sorority. Each of the colors stood for something.

I purchased a ticket.

If I were to write that the step show was highly entertaining, I would be lying. If I were to write that there was no better way to spend ten dollars that weekend, I would be lying. If I were to say that the TETs' performance increased my interest in joining their organization, Satan would offer me a job. So, for memoir's sake, I'll write out the facts.

The show started an hour and a half late. The host was confused as to which sorority was performing first. She stalled by elaborating on a joke about her pursuit of a degree from an internet college. She announced the TETs as "the beautiful, talented, first black sorority."

The TETs took the stage dressed in green, violet, and beige Girl Scout costumes. After several moments of silence, they began to step. They mocked the other sororities by showing large women onscreen dressed in the traitor colors—burgundy, sky blue, and bronze. Their voices were incredibly soft and most of their poses resembled those of a frustrated teenager primping herself in a mirror. During a stunt, one of the TETs was kicked in the face. They did a short dance to a popular rap song and much to the crowd's delight, walked offstage.

Four fraternities stepped, but the only other sorority that stepped was Beta Phi Chi. A sky blue heart beat onscreen as a few Betas ran onstage making their cameras flash out into the audience. Music began to play and more Betas ran onstage, wearing what appeared to be cream and sky blue space suits. They shouted out into the crowd when they stepped and sang a soulful rendition of their sorority's hymn. They won.

In mid-February I started consistently writing in a journal my best friend had given to me as a birthday gift. I used it as a means to capture the random thoughts I had during the day and hardly wrote anything significant unless it was about my depression. A few things about TET were jotted down from late night conversations with Renee, who would tap on my door late at night and, as if she were a spy, signal for me to meet her in the lounge or come to her room. She would always take precautions: searching for listeners, insisting that we sit far away from the door, and ensuring that her voice wasn't above a whisper.

One particular night she disregarded the protocol and banged on my door around midnight. As soon as I opened my door she made her way into my room.

"Hi. Good to see you too," I joked.

"Is your door locked?"

"Yes," I playfully clicked the lock twice to assure her.

"Okay, look. You can't tell anyone I told you this."

"Um okay I—"

"I'm serious, Whitney. No one."

"Okay, I promise."

"My friend that's on line, the one I told you about, she looks so horrible. I've never seen her look so tired and beat in my life. She told me that she's never been so exhausted and that she's never been in so much pain."

"Pain from what?"

"Could you for once *act* like you know what pledging is? Didn't your mom and aunt pledge?"

My mom and aunt pledged in the eighties. They went to two different colleges and had two different experiences. While my aunt said that she and her line sisters were humiliated on a daily basis and made to succumb to the twisted and evil whims of her big sisters, my mom was a solo pledge and her process was more of a mental test. She recited history while her big sisters picked at her with plastic claws.

"I'm sorry. Continue," I sighed.

"Well, she's got a bruise on her leg and I saw her line sister last week in a neck brace. I can't believe it's going that far. I'm still going to do it next year; I just hope it doesn't happen to me or you."

"Was she light skinned with really short hair?"

"What? Who?"

"The girl in the neck brace."

"Oh, yea. I don't know her name though."

A week earlier I had seen a girl in a neck brace. A TET was holding her books and helping her get into a car. I thought that the TET was being a Good Samaritan. I didn't know she was a suspect in a possible assault case. I didn't tell Renee.

"What are the TETs doing to them?"

"What do you mean, 'what are they doing to them'? They're pledging them. They're teaching them the secrets of the sorority, the history, and all that other stuff…They're beating them, harassing them, and making them eat nasty stuff, if you wanted a more detailed answer."

I did want a more detailed answer. I wanted as many answers as I could get. I asked Renee at least a hundred questions that night. She told me that one of the girls on line abhorred cheese and the TETs made her eat it on some nights. The TETs called and demanded that the girls do impossible things in short amounts of time, and on several occasions the girls were made to perform exercises for hours. The girls also had to buy meals and snacks for the TETs throughout the day with their own meal plans and money.

After Renee finished explaining everything that she knew, I wrote in my journal: *February 2007 Dear Journal, I just got done talking to Renee about TET again...sigh...it's all so confusing to me. Like, why the hell would anybody want to get abused to join a sisterhood? It is a sisterhood isn't it? I would never let somebody beat the crap out of me without beating the crap out of them back. I definitely would NEVER buy anybody else's food with my own meal plan or money. That doesn't make any sense...I'll try and be a serious interest next semester, but I'm not putting up with any of that. PS—should I retake Biology? Goodnight.*

III. Following Sea

Pittsburgh offered no clear days that winter. It painted every sky gray and passed out frozen raindrops anytime an angry person would look up and curse its decision. Every now and then it would raise its wind chill from the below zero digits to the above zero single digits. When it was bored, it would unbutton the clouds and reveal the sun's chest, but only for a few hours. As soon as the Pittsburghers would say, "Thanks so much for this beautiful sunshine," it would laugh and cover it back up.

When spring began, parades of rain marched down every morning and landed on streets, rooftops, and umbrellas. Ominous clouds lingered in the sky for days at a time, waiting to release more miserable rain. After what seemed like years of dull and dreary weather, beautiful days unfolded.

One of the most beautiful days came on a Thursday in March. The sun rose early in the morning and shone its rays through bulbous, white clouds. As the day drifted on, the clouds dissipated and gave way to a blank blue sky. Soft gentle winds blew through the city, embracing the Pittsburghers—begging them to realize what a wonderful a day it was.

Ice cream shops sold discounted ice cream and gelatin. Students wore short sleeved shirts and shades. People walked to their jobs instead of catching the bus. Couples lounged on park benches and played with their dogs.

I ate my lunch outdoors and lingered outside the student union as people sunbathed across the street. I skipped math class and planned to go downtown to look at the bridges, but I received a phone call from my mother, a phone call that I'll remember for the rest of my life.

"Hi, Mommy. What's up?" I said.

"How are you? Are you okay?"

"I'm okay. What's up?"

"Are you done with classes already?" her voice wavered.

"Ma, what's wrong?"

"Nothing, Whit. I was just calling to see how you were doing today."

"I'm fine. What's wrong?"

"I was just—"

"Ma, what is it!"

"J.C. died."

My father. Shot.

I cried. I sat outside on the park bench and cried.

No one stopped to ask why I was crying. It was too beautiful a day for anyone to care. They sauntered by licking their ice cream cones and listening to their IPods. I had been crying for half an hour when Renee's friend Regina stopped by.

"Whitney?" she asked. "What's wrong? Are you alright?"

I covered my face and tried to say that I was okay, but the words were locked in my throat and all I could do was sob. She sat down beside me and I managed to choke out, "My dad died."

"I'm so sorry, Whitney."

"It's not your fault," I said.

I was relieved that she had stopped by, but I didn't want her sympathy. I wiped away my tears and asked about her day. She didn't answer my question. Instead, she looked off into the distance. She sighed, "My father died when I was in high school."

"How did he die?"

"He was very sick. So," her voice trailed off.

"I'm sorry."

"He's in a better place now, just like your dad. Were you two close?"

I wanted to lie. I wanted to say, "Yes. He was the best father a girl could ask for. He was always there for me," but I couldn't, because he wasn't. I held back tears and said, "We were okay. Were you and your dad?"

"Yes, we were very close. I don't think I'll ever get over it."

We sat silent for a while—drifting into distant memories, driving ourselves into spaces of comfort. She broke the silence, "What are your plans for the summer?"

"I'm going to try and relax you know? I'm going to try and learn as much as I can about TET—"

"TET? You're interested?"

"Yea, my mom and a lot of people in my family are TETs so I've always been intrigued by it."

"Wow, your mom is a TET? I didn't know that. Did you know that the probate is in two weeks?"

"No. How do you know?"

"I'm in it," she laughed. "We crossed last week."

"Oh, well congratulations Regina!"

"Thanks, I'm so excited. Do you plan on actually trying to *become* a TET?"

"Yea, I just don't wanna get hit!"

She looked away and laughed. "Don't worry. I'll help you out."

We talked for what felt like an hour. She told me that the TETs would pick "who they liked" for the next line. She suggested that I go to all of the events, attempt to get their telephone numbers, and try to get to know as many members as possible. Before she left for piano class, she encouraged me to get rest and take time out for myself.

I watched as she disappeared into a crowd of students across the street. I sat on the bench a few minutes more, taking in the sunset. I almost went to the student union to hang out with friends, but I started crying again.

I locked myself in my room.

I remember people coming by to console me. I remember people telling me that it was going to be okay, that things happen for a reason. I remember becoming irritated with my friends for still having their fathers, for not being able to relate, for being able to say that I would be "fine" so easily. I remember becoming angry at my father for being gone for so long. I remember being sad that I would never get the reconciliation I had dreamed about for years. I remember being unable to sleep, unable to think, and unable to eat. I remember blaming myself.

Days later, I was at his funeral listening to a woman sing "The Time Has Come." My grandmother sat still—no crying, no tears. She kept her eyes on the silver casket. She kept her eyes on her son, my father.

I don't remember how long the funeral lasted. I don't remember the order of the ceremony. I don't remember every person that stood up to give anecdotes, but I do remember his line brothers.

My father had been a member of Theta Phi Theta, the first black fraternity, and each of his line brothers shared a story about their times together in college: "He didn't really have rhythm, but when it was time to step, he knew how to carry in that banner." "He was a gentle soul. All the pledges liked him the best because he wasn't as mean as the rest of us." "He was always the one who knew how to fix things—whether it was the air conditioning at a brother's house or the relationship between two friends. He knew how to fix things."

I remember laughing at their stories, envisioning myself in their memories.

After the funeral, I spent days at home relaxing. I played spades with my grandmother and aunts. I ate greens and sweet potato pie. I took time to remember all the scattered memories my father and I once shared.

It was raining when I returned to Pittsburgh. I sat on the bus, unenthusiastic about completing the remaining weeks of the semester. I had emailed all of my teachers about the funeral and received extra time to complete my work. My advisor told me that I could withdraw from classes for the rest of the term with no penalty if I wanted to, but I declined. I told him that I would get over my father's death within a week.

I sat in the dark for half an hour before turning on my bedroom's light. I started the process of forgetting: organized the books on the shelf, made my bed, and vacuumed. I unpacked my suitcase and emptied my purse. I cleaned the mirrors and straightened the wall pictures. I tucked my father's obituary into a folder and stuffed it underneath my desk. I pushed the thoughts of his death into the far corners of my mind and started to work on assignments.

IV. Rigging

The TET probate was held at night, in the hallway of a lecture building. Purple balloons adorned the walls and an array of green baskets filled with gifts stood against the wall. Nine neos, dressed in black dresses and shades, marched in a line with their arms intertwined, their heads turned up high. They began singing, "1908...1908..." until they made it to the middle of the hall. The crowd wrapped around them. Their prophytes, dressed in bright violet dresses, made their way to the front of the crowd.

The neos sang introductions for each of the black male fraternities and chanted greetings. Their recitation of history, founders, and poems was polished—not one girl made a mistake, not one girl lost her place, not one girl missed a syllable. They were robots, programmed to TET software. When they paused, an older TET fixed their hair and straightened their pearl necklaces. In between songs they posed as if they were looking into mirrors and continued their routine.

I watched in awe as the crowd became louder and louder. The prophytes removed the shades one by one and allowed each girl to introduce herself. I wished that I was in their place. I wished that it was me.

The prophytes handed each neo a handheld mirror that was encrusted in shiny green material and engraved with her respective line name and number. The neos held the mirrors in front of their faces and invited all members of Theta Eta Theta to join them in a song. When the last note was sung, they disbursed and took pictures with their friends and families.

After the probate, I met up with my friend Candace to talk. Her mother, grandmother, and aunt were all TETs.

"That was so good!" she said. "I think that's the best probate I've seen this year."

"Definitely. That's gonna be us one day."

"I hope so. I really want it. I'm going to go to all of their events."

"I'll try to, but I probably won't make it to all of them," I sighed.

"I have to. I've got to start getting their numbers."

"Regina said she would help me out this summer so I'll have to wait on that. I've got way too much make-up work to finish these last few weeks."

"That was nice of her! She looked so pretty—"

"Yea, did you hear how she said, a *thorough* number 8 is *oh so hard* to find?" I laughed. "I'm happy for her."

"I've seen all of them around before, except whoever that number four was. I've never seen that girl a day in my life before tonight."

"I only knew Regina and I've seen Cari around. I think Cari was number five, but I only know her because she stays in my dorm."

We talked about the probate for hours, analyzing every moment, hoping that one day someone would be talking about ours.

A few days later, the new TETs held their first event: Movie Night. I forgot about it and wasn't reminded until Candace sent me a text that interrupted my nap.

CANDACE: Where are you? TET movie night is about to start!

Although I didn't feel like going, I put on a blue hoodie, faded jeans, and worn snow boots. My hair wasn't done and I didn't make an attempt to fix it. By the time I reached the student union I was fifteen minutes late.

I opened the door to the event and saw a room full of interests dressed in black and white business wear. I immediately felt out of place.

I took a seat in the back and tried to focus on the film they were watching, *Freedom Writers*. It was the type of film I despised—a stereotypical inspirational film where a nice teacher moves into a bad neighborhood, saves her students from despair and failure, and helps everyone to live happily ever after. I didn't necessarily *hate* those types of films, but I had grown up in a similar neighborhood and I knew that the chances of a new teacher coming in and saving an entire class was highly unlikely. She could save three or four students. Maybe.

When the film came to an end, two of the new TETs, Sasha Irons and Latoya Riley stood near the front of the room.

"Did you ladies enjoy the movie?" Sasha asked, offering a weak smile. Faint "Yes" and "Yea" answers bounced off the walls.

"We're glad you enjoyed it," Latoya said. "We're going to ask a few discussion questions and then we can talk over refreshments. Question number one, how do you think gang violence affects the current community? Do you think it's as bad as it was five or ten years ago?"

They called on a girl in the front row to answer.

"I think that—"

"Introduce yourself please. Name, year, et cetera," Sasha interrupted.

"Oh, I'm sorry. Hi everyone my name is Samantha Russet and I'm a junior at the university. I feel that gang violence has definitely decreased a bit over the years, but it still affects the community."

Another girl raised her hand.

"Hi everyone, my name is Torina Bailey and..."

I started daydreaming. I was ready to go home and finish my homework. The excitement I felt after the probate had slightly diminished after seeing twenty interests dressed better than me. My daydream was interrupted when one of the older TETs, Ivyana, loudly announced herself as "a junior majoring in business and finance." She held her nose up high and commanded attention of the room. I tried to tune her out, but her annoying child-like voice continued to disrupt my dream.

"I feel that this is a very prevalent issue in the black community and that we as black women should take notice and work to try and improve it," she said. "I know plenty of people who grew up in poor neighborhoods who always spoke about gang violence. Like, this madness has to stop, and this movie is a prime example of a way that one person can make a difference."

Sasha and Latoya asked more questions, all of which were eventually answered by Ivyana. When they were done, they told everyone in the room to sign the attendance book if they planned on leaving at that moment. If not, "stay and mingle with us," they said in unison.

I didn't sign the book. I stood up and walked towards Candace.

"What a waste of my time," I said. "I hate that movie."

"If you really want to be a TET it wasn't a waste. I'm going to go talk to them. Come on," she smiled.

I followed her across the room and felt my heart speed up as I introduced myself to two TETs.

Their names were Kamille and Cari and they smiled after each question Candace and I asked. We asked general questions: "What's your major?" "Where are you from?" "Do you like it here at the university?" "What do you plan on doing afterwards?"

When I was in the middle of asking Cari how she felt about the clubs in Pittsburgh, Ivyana ran over and hugged her tightly.

"I love you so much!" she smiled at Kamille and gushed. "Y'all were the best line ever!"

She pulled them towards the back of the room where the rest of the TETs had assembled themselves.

They started taking photos of each other and laughing about how well their event had gone. They ignored the interests, and while those unfortunate dressy souls continued to watch the TETs enjoy their lives, I left.

Later that week, the TETs held a panel discussion about diseases that affected females in the African American community. I wore a wrinkled black top, jeans, and a pair of Jordan's. I sat in the back once again and listened as the TETs presented topics to the panel—a group of women who used as much medical jargon as possible, annoyingly confirming the fact that they were highly educated. The interests that were sitting in the audience asked the panel questions like, "If I had HPV could I die?" "Is HPV like HIV?"and "Could you repeat everything you just said?"

An hour and a half passed. A lesbian began talking about her experiences with different illnesses and the interests had a field day probing her for elaboration. With a math exam awaiting me at eight the next morning, I made a mental note of the fact that lesbian women didn't have to take birth control and left.

After I finished finals, I went on Face book and added each of the new TETS to my friend list. I looked through their photos, browsed through their friend lists, and read their wall posts. I copied down each of their names, their line names, and their numbers into a black notebook:

1.) Kamille Jackson "Close Call"
2.) Sasha Irons "The Challenger"
3.) Latoya Riley "Cheater, Cheater"
4.) Julia Benson "The Cosigner"
5.) Cari Jones "Retrospect"
6.) Britney Lynn "Supermodel"
7.) Nicole Ballard "Kraft"
8.) Regina Addison "Musical"
9.) Tiffany Stringer "Hollywood"

V. Bear Away

In the summer, I did basic research on all of the black Greek lettered organizations. I kept two notebooks: one for information regarding Theta Eta Theta, and one for the other organizations.

There were nine black Greek lettered organizations that made up what was considered the "divine nine"—four sororities and five fraternities. Theta Phi Theta, the first black fraternity, was founded in 1906 by seven distinguished gentlemen at an all white university. In 1908, the first black sorority, Theta Eta Theta, was founded at a historically black university. In 1911, two other fraternities were established—Nu Alpha Pi at an all white university in Indiana, and Rho Gamma Chi, the first black fraternity that was founded at a historically black university. In 1913, members of Theta Eta Theta who were dismayed by the original vision of the sorority founded their own sorority, Mu Beta Xi. In 1914, the fraternity Chi Beta Omicron came into existence and six years later, in 1920, a new sorority was born: Beta Phi Chi. The last black sorority, Pi Upsilon Tau, was founded in 1922 by a group of educators in Indiana at another all white institution. And the last black fraternity, Xi Lambda Psi, was founded in 1963 at a historically black university by a group of men who were social activists amongst the African American community.

Each organization had a rich and divergent history. They each had different goals and principles, but they all expressed a desire to work together to achieve betterment in the black community. I outlined their goals and wrote down interesting information that I found on each of them. After all of my reading, I felt that Theta Eta Theta was the best choice for me.

My aunt kept telling me that becoming a TET was expensive and that I might want to consider saving $900. But after quitting seven jobs that were doled out to me by a temporary agency and failing to secure an internship, I resolved that I would simply beg my mom to fund my TET endeavors.

I became a professional bum for the rest of the summer. I slept until the afternoon, stayed up late writing, and hung out with friends. I also spent more time talking to one of my guy friends, Antonio.

Antonio was an aspiring artist. He wanted to go into the music industry and make music that actually made sense. We had been friends for both semesters; he had been a perfect gentleman. After my father passed, he insisted that I spend nights in his room. I slept on the bed and he slept on the floor. He asked if I was feeling okay about everything, if I was going to be alright. To save myself from a deep conversation, I lied and said yes.

We talked on the phone almost every night that summer, but we never completely opened up to each other. We discussed surface matters—our daily activities, high school past times, and future plans.

He thought that my family was rich since I could afford to not have a job during the summer and didn't have to take out any loans for school. I tried to explain to him that we were financially stable, but we were far from being rich. I told him that before I reached middle school we had been on welfare and lived years in a poor, crime-ridden neighborhood. He didn't believe me.

"Quit lying, y'all were never broke. You don't know what it's like to struggle. I struggle every day," he said.

"I'm telling the truth. My dad wasn't around a lot when I was younger and my mom had to do everything herself. She really couldn't afford much."

"Isn't your mom a nurse?"

"Yes, but—"

"Wasn't she a nurse back then?"

"Yes, but not always and—"

"Exactly. Just because she didn't buy you everything you wanted back then like she does now doesn't mean that you struggled."

I didn't bother with a rebuttal. It wasn't worth it. I kept the elements of my past inside and hoped that one day I would be able to tell someone the entire truth. I knew that Antonio wasn't that person, but as the summer days wore on and we began to talk more, I thought that things would change. I developed feelings for him and felt that we were becoming compatible. I thought that he was starting to sincerely care about me.

He was interested in Rho Gamma Chi, a black fraternity that was stereotyped for its outrageous sexual manners and outlandish behaviors at parties. He'd already befriended all of the members at our school and asserted his interest since the first semester. When I asked him why he wanted to be a Rho, he scoffed, "Because Rho is the only organization that emphasizes brotherhood."

"Don't they *all* emphasize brotherhood?" I asked.

"No. The frats at our school are more into *quantity*, not quality so they just have a bunch of people in their organizations that don't even fuck with each other. Rho only picks people who they would actually consider brothers."

He always took Greek life so seriously, as if it were a matter of life or death. Granted, I wanted to be a TET, but it wasn't always at the forefront of my mind. I once asked Antonio if he knew anything about the TET process, if pledging was as bad as I heard it was.

He laughed as if I had told him an incredible joke. "The TETs think they go hard in their process, but they don't. They don't even know what a process is."

"Do they really beat those girls though? Like, I really can't see that happening."

"You sound really stupid right now. Why can't you see that happening? You think pledging is going to be fun? Have you done *any* research?"

"Yes. And the rules said—"

"Whitney, they don't follow those rules. Stop playing dumb. Yes, you're going to get hit. Yes, you're going to get beat, and you'll be a better person for it."

"I just don't see how being abused makes you a—"

"Well, maybe pledging isn't for you. Maybe you should do graduate chapter. Maybe you shouldn't do TET at all. I hope you don't say any of this stuff when you talk to the TETs because you'll fuck up your chances for sure."

I was quiet for five minutes. I told Antonio that I would call him back. I didn't.

I was angry, but I saw where he was coming from. I needed to have some idea of what I might be getting myself into. I tried to do more research. I found nothing that I hadn't already read before. There was the list of facts on Wikipedia, the brief history summary on the national website, and the short paragraphs on random sites that outlined the founders' lives.

I googled, "pledging black sorority," and news reports about a few girls came up: Two girls had drowned after attempting to pledge a chapter on the west coast, one girl had sued the sorority because of a hazing incident, and others had filed claims about being harassed. I remembered what Antonio had said about those girls, how they "knew what they were getting themselves into," and how "they didn't want to be paper in the first place and shouldn't be suing the sorority for their own mistake in judgment."

I googled "I pledged a black sorority," "Pledge process for black sororities," "Pledge process for TET," "TET process," "I was not a paper TET," "How to be a TET," and the results were just as dismal. There was nothing concerning the pledge process except threads of Greek chat forums that had been written years ago.

One morning I got a text from Regina.

REGINA: Hey Whitney, I hope you're summer is going well. Here are two of my LSs numbers. Tiffany (123-555-0987) and Julia (333-555-6543) they're really cool, don't be scared to talk to them. Have a nice day! :o).

I didn't understand why I would ever need to call someone I didn't know. What could we possibly have to talk about? What was there to say? What was the point?

I went back and forth asking myself those questions, but Candace and Renee insisted that I call the TETs. They said it would bring me steps closer to being on line and that I would be far ahead of other interests when we returned to school. It took me two weeks to muster up the courage to call Tiffany on a Saturday afternoon. My heart jumped each time her phone rang.

"Hello?" she answered in a nasally tone.

"Hello, is this Tiffany?"

"Yea, who is this?"

"This is Whitney...Regina gave me your number. I was wondering if you had time to talk?"

"Oh, yeah I have time. What's up?"

"Well...How has your summer been going?"

"It's going fine."

"Have you done anything exciting?"

"Not really. I've just been hanging out with my friends when I can."

"Yea, me too since I haven't had much success with working."

Silence.

"Do you have any big plans for the summer?" I asked.

"Um, me and my LSs are going to go to a Greek barbeque later and we'll probably do a few road trips here or there but nothing really *exciting*. I'm just happy to be getting a lot of sleep."

"Oh, okay. What's your major?"

"I'm a communications major and I'm taking classes in foreign language and drama."

"What do you plan to do with that?"

"I don't know yet—something good though," she sighed.

Silence.

"That's sort of how I feel about my major. Most people say the only thing I can do with it is teach, but I don't think I want to do that."

Silence.

"Where are you staying next year?" I asked.

"I'm staying in an apartment a bit far from campus."

"Are you going to do an internship next year?"

"I'm just going to try to make good grades."

Silence.

"Well Whitney, it was nice talking to you," she said. "I have to take a nap, but feel free to call me anytime."

I said goodbye and hung up with no intentions of ever calling her again. I decided that I wouldn't call Julia either. I was just going to enjoy the rest of my summer and worry about Theta Eta Theta in the fall.

In June, Candace and I went to Jersey to vacation with two of our friends who were twins. When I arrived, the first thing I wanted to do was sleep, but the three of them persuaded me into staying up and going to a party in New York City.

I'd never been much of a party person; I was too much of a square. In fact, if someone had given me the choice of writing a ten page paper about the influence of Shakespeare's sonnets on the modern song or going out to a party, I probably would have chosen to write the paper and added eight more pages for fun. Nonetheless, I obliged.

We waited in line amidst the cold night air for about half an hour and when we finally made it into the club, the room was crowded and smelled like a mix of sweat, alcohol, and marijuana. I was about to start dancing, but my stomach began to churn and I ran off the dance floor.

By the time Candace and the twins found me, I was vomiting behind an ATM on some stranger's jacket. They collectively decided that it was time to leave.

On the weekend, we spent the day shopping in Manhattan. When Candace and I saw violet and emerald handbags and clothes, we would get excited and talk about how much better they would look on us if we became TETs. On the last night of the trip, before Candace went to sleep and after she'd had a little too much alcohol, she said, "Night, future LS."

A week after the trip, I called Antonio and things went back to normal. We acted as if the argument had never happened and filled each other in on what went on during the past couple of weeks. The more I talked to him, the more I considered sleeping with him. Although we weren't together and he didn't know me as well as I wanted him to, I thought that sex would bring us closer together. I thought that if we had sex he would listen to me and be the friend I could always depend on, the friend who would always be there.

We texted each other several messages loaded with sexual innuendoes the last month of the summer, and I looked forward to losing my virginity to him. He told me that he liked me. He told me that he cared about me. I believed him.

I arrived in Pittsburgh for my sophomore year a week before the official student move in. I had a freshman mentor conference to attend and the university allowed all of the participants to move in early. My family waved goodbye from the gray trailblazer once more and left me to complete another semester alone.

I began decorating my room. I put up black and white photos of Hollywood legends on my wall. I pulled my gold comforter on the bed and accented it with decorative red and gold pillows. I filled cherry colored vases with faux white lilies and tacked my name in black and gold letters at the top of my wall. As I was cutting the paper shapes that were going to embroider my mirror, I got a text.

ANTONIO: Whatchu doin?
ME: Decorating my room, you?
ANTONIO: I'm setting up my room too...I'm coming over tonight.
ME: Aren't you going to ask? Lol
ANTONIO: Nope...I don't have to lol

I laughed and continued decorating. Tiara and Alexis came by to help me organize my closet. I told them how excited I was to see Antonio later, and filled them in on how much we had talked over the summer. They kept me company until late at night and told me to make sure that I got a kiss from him. At 11:30, I called him. "When did you plan on coming?"

"I'm eating right now. I'm going to come right after I eat."

An hour passed. Two hours passed. I called him and told him that I was going to sleep. "I'm still coming, but if you fall asleep I'll call to wake you up," he said.

I should have turned my phone on silent. I should have drawn my blinds, turned off the lights, and gone to sleep. But I didn't.

At 3:15 Antonio called.

"I'm downstairs," he said. "Wake up."

I got out of bed and went down to the lobby. I signed him in, not mentioning how late it was, not questioning why it took him more than three hours to eat. I told him that I was tired and that I was going to sleep. I suggested that we eat breakfast together later. When we got inside my room, he hugged me tightly and said, "I missed you." "I missed you too," I heard myself say.

He kissed me. I kissed him back. We walked over to the bed and he lay down on top of me. He held my face in his hands and said, "I'm sorry I was so late." Sliding his hands under my shirt, he unclipped my bra.

"Take your shirt off," he said. I obliged.

He pulled his shirt over his head and took off his shorts. I watched as he unbuttoned my flannel pants and slid them off of my body.

There I was, completely naked with a guy for the first time.

He caressed me and whispered, "Do you feel okay?" but he didn't wait for a response. He started fondling my breasts and exploring my body. He rolled over and pulled me on top of him.

He told me to turn around. I moved my body and felt his tongue moving between my thighs. I positioned my mouth on top of his penis and kissed his shaft. He begged me not to stop.

I realized that I was uncomfortable; something wasn't right. As he caressed my thighs, I lapsed into a memory.

On a night in June I was on the phone with Marcus, one of our mutual friends. He was telling me about an argument he'd had with his ex-girlfriend, explaining why he hated being in relationships. He applauded the fact that I had never been in a serious relationship and told me to keep it that way until I was absolutely sure that the "lucky guy" really cared about me and could be trusted.

I told him that I was starting to feel that way about Antonio. I told him that I didn't want to be in a relationship with him, but I felt that he really cared about me. He exploded in laughter, "Antonio? Are you serious? Tell me you're joking!"

"No, I'm serious. I'm really starting to like him!"

His tone changed. He sounded concerned, "Wait…Real talk? Like, are you for real?"

"Yea, Marcus I'm serious. Why is that a problem?"

He sighed.

"Marcus?" I wanted a response.

"Whitney, I'm telling you…leave Antonio alone. Don't expect anything from him. He's not what you want."

"I don't want a relation—"

"No, you don't understand. Don't catch feelings for him; it's not going to end how you think."

"What are you talking about?"

"Okay...I'm not tryna' throw salt in his game or anything but, you're my friend, and I really don't want you to get hurt, so..."

"So?"

"So, between me and you...first semester, me, him and some otha' dudes you know had a competition to see who could bag the most girls...He won."

"How many?"

"Eight."

"You're lying, he—"

"Nope, I'm definitely not. I really thought I could bag way more bitches than him, but hey, somehow he pulled that shit off."

"Why would y'all do something like that?"

"It's college, Whit. It's not like any of the girls were like you or anything. They were hoes. We were just supplying their demand."

I laughed, "I guess."

"Yea, but, please don't buy into the hype. You might really like him, you might really have feelings for him, but he's not...He's not who you think he is...trust me..."

"We talk all the time and—"

"I'm telling you Whitney..."

I needed proof. I told Marcus that I wouldn't say anything to Antonio about our conversation, but I needed to know more. He told me that towards the end of the fall semester, Antonio had talked to one of my floor-mates. I had already known that: Antonio told me that he wanted to be in a serious relationship with her, but since she just wanted to be physical their bond eventually fell apart.

"And you believed that shit?" Marcus asked.

"Well yea. I didn't have a reason not to."

"Wow, you're way too naïve. He used that girl. She wanted to be in a relationship. He didn't. I mean it was crazy. I felt so bad watching her get strung along for months, but he was my boy so I couldn't say anything. One day he just told her 'I'm tryna' concentrate on my schoolwork, I don't have time for you anymore' and that was it."

"Really..."

"Yep. Just don't let that happen to you…"

I snapped out of my memory and felt Antonio planting kisses on my neck. I pushed him away.

"What's wrong?"

"Nothing. Can I ask you something?"

"Anything," he kissed my forehead.

"Did you ever… have a competition… to see who could sleep with the most girls?"

He slid his fingers between my thighs, "No, I would never do something like that."

My heart sank.

"Why did you keep in contact with me all summer?"

He pulled my legs up and wrapped them around his waist, "Because I liked you."

"Do you care about me?"

"Sshhh, stop asking questions you already know the answers to," he said as he kissed his way up to my chest.

I could feel the tears welling in my eyes, but I didn't let them fall. I returned his kisses and pressed myself against him. He whispered in my ear, "Remember those late night phone calls? How you said you wanted it?"

"I can't…I'm not ready."

He kissed me, "I'll be gentle."

"I really can't, I'm sorry."

"Just let me put the tip in."

"No…I can't."

"Just the tip," he squeezed my breasts.

"I'm sorry Antonio…I can't do it with you."

He turned over on his side. He said goodnight. I didn't respond. I didn't sleep. I lay in the bed looking at the ceiling, feeling used. He didn't really care about me. He had put on a show for a year and a summer, and I had refused him the finale.

I couldn't look him in the eyes when he woke up. I asked him, "Do you think I'm a slut?"

"No."

"Do you think I'm a hoe?"

"No."

"I'm sorry to ask you that, I just can't believe I did that."

"Did what? We didn't do anything."

"I know, it's just…I never… I never—"

"You've known me for more than a year now. You're not a slut, you're not a hoe—you're still a fuckin' virgin. Just forget about it. Everything's cool."

I signed him out five minutes later. We didn't speak on the elevator. We didn't say goodbye.

I banged on Alexis's door. I told her everything. I told her how stupid I felt for being so naïve. I couldn't believe that I trusted him that much. I couldn't believe that I had almost given him my virginity, and it would have meant nothing to him. I cried for days.

Alexis tried to make me feel better, suggesting that I accompany her and her mom on a shopping trip. She told me to go out and try to think about something else. I couldn't.

I went to the conference pale and disheveled. I tried to conjure up new activity ideas for incoming freshmen during the brainstorming session, but all I could think about was that night. I was so out of it that I almost failed to realize that I had been assigned to work with an older TET for the rest of the year.

Antonio was at the conference as well. He barely acknowledged me. He gave a slight head nod when he saw me in the hallway, but he didn't speak. He talked to everyone else in the room. He made jokes and participated. He was unaffected.

The hardest thing to do after the conference was to tell my other close friends about the ordeal. I sat in Renee's room and used half a box of Kleenex when I retold the story. I cried over lunch telling Candace. I ruined a day of shopping with Tiara by shedding tears in the middle of Target.

I felt like a fool.

All the hours dedicated to trying to become a part of his world, all the questions asked and answered, and I didn't know him any better at all. I only knew his façade. He chose what parts of himself he wanted me to see and unfortunately that wasn't much. I was even given a chance to back out. I had been warned, but I didn't listen. It was my fault.

VI. Know the Ropes

At the student activities fair I went up to the TET table. Two of them were sitting behind the table: Britney Lynn and Julia Benson.

"Good afternoon, ladies," I said.

They stared at me.

"How are you doing today?" I asked louder, unsure of if they had heard me the first time.

They said nothing. Julia smiled and pushed a green spiral notebook towards me. "Take all the info you want and sign the book please."

They began debating on what restaurant they had a taste for while I picked up three of the brochures that were on the table. I mumbled "Goodbye, ladies" and stepped away. I watched as other interests walked to the table and received the same treatment that I was given.

I looked at the information I took from the table and noticed that they were hosting a few events the week classes began. I wrote down the events in my planner, but I couldn't focus on anything TET related because I was still having trouble getting that night with Antonio off my mind. I tried to get his attention by sending him angry text messages, but he rarely responded and when he did, he would say, "I'm busy," "I'm in the studio," or "I'm eating." On the night he finally responded without an excuse he said, "What do you want?"

I told him that I wanted to talk to him, that it was important. I asked if he could call me later that night before 2 a.m. He called at 1:57.

I told him that I had felt really uncomfortable that night, that I felt used because of the way he had started to treat me, and that I still wanted to be his friend. I explained to him how we used to talk every day in the summer while we were in different states, and now that we were in the same state he acted as if he couldn't utter a mere "Hello" when he saw me walking down the street. I said all of this over the course of thirty minutes, and his two second response was, "You've been talking in circles, but okay."

I forced myself to see that he didn't care and realized that it was time for me to stop caring. I allowed the last stream of tears to fall and I didn't cry about him anymore. I deleted his number, temporarily blocked him from my Face book account, and trashed any texts that I had ever sent to him.

He didn't exist anymore.

Sometime in September, I found myself at a meeting for the TETs' new yearly project, Book Club. In an attempt to fit in, I wore black slacks and a white button down shirt. I combed out my curls and made sure that my hair looked sleek. There were twenty other interests, dressed in black and white business casual, all dreaming that they too would one day be TETs putting on an event. With my depression becoming harder to fight each day, I dreamed about becoming a TET more often and within those few minutes, I was actually happy.

"Good afternoon ladies," Regina announced.

"Good afternoon," we answered.

"On behalf of the Epsilon chapter of Theta Eta Theta Sorority, Incorporated, I would like to welcome you all to our second book club meeting. We're going to meet every other Thursday for the rest of the semester and talk about the book we've selected. For those of you who don't know who I am, my name is Regina Addison and I'm a junior at the university," she turned towards Latoya.

"Hi everyone. My name is Latoya Riley, I'm a senior at the university, and the woman sitting behind us is Tanya. She became a TET in 2004 and she's here to help us take orders for the books. But before we do that I'd like each of you to introduce yourselves. Give us your name, your year, and one interesting fact about yourself."

"No, no, no," Tanya stood up. "I don't think so. Instead of one interesting fact about *you*, I want to hear an interesting fact about *my* organization. Go."

Renee stood up first. "Hello everyone, my name is Renee Royalton. I'm a junior at the university, and an interesting fact about Theta Eta Theta—"

"*Sorority Incorporated*," Tanya snapped.

"I'm sorry. Theta Eta Theta Sorority, Incorporated. It was founded in January 1908."

"Okay next," Tanya motioned for Renee to sit down.

"Hi all. My name is Amber Jackson and I'm a sophomore at the university. An interesting fact about Theta Eta Theta Sorority Incorporated is that its official plant is the ivy."

"Next."

"Hi. My name is Candace Blake and I'm a sophomore. An interesting fact about Theta Eta Theta Sorority, Incorporated is that its official motto is achievement through sisterhood."

I was shaking in my seat. Everyone that stood up to introduce themselves had taken my fact. I had only memorized five. I hoped that the TETs would overlook me and not make me give one.

"Hi, my name is Jasmine Henderson and I'm a sophomore. My interesting fact about Theta Eta Theta Sorority Incorporated is that it's made up of *very* strong and *very* intelligent women."

"Sit down please," Tanya rolled her eyes.

There were five people remaining. I made up a fact. "Hello everyone. My name is Whitney Gracia Williams and an interesting fact about Theta Eta Theta Sorority Incorporated is that there are chapters in Peru and China."

The TETs scratched their heads and the remaining interests introduced themselves and gave their facts.

"Yea," Tanya said after the last fact. "Some of your facts were *wrong*. You need to go home and research my organization for your own benefit. Research, research, research, thanks. Neos go ahead and continue with the book club instructions."

Latoya cleared her throat. "Well, as Regina said we're going to meet up every other Thursday. We have room 365 reserved in the cathedral and our meetings will start at exactly 8:08. You don't have to dress up or anything. It's gonna be real chill and we'll try to read four to five sections between every meeting. This year we're trying to do something new with our chapter and we think this is one way to do that. Regina, could you introduce the book please?"

"Sure. This semester we'll be reading *My Sister's Keeper* by Jodi Piccoult."

"This is one of my favorite books," Latoya smiled. "You all are going to love it. We'll call you up one by one and if you want us to order one for you, come up and we'll put a check by your name. When the books come in, you'll get an email about where you can pick it up. If not, just let us know that you plan to buy it later or get it from somewhere else. It's thirteen dollars."

I let them put a check by my name and waited for Renee at Quaker Steak and Lube. Fifteen minutes later she showed up out of breath.

"Did you run to get here? Dinner isn't that serious," I said.

"No. I was talking to Tanya about how happy I am about book club."

"And you're out of breath because?"

"Because you suggested that we eat all the way over here, damn near off campus! I was on my way a while ago, but I had to go back and help one of my residents get back into her dorm room. I didn't want to be too late."

I laughed. Since Renee had become a resident assistant in a freshman dorm, she was always on call for the simplest of incidents.

"Are you really that happy about book club?" I asked.

"I'm just happy that the Epsilon chapter is finally *changing*. Those bitches that were in the chapter before Regina and them never thought to do a book club. They were too busy being stuck up, drinking, and hoeing around."

"I just hope that book club doesn't ever start to feel like a waste of my time."

"Me too, but I don't think it'll feel like that. With people like Regina being active, it should go well. They know that their prophytes weren't that accommodating at events and I think they're trying to change that. I think the chapter is finally going to be really good."

"I hope so."

"Do you plan on calling Tiffany again?"

"Um, no."

"Why aren't you going to?"

"One, because I don't *feel* like it. Two, because I really don't see the point. I really want to be a TET, but according to that website I don't have to do anything but go to events. That's all I'm going to do."

"Whitney, they're not going to pick you if they don't *know* you. Like, you're *supposed* to call and get to know them."

"Why?"

"Look, I honestly don't know. I didn't know that all this stuff was required last year. I thought just like you did. I'm learning just like you are and I think it's in your best interest to call. Do you know how many interests would kill to have *two* TET numbers? I only have Regina's and Tiffany's and they don't count because I knew them before."

"Tiffany? Please. That was the most awkward conversation I've ever had in my life! She didn't say anything! She didn't learn anything about me, and what I learned from her I could've learned from her Face book page!"

"Then what's your excuse for not calling Julia?"

"I don't know her, Renee. Like, if somebody that I didn't know randomly called to talk to me I'd probably hang up."

"They'll know that you're an interest Whitney. You should really get on the ball. I heard that they're going to have another spring line."

"Yea, yea, yea," I said as I munched on hot wings. I'd had enough interest talk for one day.

"I know where Ivyana has class on Tuesdays, so I might show up and ask her for her number."

"Stalking? Is it really that serious?"

"Yes, it is! You don't understand. If you really want this as bad as you claim to want it, you'll do anything to get it. Asking them for their numbers and calling them isn't going to kill you or me. It's harmless and it's going to help us get one step closer to being on line."

"Yea, and I'm still not feeling that whole abusive thing for weeks either."

"Don't worry about that now. Worry about that if you get picked."

I stuffed down more hot wings and changed the subject. I started talking about how I had been extremely sad for the past few months and didn't understand why. I told her that most of the time I acted as if everything was fine when I was out in public, but I was a mess on the inside. She told me to get more involved in campus activities and go out to more social events. I thanked her for her advice, but I didn't take it.

I stuck to my normal routine—classes, writing, and the occasional group event with my peer group leader, Deborah. She was a TET who had crossed in the fall of 2005. Although I was interested in being a member of her chapter, I didn't bring up my interests with her. Instead, I talked to her about all the things we had in common: Both of our mothers were registered nurses, we both had full scholarships to the university, and we both lacked experience with the opposite sex. I thought that if she saw me as a genuine person and not just as an interest, my chances of becoming a TET would increase.

Every semester all the Greeks on campus came together to host "Meet the Greeks." It was held in two separate rooms: one for the white Greeks and one for the black Greeks. The room for the white fraternities and sororities was set up like a social mixer. Each organization had its own table and interested candidates could walk around eating free pizza while they browsed their options.

In the room for the black Greeks, the room was set up like a court hearing. A panel of members from each organization sat at the front of the room, while the audience's chairs were arranged in long, pew-like rows. Each organization had its own table, but since only eight of the organizations were active on campus, the tables were spread out along the walls of the room. The free pizza sat on tables in the back and would not be offered to the prospective candidates until after the panel discussion, when it was cold and hard.

I hated "Meet the Greeks." It was like a game show where the panel competed to see who could give the vaguest answer. If a person had a question to ask, he or she would write it down on a slip of paper, put it in the question bowl, and wait for the moderator to pull it out and read it off to the Greeks. If a question read, "Do you all haze or pledge?" the answer would be a variation of, "There is a strict anti-hazing policy in place and there are consequences," "I don't know what *pledging* is," or "all of our organizations are non-hazing organizations and we suggest that you go on our websites to see our respective stances on hazing."

If a question read, "How much does it cost to join?" the answer would most likely be, "monetary costs are no cost at all when it comes to how much time, energy, and effort you'll need to put in." If a question read, "What do I need to do if I want to become a member of a sorority," the answer could be one of two things: "Do your research and go to events" or "Let your heart lead you to do what it believes, work hard, and don't do it for the colors." The ultimate question would read, "How long does it take to become a member of a sorority or fraternity?" The answer would be, "Every organization has a different time period. It depends on how much effort you put into the organization you wish to join."

As I sat in my third "Meet the Greeks" affair, I shot "Are you serious?" faces at Candace. We rolled our eyes at the vague responses and clapped in the rare event that a panel member completely answered the question. When the event came to a close we both walked over to the TET table, attempting to get face-time. I walked over to Tiffany and introduced myself.

"So, *you're* Whitney! Well, finally good to meet you in person. How was the rest of your summer?"

"It was pretty good. How was yours?"

"It was great, do you have any questions?"

"Um, well…How has TET changed your life?"

"In the best way ever. Now I have supportive new women in my life and I have the ability to network with thousands of other women from all over the world. Oh wait, excuse me for a minute."

She walked away and joined a group of her line sisters across the room to take photos.

I left.

For the first official book club discussion, I headed to the cathedral dressed in a graphic tee, jeans, and tennis shoes. Although we were told that we could dress comfortably, all the other interests were still wearing business casual.

This time, Latoya and Regina weren't the only TETs at book club—Sasha, Julia, Tiffany, and Britney were all gathered at the front of the room. At 8:08 Julia coughed. "Okay well, welcome to Book Club. Let's go around the room. Give your name, your year, your major, and an interesting fact about Theta Eta Theta Sorority, Incorporated."

I was prepared this time. I had spent two nights in the library going through the university's archive of yearbooks, looking at old chapter photos, and trying to find out what type of service programs the chapter completed in the past. I searched for press releases on the internet and went through the school newspaper's online records. I'd even bought a black Greek history book at Barnes and Noble and memorized fact after fact.

Once again, each of us doled out information about the sorority. At the end of the recitations and history points, Latoya asked, "So, what do you ladies think of the book so far?"
INTEREST #1: I love this book, and I think that the dynamics between the characters, especially the younger sister and the mother are really interesting. I can't wait to read on.
INTEREST #2: Yea, I agree, it's really deep. The poems that the author incorporates at the beginning of each section are *amazing*.
RENEE: (in the phoniest voice ever) Yes, and I can see that this is going to be a very complex story, like the characters are already so *developed.* The premise of the book in general is just *so thought provoking.*

It became apparent that each interest just wanted to impress the TETs by attempting to sound insightful. There was tension in the room and I hated it. I hated listening to Renee change her voice to sound fake when she answered questions. I hated watching interests raise their hands frantically as soon as a question was asked just so they could attract attention, and I hated that I was underdressed once again. I didn't participate in the discussion. I drifted off into thoughts about school.

"Did you know that Amber Jackson had to clean Ivyana's house?" Renee asked me one night.

"What? What do you mean she *had* to? Doesn't Amber have to call her every night already?"

"Well, yea. Ivyana called her and told her that she needed to come over and clean up. Amber thinks that if she doesn't do what Ivyana says she won't get picked for the next line."

"What? That doesn't even sound true!"

"I'm tellin' you, Whit!"

I didn't want to believe Renee. Amber Jackson was my old Biology study partner. We had discussed everything from dating to classes to the fact that both of our mothers pledged TET in undergrad. She was friendly and talkative, but she was dating a member of Nu Alpha Pi named Mike, Ivyana's ex-boyfriend.

"Well, if it is true, do you think Ivyana's just using it as leverage since Amber is dating her ex?" I asked.

"Yep, that's what it seems."

"That's crazy. Are you sure that's true?"

It was true. Amber had been doing more than cleaning Ivyana's house. Ever since she'd shown up to a Greek party in a violet dress, she'd been Ivyana's personal assistant. She'd been printing out her papers, bringing her coffee to class, and treating her to lunch every week. Since she was "wrong" for dating Ivyana's ex, Amber had to make herself seem like a good person in Ivyana's eyes by doing everything that Ivyana said. From what she had been telling Candace and Renee, it seemed to be working.

I didn't understand why Amber would clean Ivyana's house or buy her coffee. It didn't make sense to me. I also had no idea why Renee and Candace were calling the TETs and trying to get their numbers (Renee had five numbers, and Candace had two). I had Tiffany's, Regina's, Julia's, and Deborah's but I didn't plan on calling them. I was just going to continue going to book club, attending their campus events, and saying "Hi," whenever I saw them on the street.

Candace and Renee talked about TET all the time. In my journal I referred to their endless conversations as "interest yakking." Every conversation was centered on prospective interests, pledging predictions, or anything remotely TET related.

Interest yakking had no purpose. No essentially new information was added. There was just the recitation of the same topics and assertions in a different order. In the rare occasion that there was new information to discuss, it added another hour to an already five hour long conversation.

One day while they were discussing which TET numbers they needed to get, Renee turned to me and asked, "So Whitney, have you called Tiffany again?"

"I told you *no* like two weeks ago," I sighed.

"Exactly. It's been two weeks and you still haven't spoken to her since the summer."

"What's your point?"

"Are you trying to be an interest or not?"

"I'm an interest right now. I just have a lot on my mind and my aunt told me not to call them."

"Well, just so you know, they're not going to consider you if you don't call at all. That's what Regina and Tanya told me. I understand that you have a lot on your mind or whatever, but it's about to be October. If they're trying to have a spring line you're going to have to do more than just go to events if you want to make it."

"Okay I just—"

"Whitney, there are like twenty-something girls who want to be TETs. Amber is already doing stuff for Ivyana and other people have started calling them too. And you might want to consider dressing up a bit at events because they look at things like that—at least that's what they've been telling me. I'm not trying to come at you, but you're my friend and if you want to be a TET that bad, I just think these are some things that you should know."

"Well, thanks," I said and continued to listen to her and Candace talk about whose numbers they needed to get.

I really did want to be a TET. But when I dreamed about Theta Eta Theta, I dreamed about volunteering, co-hosting events with both black and white sororities, and being able to belong to a dynamic group of women who were proactive in the community. I never once dreamed of being maimed and abused for weeks at a time.

Yet, at one point I had a change of heart. I thought that there had to be some type of meaning behind the process, that surely it wasn't pure monetary and physical abuse. I thought about all the conversations I'd had with other interests, all the times that I'd tried to rationalize the process. When I asked Amber if she was willing to get slapped to join, she cheerily responded, "Yea, I'll get slapped." When I asked if she was willing to get beat up, she said, "Yes, I'd do anything," without hesitation. Candace expressed the same feelings and Renee never thought twice about anything regarding the process.

I spent several nights searching for books on the internet that could possibly give me a glimpse of someone else's pledge experience, but I didn't find any. All the books were about the history of sororities, hazing incidents that occurred over the years, and fictional assumptions. I purchased ten books, and after I read each book I was disappointed. They didn't tell me anything helpful. The third person narratives of secret worlds, secret lives, secret underground processes, and faulty storylines made my head hurt.

I realized that there was no book that would answer my questions. I was going to have to put my logic to the side. I thought about my mom and my aunt, about the memories they'd revealed to me over the years, and how I wanted that to be me. I thought back to my father's funeral, remembering what his line brothers had said to me after the funeral—how "happy" my father would be if he could look down and see that his daughter was a TET.

I thought that I could extend the familial legacy and gain some kind of connection with my mom and my aunt, especially if I pledged the old school way. I knew that I had the passion to do great things within the organization if I were given the opportunity, and after awhile I pushed my judgment about the pledge process away. I forced myself to think that if other girls made it through the process unscathed, then so could I. I wrote, *Theta Eta Theta...all or nothing,* in my journal and decided that I was going to do whatever it took to get into the Epsilon chapter.

The next day I called Julia at 5:00.

"Hello?" she answered.

"Hello, is this Julia?"

"Yes, this is she. Who is this?"

"This is Whitney...Whitney Gracia Williams."

"How did you get my number Whitney?"

"I got it from Regina over the summer..."

"Hmm, okay. Well, I'm kind of busy now. Could you call me back at 7:08?"

"Okay."

Renee called me thirty minutes later. "Why did you tell Julia that Regina gave you her number?"

"Because she asked me how I got it."

"Well, Regina just called me really upset because Julia asked if it was true and she said no. Then she had to call Julia right back and say yes, because she forgot that she had given it to you because it was so long ago."

"Was I not supposed to do that?"

"I think you were supposed to call in the *summer* when she first gave it to you."

"I didn't know."

"I think you were supposed to be discreet."

"How is telling her own line sister what she did indiscreet?"

"Girl, I don't know. I guess you should have made up a lie."

"As soon as I think this can't get any more illogical, it gets even dumber."

"I'm learning too...You just have to understand that that's how it works."

"So should I call and apologize to Regina? Should I even try to call Julia back?"

"I don't know. I really don't know."

Renee started telling me about the conversations she'd had with other TETs during the week and how "inspiring" they were. She said that she was going to try and set up lunch dates in the next two weeks. After she finished explaining how happy she was about the "oh-so-changed" Epsilon chapter; I got off the phone with her. I wasn't going to let one mistake discourage me. I called Julia back later.

"Hello?"

"Hi, is this Julia?"

"Yea, this is me. How are you Whitney?"

"I'm fine. How are you?"

"I'm great. What's up?"

"I was just calling to ask how your day was going."

"It's going fine. I have a few papers due next week, so I'm trying to get those out of the way."

"What's your major?"

"Right now I'm doing Communications and English Writing, but I'm kind of getting bored with the writing so I may just minor in that and take more advanced communications courses. What's yours?"

Julia and I talked for about an hour. She was friendly and acted as if she was genuinely enjoying the conversation. She instructed me to call her in two days at 8:08.

When she picked up two days later I said, "Hi Julia. How are you doing today?"

She laughed. "Could you call me back and properly address me?"

"Okay," I hung up and redialed her number. "Hi Julia, how are you—"

"Nope. Try it again," she hung up.

I called again. She said hello. I said, "Hi Julia, this is Whitney—"

"Nope. I'm going to give you two minutes. *Think* about it."

I didn't know what to do. I called Renee. "Renee, Julia just hung up in my face because I didn't address her right. I didn't know there were rules about that. What am I supposed to say?"

"You have to say, 'Hello may I speak to.' Tanya just told me that yesterday."

"Okay, thanks. I'll call you back later."

I called Julia again.

"Hello?" she answered as if I was calling her for the first time.

"Hello, may I speak to Julia?"

"Yes, this is Julia. May I ask who's speaking?"

"This is Whitney."

"Hello, Whitney. That's how you are to respond when you call any of my sorors from now on. You never know who might have my phone, so you need to *ask* to speak to me every time. My prophytes were big on establishing protocol. You're lucky you're talking to me first and not them, because they probably wouldn't have given you a second chance—let alone all those chances I gave you, especially since you got my number so easily."

"Okay…"

"How was your day?"

"It was okay. How was yours?"

"It was fine. I didn't really do too much today, just chapter business. Do you have any questions?"

"Um, what made you want to become a TET?"

"Good question. My dad is a member of Theta Phi Theta, and when I was little I used to go to their events with him. This one time when we went to an event, there were women from Theta Eta Theta and I asked him who they were. And he explained to me what a sorority was and told me that Theta Eta Theta was the sorority that set the standard for the other black sororities, just like Theta Phi Theta set the standard for the other black fraternities. So, naturally when I got older I did my research, found out what TET was all about, and decided that it was what I wanted to do."

"When you were applying for colleges did you check to make sure there was a chapter?"

"Oh yea, definitely. Besides finding a school that had my major, I really wanted to be able to find a school where I could join. And I'm so glad I chose to come here because I'm part of a single letter chapter that is almost ninety years old. Like, to have an active *single letter* chapter with such a strong history is really rare, and I'm so happy about that. Do you have any other questions?"

"Well, not really but—"

"Whitney, Whitney, Whitney," she sighed. "I'm going to help you out a little bit. If me or any of my sorors *ever* ask you if you have other questions, then you need to ask more questions. I'm just going to assume that you're calling me because you want to be a member of my organization. That means you need to be trying to get to know the people *in* the organization, like myself, and try to ask about us as much as possible. So, I'm going to ask you again. Do you have any more questions?"

"I…In what way has the organization been beneficial to you?"

"Well, besides the networking with numerous women, I feel like me becoming a part of this sorority has helped me to break out of my shell a bit. Like, I do a lot with programs and I'm able to express my creative ideas and carry them out in an environment where everyone supports me. Can I ask you a question?"

"Yes."

"Why do you want to be a member of my sorority?"

"Well, I've been intrigued by it my whole life. My mom and aunt are members so I was always able to see them do things for the organization. My dad was a Theta too, and when I went to his funeral and saw his line brothers speak about him, it made me feel like the lifetime bond was genuine and I really want to be a part of that."

"Have you researched my sorority?"

"Yes."

"If I were to ask you what our platforms are, would you be able to list them?"

"Yes."

"Okay. Well, you don't have to list them now, but I will say that we are really bent on interests doing their research and not just doing it for familial ties. I'm not saying that you are, but I just want you to know that research is important. I'm already a TET and I try to find new things to learn about my organization on a weekly, if not, daily basis because I'm that passionate about it. Long story short, we're looking for passion and dedication, nothing more, nothing less. If you really want to be a part of Epsilon, you're really going to have to go above and beyond."

My heart skipped. I was going to have to prove myself.

On a Friday afternoon, Julia and I met up for lunch. We sat in a booth near the back of the campus cafeteria. After sharing small talk for thirty minutes, she said, "So, what do you think—rather, what have you *heard* about the Epsilon process?"

"You mean, what happens when you all pledge?"

"Yes."

"Um, you get paddled with wood, you get slapped, you have to do all types of physical activities…Eggs and other things are thrown at you....You have to eat things you wouldn't normally eat...Umm you get beat," I trailed off, trying to remember what I had heard from other interests.

"Well Whitney, much of what you said isn't far from what we do in the Epsilon chapter, but I can assure you that it's done with caution and it's all worth it in the end. And if you're lucky enough to get picked, you'll get to see what I mean."

I was at a loss for words.

"Do you have any questions?"

"Um," I stalled. My brain was still processing the fact that she didn't deny any of the things I listed. I forced myself to think *"all or nothing"* and asked, "Is there anything you regret doing during your process?"

She looked off to the side, as if she were considering a deep thought and didn't speak for a few seconds. She shook her head slowly and then, as if she was the happiest person alive said, "Nope! No regrets, whatsoever!"

"Oh, okay. Did you ever get sick?"

"Did I? Ha! Yea, I did, but I can't really talk about that at this stage. Do you have any illnesses?"

"Well, I have depression and—"

"Oh! Depression, I had that. It's not a big deal though. I took medicine for it. Is yours clinical?"

"I don't think so."

"Well, have you been to the counseling center before?"

"Yea, but the guy I talked to didn't help me at all."

"I think I know who you're talking about. You need to go see Sylvia. She's amazing. I don't go to her anymore, but when I did she helped me to get through a lot of things."

"I'll ask for her if I ever go again."

"Good. Do you see my LSs at that booth over there?" she pointed her fork.

"Yes."

"You should probably be asking for their numbers right now."

"I'm allowed to ask for that when they're all together?"

"Yea, like you have to *use your resources*, Whitney. Three of them are over there right now. Uh, are you going to get up?"

"Oh, sorry. Excuse me for a minute," I slid out of the booth and walked over to where three of her sorors were eating. Latoya and Cari stopped mid conversation when they saw me approaching. Kamille kept looking down at her food.

"Good afternoon ladies."

"Good afternoon," Latoya smiled as she shifted in her seat.

"My name is Whitney Gracia, and I was wondering if I could have each of your numbers?" I pulled out my phone.

"My number is 555-243-5589," Kamille looked up.

"My number is 555-371-9015. Use it." Latoya said.

I looked towards Cari and she sighed. "You can have my number *after* you talk to Latoya. When you talk to her ask her for my number."

"Okay, thank you ladies for your time," I smiled and walked back to Julia's booth.

"Now that that's over with, tell me what you plan on doing with your future."

I was supposed to call Latoya at 3:00 one day. I didn't remember until 3:01, but I decided to call anyway. She didn't answer. I called two more times, and on the second time she picked up.

"Hello?"

"Hello, may I speak to Latoya?"

"This is she."

"Hi Latoya, this is Whitney. Are you available to speak?"

"Yes, I am."

"Okay, how has your day been going?"

"It's going well, how's yours?"

"It's going fine, are you excited about graduating in the spring?"

"Yea, I'm trying to make sure I'm on track for that. If I'm not, I'm pretty sure that I'll only be one or two classes short so I'll still get to walk and I'll finish the other classes in the summer."

"What's your major?"

"I'm majoring in Developmental Psychology."

"Do you know what you're going to do with that?"

"Um, um, I'm not definitely sure yet but maybe I'll teach or go to graduate school. I'm not completely sure yet."

Just as I was about to ask another question, my mom called the other line. I had missed her calls all week and couldn't afford to miss another one. I asked Latoya if I could call her later in the week since "something just came up." She approved and I clicked over.

Later that day, Julia called me. "Whitney, why does my ace have no idea who you are?"

"I don't—"

"Have you called her yet?"

"No, I was going to."

"It's almost been a week and a half. Are you still an interest? If you aren't just let me know so I can stop wasting my time entertaining your questions. I've talked to you twice this week, you have yet to call Kamille, and it's making me look bad."

"I'm sorry, I'll—"

"You need to call her between today and tomorrow. At 9:08 tomorrow you need to call me and give me one interesting fact about my ace."

Click.

I waited about two hours to call Kamille and spoke with her for about forty five minutes.

I was shaking in my seat at book club the next night, nervous about calling Julia with an interesting fact. I sat and suffered as the other interests showed their annoying attention seeking insight on the book. When I checked the time it was almost 9:00 and there were two more discussion questions that had yet to be addressed. Julia had left the meeting earlier, and I figured she wouldn't mind if I called her late since she saw I was in attendance at book club.

At 9:02 my phone vibrated.

JULIA: You still need to find a way to call me at 9:08! Be discreet!

I didn't know what to do. I was too far from the door to causally get up and act as if I was going to the restroom. All the other interests were watching each person's every move, so they'd probably wonder why I left. I could pretend to sneeze and then get up and leave and return with a piece of tissue after I made the call. I could—in mid thought, Latoya announced that book club was going to be cut short and that the remaining questions would be addressed at the next meeting.

As the interests swarmed around the TETs to mingle, I slid out of the room to call Julia. I went up three floors and stood inside an empty classroom. I made sure that no one was walking down the hallway and called.

"Hello?" Julia answered.

"Hello may I speak to Julia?"

"Hi Whitney. Do you have what I asked you for?"

"Yes. An interesting fact about Kamille is that her favorite Disney movie is *Beauty and the Beast*."

"Okay, thank you."

VII. Close-hauled

On October 16, 2007, I turned nineteen. I received text messages and calls all day from people wishing me a happy birthday. Even Julia called me.

I always felt that my birthday was the most important thing that happened in October, but this birthday was different. I was still depressed.

When I went to meet my friends in the cafeteria later that day, I saw Candace and Deborah leaving. Candace walked past me; Deborah approached me outside the entrance.

"Hey," she said. "I finally got my phone fixed, so we can text each other messages about the freshmen group if we need to."

"Okay, I'll remember that. Um…Do you have any free time tomorrow? I was wondering if we could meet up."

"Tomorrow sounds good. How about here at four?"

"Okay I'll see you then."

I texted Candace once Deborah walked away.

ME: So how did it go?
CANDACE: It went okay I think. She was a bit more upfront and intimidating than I expected though.
ME: Really?
CANDACE: Yea, like she was straight to business. She didn't think I understood the process well enough and she asked question after question and it took me a while to come up with answers. I hope she doesn't think I'm slow.
ME: Wow, she doesn't seem like the mean type…
CANDACE: Not mean—she's just really intimidating and in search of straightforward answers.
ME: Deborah is scary :-(

Half an hour later, Candace and my other friends surprised me with a cake and balloons. I blew out the candles, and after I cut the cake I asked Candace if she received my last text about Deborah being scary. She acted as if she had no idea what I was talking about. I went through my phone's outbox and realized that I had actually sent that text to Deborah.

I immediately sent Deborah a text that said, "Oops! I'm sorry, I meant to text you about an event for the freshmen group called 'scary evenings' for next weekend."

That was the worst lie I could have ever come up with, but it was the only thing that I could think of. I was terrified of meeting with her the next day, but I tried to enjoy the rest of my birthday.

I failed.

Despite opening presents and listening to nine different renditions of the happy birthday song, I couldn't think about anything except the next day's meeting with Deborah. I thought my chances of becoming a TET were ruined. I wondered if she would even show up.

The next day I stood outside of the dining hall at 4:00 waiting for Deborah. Five minutes passed. Ten minutes passed. I scrolled down to her name and pressed the call button on my phone.

"Hello?" she answered.

"Hello, may I speak to Deborah?"

"This is she."

"Um, hi this is Whitney. I was wondering if we were still meeting up today?"

"Oh, right. Come outside of the towers and meet me on Fifth Avenue."

I walked outside, but I didn't see her. I stood on the student patio for five minutes and noticed her crossing the street. She came up to the patio, looked at me, and kept walking. A few seconds later she stopped and motioned for me to come to her.

"Someone wants to talk to you," she handed me her phone.

"Hello?" I said.

"So you think my LS is *scary*?"

"No, I—"

"That's what you *said*!"

"I didn't mean to—"

"You didn't mean to? If you didn't mean to, you wouldn't have said it! My LS might be feeling sensitive and she might have taken that to heart. Did you *apologize*?"

"No, I—"

"NO? Oh my god, what's your name?"

"Whitney."

"Okay, *Whitney*. Give my LS her phone back."

I handed Deborah her phone and walked five steps behind her while she finished talking to her LS. We turned the corner to go down another street. When we reached the light, she snapped her phone shut. "Tell me why you felt the need to send me a text that said 'Deborah's scary.' And please don't feed me a bullshit excuse about how it was supposed to be about our peer group."

I sighed. "Well, I was asking my friend how her meeting with you went, and she just said that you were a straight to the business type person, and I interpreted that as intimidating, not necessarily scary."

"But then you added a sad face? What was that supposed to mean?"

"I'm really sorry. I didn't mean it like that."

"Hmmm."

We kept walking. She didn't say anything. We walked past the library, through the park and past the arts building.

She cleared her throat after we made it near the Carnegie museum, "You know, I actually liked you. When Julia told me that she had spoken and met with you I didn't know how to react. On the one hand, I was like 'Oh, yea Whitney seems cool. She seems like a nice girl.' But on the other hand, I was like 'Why didn't Whitney ever express her interest to me?' I mean we've been here for what—six weeks or so? I've seen you at our freshmen group events, we've ridden the bus together to get stuff for the events, and now all of a sudden I'm *scary*? I don't know what to think of you now, but I have to give everyone—no wait, I don't *have* to give you anything, but I like to give everybody a chance."

She led me over to a wooden table that was underneath a row of trees. She took off her purple and green scarf and began wringing and twisting it between her hands.

"So, let's get started. Why do you want to be a member of Theta Eta Theta Sorority Incorporated?"

"Well, my mom is a member of the sorority, and my dad was a member of Theta Phi Theta so I've grown up seeing the positive things that the organization does, and I want to be a part of that. I also want to be a part of a sisterhood and have women who I can depend on no matter what."

"Why do you want to join the *Epsilon* chapter?"

"Because the Epsilon chapter is very active on campus, and you all do a great deal of community service."

"But you could join any other organization on campus and do lots of community service. There are also hundreds of other organizations that are very active on campus. What's so special about us?"

"I just feel that there's no other group on campus that I could join that shares my ideals about service and sisterhood and offers lifelong membership."

"Actually, there are *three* other sororities that offer lifelong membership. Why not Mu Beta Xi? Why not Beta Phi Chi? Why not Pi Upsilon Tau?"

"Well, I feel that Theta Eta Theta set the standards for the rest of the black sororities. Like, if it hadn't have been for Theta Eta Theta, the members who left to form Mu Beta Xi wouldn't have had a model to follow. And besides that, I just feel that the programs that Mu Beta Xi has are focused on five set issues, whereas Theta Eta Theta changes its platform every four years. As far as Beta Phi Chi goes, I think that it's a wonderful sorority and they do a lot of great things, like March of Dimes and community service with children, but I know that my heart doesn't love that organization. For Pi Upsilon Tau, I feel that their main focus is education, and while that's a great platform to have, I'm just not interested."

"Hmmm, okay. When did your mom cross?"

"Spring '84."

"Is she active?"

"No."

"Is anyone else in your family a member?"

"My aunt, my cousins—"

"Is your aunt active?"

"Yes."

"Hmm. Did either of them, like your mom or your aunt, tell you anything about their processes?"

"Well, my mom never really goes into too much detail, but my aunt and cousins told me things about having to eat raw eggs and do all kinds of stuff."

"What kinds of stuff?"

"Stuff like work out, dress alike, eat grapes out of the toilet, get pushed and shoved, eat things like—"

"Okay, that's enough. I just wanted to know if you had any idea about what you were possibly getting yourself into. Do you talk to your friend Candace about this stuff?"

"Yea."

"Does she know what might happen to her if she's selected for a process? She told me her grand mom pledged, her aunt pledged, and her mom did grad, but does she have any idea what *pledging* is? I felt like she had no clue yesterday."

"I think she was just nervous."

"Well, how do *you* feel about pledging? What is the purpose of pledging?"

"I think the purpose of pledging is to learn information about the organization and to form a bond between the new members, to teach them how to work under pressure and to instill selflessness and sisterhood."

She unfolded her scarf and playfully dragged it along the table's surface. "Do you know what we're sitting on? What kind of material is this?"

"Um, wood."

"How do you feel about that?"

"I—"

"Do you think taking wood is a necessary part of pledging?"

"Well, I think that in order to build trust on a line, there has to be some sort of stressor put on the system so…"

"Good. Being paper is not what Epsilon is about. I was originally brought in paper and it was the worst feeling in the world. There were fourteen of us and we were going to pledge but there was a whole lot of mess and confusion so we crossed in three days. But that wasn't enough for me. I didn't feel a bond with any of them. It felt like we were just members of a club doing community service, not a *sisterhood*. So, me and six other girls went back and pledged and I'm so happy I did that. We don't always get along, but I know that at the end of the day all those girls have my back."

"Do you still talk to the girls who were on the paper line?"

She laughed. "Actually, like a few weeks after I crossed with my real LSs I was at the mall and I saw this girl that looked really familiar. I couldn't figure out where I knew her from so I kind of snuck glances of her here and there. Then I realized that she was one of the girls who was on the paper line with me. Me and Ivyana laughed a long time about that. Anyway, if you're really serious about being a member of my organization and this chapter, you're going to need to work a lot harder. You've only spoken to three members and there are more than three of us in the chapter. Do you have any other questions?"

"Well, if you don't mind my asking, were there two separate probates? Like, did you have one when you crossed as paper and one when you pledged?"

"No. We got done like right around finals week and we were all too tired for a show. Being 'made' was enough."

"Do you think the process helped you to become a better person?"

"Definitely, there's no other process like it on this campus. I don't know how many times I've looked back and said, 'I'm so glad I was lucky enough to have a process.' It challenged me to do a lot of things. It pushed my mind and body to the limit. You'll be amazed at how much you can accomplish if you get picked. It's surreal, especially since our process is so demanding. My prophytes made us work extra hard and I respect them so much for that. That's why we prefer small lines. There's no way to facilitate a bond with twenty or more girls on a line."

"Can I ask you a question about your prophytes?"

"Sure."

"I'm not trying to sound like a Face book stalker or anything, but I noticed that there were like fifteen or sixteen girls that crossed before your line, but only six of them have wall to wall conversations and lots of photos with each other. Is that because they went back and pledged too?"

"Wow, I didn't see that coming. Technically, I guess you could say that. If you ever get the chance to talk to them one day they might give you the entire story behind that. On another note, I meant to bring this up earlier but you need to be careful in how you talk to my sorors and how you address them. We all know everything that an interest says or does to one of us in a matter of minutes. Meaning that if someone tells you to call at 3:00 and you call at 3:01, that's not making a good impression. When it's time to evaluate things we keep stuff like that in mind. Do you understand?"

"Yes."

"Good. How do you feel about Amber Jackson?"

"She's cool."

"How well do you know her?"

"We used to study for Biology together last year, but now that we're not in the same class we don't talk as often."

"I see. Well, maybe you all should start talking again. You know, help each other out. Tell her that she doesn't have to speak so loudly when she talks to one of us."

"Okay."

"Are you friends with Vanessa?"

"Yea, we're okay," I said, although I only knew that Vanessa was a sophomore who was genuinely insightful when she spoke, and always answered every question in a politically correct manner.

"You should tell her that asking for one of my neo's numbers in the campus computer lab is not the way to be discreet. That was a bad idea; you never know who is watching. You interests should be trying to put your best foot forward individually, but it doesn't hurt to help each other out here or there. You know Whitney, I think I might actually like you as an interest, but that doesn't mean I'm going to be extra nice to you since we're in the same peer leader group. You're going to have to find a way to get more of my sorors numbers because you're way behind in the game; you're going to have to work harder. Don't do anything stupid like wearing our colors or any other organization's colors to our events, or going around telling everyone that you're interested. I need to see you at *every* event, I need to hear about how well-researched you are from my sorors, and I need to get the impression that you're capable of following directions and being trusted."

"Okay, I'll try to—"

"No, don't *try*. Do it."

After talking to Deborah everything made sense. The process was necessary. I wanted to pledge, I wanted to earn my letters, and I wanted to be respected.

I became obsessed with everything regarding Theta Eta Theta and the Epsilon chapter. I stayed up late every night, interest yakking with Candace and Renee. I started to ask for the TETs' numbers when I saw them walking around campus. I wrote down everything they said into my journal, committed interesting facts to my memory, and incessantly dreamed that one day I would be a TET.

During the week of October 22, 2007, the TETs held a week devoted to breast cancer awareness: Monday was the breast cancer forum, Tuesday was crafts night, Wednesday was the yogurt eating contest, and Friday was movie day with a pink rally in the afternoon. In addition to those events, on Monday and Wednesday they planned to sell pink breast cancer wristbands in the student lobby.

I signed up to participate in both of the tabling sessions, thinking that all I would have to do was sign the attendance book and buy a couple of wristbands since the TETs preached discretion so fervently. Yet, I quickly learned that logically thinking about anything regarding the Epsilon chapter was pointless.

I arrived to the table, dressed in a hoodie and gray painter's pants. Renee, Candace, and four other interests, who were all nicely dressed, stood in front of it yelling at the passersby, begging them to buy bracelets.

Julia was the only TET present and she sat behind the table reading a book, only lifting her head at a point of sale to put collected money into the box. I sold about ten bracelets before asking Renee, "If no one's supposed to know that we're interested, why the hell are we standing in front of a table that says Theta Eta Theta and selling pink bracelets?"

"Hey, you gotta do what you gotta do," Renee sighed.

"That wasn't the question I asked you," I laughed.

"I don't know girl. Just lie if somebody walks by and asks you about it."

"They made the interests do the selling last time remember?" Candace chimed in. "Why would you expect this time to be different?"

I flashed back. In September the TETs had held a fundraiser for Rita's ice cream discount cards. I probably didn't notice that we were doing the actual selling because a few of the TETs were selling as well. Or maybe I didn't notice because I was too intimidated by Tanya, who came up to the table on three separate occasions just to say, "I hope you all know what you're getting yourselves into." She also threw out hints about missing Theta Eta Theta events, saying, "If you ever can't make it to an event and you consider yourself a *serious* interest, I suggest you email the sorority account to let us know. Leave a paper trail. If your name isn't in the signature book, it needs to be in our inbox."

Minutes later, Amber Jackson and Ivyana walked into the lobby. Ivyana smiled at each of us and said, "They should get here soon," to Julia. She wrote down a few characters on a sheet of paper and handed it to Amber. "Could you go to the computer lab and print off more flyers? This is my username and password. Use this so you don't have to use up your own paper."

"Okay, be right back," Amber said as she walked away.

In that moment, I wanted to be in Amber's shoes—doing things for the TETs so that I would make line. There she was, calling Ivyana every night and running small errands, while I had yet to speak to Ivyana, let alone get her number.

I knew that asking for Ivyana's number at an event in front of other interests was out of the question, so I continued to solicit bracelet sales for the rest of the afternoon.

Subject:	Missed Event (Paint for the Cure)
From:	wgw██████edu
Date:	Tue, October 23, 2007 4:27 pm
To:	██████1908@yahoo.com
Priority:	Normal

Options: View Full Header | View Printable Version

Hello ladies of [Theta Eta Theta] Sorority, Incorporated,

I will not be able to attend tonight's event "Paint For The Cure," due to a mandatory forum for [freshmen peer] leaders, of which I am a part of---
I hope tonight's event goes well, and I am looking forward to the rest of this week's events---
Have a great day,
Whitney Gracia

VIII. Adrift

I remember waking up with a migraine, an unrelenting ache in my head that became more painful with each new thought. I remember crying, crying for no reason at all.

I went to the campus counseling center and asked to see a therapist. The receptionist didn't look up at me when she said that they were full for the day and that she would gladly schedule me for an appointment for the next week.

"No. I need to see someone *today*. It's important," I heard myself say.

She looked up at me, probably noticed that my eyes were bloodshot, that there were tears streaming down my face and said, "Okay, how about in an hour? Sylvia is the only one available today."

"That's fine," I said and walked to the nearest stairwell. I didn't want to be around anyone. I needed to be alone. I sat in the stairwell and waited.

Sylvia introduced herself to me later and led me into a small office. She closed the door and said, "So, what's going on Miss Whitney? Why are you here today?"

"I think I'm depressed."

"Okay. Is there something that has happened recently that brought this about?"

"I don't know."

"Alright, well walk me through this year. Tell me some of the major things that have happened in your life."

"I lost my father last semester."

"I'm sorry to hear that."

"It didn't hit me until last month. Like, I went to his funeral, I was there and I saw him. I saw his body in the casket, but it didn't...It didn't hit me that he was really gone until last month," she handed me a box of Kleenex. "And um, this guy I used to really like hurt my feelings this semester, and I'm just out of it. I can't really concentrate in any of my classes, except the writing one. I just don't care about a lot of things anymore. This is going to sound really dumb, but the only thing I'm actually excited about is TET."

"Oh, you're a member of that sorority?"

"No, I'm trying to be."

"I see. Well Whitney, you definitely seem to have a lot going on. Tell me a little more about your dad."

"What about him?"

"Did you have a relationship with him?"

I hated that question. I hated knowing the answer and I hated having to say it aloud.

"No."

"Were you all ever close at any point? Like during your childhood?"

"I didn't have a childhood."

"What do you mean?"

"My childhood ended when I was nine."

"Do you feel like he was a contributing factor to—"

"He walked out on us. He left us and he never came back. He promised that he would show up for birthdays and holidays, but he rarely did. At one point he was there for me, but not when I needed him the most. And now he's gone for good."

"Do you feel that he's a factor in your depression? Do you ever think about him?"

"Now that he's dead, yea. I wonder 'what if' a lot."

"Well, before he died did you think about him?"

"I hated him. I wrote this poem about how I'd never forgive him and I put it on Face book. He was shot to death the same day I posted the poem."

"You don't think it's your fault do you?"

"I don't."

"When you found out he died, did you cry?"

"Yea, for a week. Then I moved on."

"I see. And what about this guy that hurt your feelings this semester? Are you hurt because it didn't work out?"

"I guess I'm hurt at the fact that I trusted him so easily. I shouldn't have done that. I just wanted a supportive male friend because that's always been a void in my life. I usually don't trust guys that easily. But since I liked him, I let my guard down and my emotions got screwed up."

"Can you be more specific? What exactly happened?"

I sighed. "We pretty much talked all summer. I liked him a whole lot, but then I found out he'd messed with a lot of other people and he lied to me about it. He didn't care about me half as much as I cared about him. I almost had sex with him and I'm glad I didn't, but it still hurts because he doesn't understand why I'm upset. I trusted him too much."

"Did you ever try and talk to him about it?"

"Yea, but he doesn't care and I don't care to talk to him about it anymore."

"Did you ever grieve about your father for more than those few days you cried last semester?"

"No. I didn't want to think about him."

"Is your mother remarried?"

"Yea."

"Do you feel like your stepdad is a good father figure?"

"He is, but—"

"But what?"

"I don't want to talk about it."

"Alright, well tell me about what has been making you happy. Tell me about the sorority."

"Okay, I wouldn't necessarily say 'happy' but it keeps my mind off everything else. I mean, a lot of the things involved in being an interest are stupid, but they keep me going."

"What kind of things do you have to do?"

"I just have to call them and get to know them. Like, since they were founded in 1908, I have to call them on the 08, or 38, or on any eight. And I just have to meet up with them over lunch so they can get to know me better."

"So you really want to be a member?"

"Definitely."

"Why?"

"Well it's been in my family and everyone always had such nice things to say about their experiences so I want to be a part of it too. Plus, I do community service a lot and since that's one of the major things that they focus on, I think I'd enjoy it very much."

"I have somewhat of an idea about what goes on in sororities. Do you think it will trigger more depression if you get chosen for the pledge process?"

"I really don't think so. I think I'd be happier because I would be getting what I wanted."

She asked more questions and I found myself wanting to tell her everything that I had been feeling since freshman year, but I couldn't bring myself to say it right then. I couldn't bring myself to admit to anything. She seemed genuine, but I knew that one therapy session wasn't enough to make me completely trust her. I promised her that I would come back regularly for the rest of the semester.

In the last minutes of the session, she asked if I had a hobby that would ease my mind and help me to pinpoint why I felt the way I felt. I told her I liked to write and she suggested that I use that method to get my feelings out.

10/31/2008 Dear Journal, My father used to be great. Before he was dishonorably discharged from the military, before he was strung out on cocaine, before he started stealing—he was a good guy. When he left, I didn't think about him too much unless he said that he was going to stop by and he usually let me down. The drugs changed him. They made him yell at me, they made him hit me, they made him hurt me.

But he used to be a good guy.

IX. Grounding

Subject:	Missed Bookclub meeting
From:	wgw████████edu
Date:	Thu, November 1, 2007 3:40 pm
To:	████████1908@yahoo.com
Priority:	Normal
Options:	View Full Header	View Printable Version

Hello ladies of [Theta Eta Theta] Sorority, Incorporated.

    I will not be in attendance at the Bookclub meeting tonight due to my [freshman peer group] group event at Alumni Hall. I am enjoying the book, and will contribute to the discussion at the next Bookclub meeting.

Have an amazing day,
Whitney-Gracia

It was November and although I was depressed, I was hoping that I was putting in enough work to be considered for sorority membership. I was navigating my way through the game of being an interest. I taped a list of the fourteen Epsilon chapter members and a calling chart to the back of my closet wall. I stalked them outside of lecture halls, parking lots, and coffee shops to get their numbers. I called each of them multiple times during the week, wrote down all of their interests and activities in my notebook, and attempted to meet each of them in person.

I even developed a system: With the exception of a few TETs, I absolutely abhorred talking to them on the phone. So, after about ten minutes of talking, I would say, "I was wondering if you wanted to go out to lunch with me sometime this week?" The answer would always be "yes," a time and place would be set, and the phone conversation would come to an end.

I had spoken with everyone except Ivyana and Sasha. I still didn't have Ivyana's number and whenever I called Sasha she would blatantly hit ignore, or pick up and say, "I don't feel like talking on the phone," and hang up in my face.

Candace, Renee, and I pieced together more information about the pledge process and the Epsilon chapter history from upperclassmen and other black Greeks. We learned that "pre-pledging" meant going to late night study sessions, and that if interests were selected for study sessions, they would likely be on line when pledging began.

The Epsilon chapter had been previously suspended for hazing a couple of years ago, and the current graduate advisor had actually pledged in the chapter during the 1970s. While we were never told exact details about the pledge process, it was made clear that the Epsilon chapter "went hard."

One day while I was meeting with Latoya at a coffee shop, she brought up the fact that I hadn't spoken to Ivyana. She said, "It's good that you've been speaking to most of my line and calling us, but Ivyana is my prophyte and she has a lot of say in who gets into our chapter and who doesn't. Why haven't you talked to her?"

"I don't have her number."

"Why?"

"Every time I see her she's busy."

"What do you mean *every time you see her?*"

"Well, for the past three weeks I've waited inside the New Balance store that's right next to the business hall every afternoon. On some days I wouldn't see Ivyana come out of the building, but on the days that I did she'd be walking with someone else, talking on her phone, or around too many people. That's kind of why I don't have her number yet."

"Ummm, you know what? I'm just going to give you her number okay? I'll tell her that I gave it you when I talk to her tonight."

"Okay."

I called Ivyana as soon as I returned to my room and left a voicemail. I called her for a week straight and she never answered.

One Wednesday while I was eating before class, she called me.

"Hello?" I answered.

"Hi. May I ask who this is? I've noticed this number on my caller ID for the past few days."

"This is Whitney."

"Whitney who?"

"Um, Whitney Gracia Williams."

"Oh. What do you want? And how did you get my number?"

"I was wondering if I could meet with you to talk. I got your number from Latoya. Is that alright?"

"No. I would have preferred that you got it from me personally, but you already have it and there's not much I can do. Where are you?"

"I'm in the cathedral."

"Do you have a class soon?"

"No," I lied.

"Good. Meet me at Market Central now."

Click.

I put my tray away and rushed over to the cafeteria. Ivyana looked annoyed when I arrived. I swiped my card so that she and I could enter.

"I want to sit in a booth," she said.

After following her around the dining hall for a few minutes, she picked a table and looked back at me. "Here's one, but it's dirty."

I resisted the urge to roll my eyes and used a napkin to knock the crumbs onto the floor.

"Thanks," she said as she slipped out of her jacket. "Be back in a minute."

I went to the fruit station and filled my plate with pineapples. I thought about the excuse I would have to give my teacher for missing that day's class, and hoped that my meeting with Ivyana would be brief. When I returned to the table she was sitting down with a bowl of stir fry.

"So, how is your day going, Whitney?" she asked.

"It's going well. How's yours?"

"It's fine. What's your major?"

"English Writing for now but I'm going to double in Communications eventually and maybe minor in Film."

"What do you plan on doing with that when you graduate?"

"Well, I want to write screenplays so I'm hoping to go to grad school and develop my screenwriting skills better."

"That's interesting," she said dryly. "Why do want to be a member of Theta Eta Theta Sorority, Incorporated?"

"I want to be a member because I—"

"Better yet, save that. Tell me everything you know about my organization."

"You mean the chapter or the national history?"

"Whatever you know."

"Um, well I know that there were twenty founders—"

"There were *twenty* founders? *Really*?"

"Technically, no…Weren't there nine? Yea, there were nine in the original group and seven were invited to join without initiation and weren't there four incorporators?"

"Are you *asking* me or are you *telling* me?"

"I'm telling you. Sorry."

"Continue."

"Okay, um, it was founded in January 1908, and incorporated in 1913…The first national president was—"

"What year was my chapter chartered?"

"Um—"

"*Um* is not a year."

"1918."

"Okay. I know that you've spoken to a lot of my other sorors, and from them I've gathered what type of individual you are so there's really no need to get into any of that. Do you have any experience with programming?"

"Yea, when I was in high school I helped to coordinate events."

"So you have *no* experience with programming."

"No, I do. Right now I'm involved with the freshman peer leaders group and I have to come up with events and set up an itinerary and budget and find ways to advertise it so that the students will come out."

"So you have *minimal* experience with programming," she sighed. "What do you think it means to be a TET?"

"I think it means that you have high morals and are not only passionate about academics and community service, but you have a deep desire to be part of a group of women who are supportive and like a family."

"Do you think you'll be able to keep up with the image that me and my sorors have on this campus?"

"Yes," I said, immediately regretting that I was wearing a blue hoodie with blue and white Air Force Ones.

"Good, because we have an image to uphold and if you're *lucky* enough to get into my chapter I don't need you to be walking around looking busted. Tell me, why did you feel that you had to get my number from Latoya? Why couldn't you get it from me?"

"I attempted to get it from you, but I couldn't."

"Why? I don't remember you ever asking me for it."

"Well, I know you have a class in the business hall in the afternoons. I stood inside of the New Balance store that's right next to it and I waited for you to come out for three weeks straight. Every time I saw you, you'd be walking with someone else or on your phone and I didn't want to be indiscreet. So, when I met with Latoya last week and she asked if I had talked to you, I told her why I hadn't and she gave me your number."

She put her hand on her chest and laughed. "That's hilarious, but that's really creepy Whitney—really *really* creepy. But, it worked in your favor I guess. Have you ever eaten the stir fry here?"

I spoke to Ivyana for a half hour more, asking questions about her plans after graduation and listening to her talk about the difference between genuine and generic stir fry. She said she hoped to see my name on her call log more often and that I should consider dressing up when I came to events. After receiving a phone call, she told me I was free to leave.

On my way out I saw Teresa, another interest, walking into the dining hall.

"I still don't have Sasha's number," Candace moped over dinner.

"It's not like she answers her phone anyway. I thought you went to go get it today though."

"I did. I stood across the street from her daycare job in the rain for the second time this week. I stood out there for about two hours and she never came out. What's worse is that one of the parents walked towards me and was like, 'Excuse me, are you okay?' And I was like, Yea, I'm just waiting on my nephew to come out."

"I think you should just take the 'L' on that one," I laughed. "That was creepy."

"You should talk. I'm still kind of worried that they won't pick me because of that comment I made to Julia and Britney a few weeks ago."

"When you said getting hit was your worst case scenario?"

"Yea! Ugh! I hope that doesn't mess my chances up! I know I'm going to get hit if I make the line. I was just nervous when I met with them. Julia can be intense sometimes. Did anyone ask you what your worst case scenario was?"

"Yea, Deborah did. I told her it would be being made to jump off the top of a building."

Candace shook her head. "You would say that. Have you made calls today?"

"I called Tiffany and thanked God it went straight to her voicemail."

"You're horrible, Whitney."

"I know," I laughed.

It became apparent that Candace, Renee, and I had different methods of being interests. While Candace called the TETs consistently and kept a record of each call, the length of every conversation, and everything that was said to her in a hidden document on her computer, Renee relied on calling three times a week or more, dressing up when she met with them, and leaving long, "thoughtful" voicemails in the event that they didn't answer her calls.

In fact, one night while we were all discussing TET in Candace's room, Renee made a call to Ivyana. When Ivyana didn't pick up she said, "Hi Ivyana, this is Renee Royalton. I was just calling to speak with you. I hope you're enjoying your day and I just wanted to let you know that they're serving hummus today in the cafeteria. I know you like hummus, so you'd probably enjoy your meal if you ate there tonight. Have a nice day, goodbye!"

I, on the other hand, considered myself to be "the worst interest ever." I called frequently and went out to lunch dates, but I couldn't bring myself to dress up for book club or weekly events. Still, I felt that my chances of being selected for the rumored spring line were decent. I had only made a few mistakes and the TETs were only occasionally rude to me.

For other interests, this wasn't the case: Amber Jackson was repeatedly ridiculed, harassed, and made to buy things for Ivyana. There was an interest that was made to delete all of the TET numbers because the TETs told her that she was wasting her time. There was another interest the TETs blatantly ignored at book club, despite all her attempts to impress them. And then there was Vanessa, the girl Deborah asked me to help out weeks earlier. She had been going around under the assumption that the TETs would never harm an interest that pledged.

Late in the semester Vanessa came up to me in the dining hall. "Whitney, you're interested in TET right?"

"Yea, aren't you too?"

"Yes, but I'm really confused about some things."

"What do you mean?"

"I heard that they have some type of process where the girls actually get hit. Do you know if that's true or not?"

I looked over my shoulders and motioned for her to sit down with me at a table. "It's true."

"Like, they get beat up?"

I sighed. I told Vanessa everything I had learned about the Epsilon process. I told her the process was necessary and the Epsilon chapter was into building strong bonds with every line that came through.

At the end of our conversation I told her that she needed to start talking to the TETs. Although Candace suggested against it, I promised Vanessa that I would help her to get their numbers.

I attended event after event, book club after book club. I continued to call and meet with the TETs every week, but there was still no announcement of an interest meeting or a formal rush.

Phone calls and conversations became redundant. Book club became a chore. Tiffany and Sasha would show up late, interrupt the discussion, and ask questions about the assigned readings because they hadn't read the book. They would talk over certain interests and ridicule people's interesting facts.

There were no community service projects, there were no enjoyable events. Each event was geared towards intimidating interests, and each interested candidate was always on her best behavior.

In December, the TETs started hosting study sessions. I became excited. I thought that these were the study sessions that occurred during pre-pledging. They weren't.

We were all asked to give an interesting fact at the beginning of each session, and we studied and chatted over refreshments. At the last study session of the semester, Sasha closed the door to the room and said, "A lot of y'all have been calling and meeting up with us a lot this semester. But just to let y'all know, some of you all are going to be disappointed in the results next semester. Have a good break."

I was tired of being an interest. Over Christmas break I called all of the TETs twice in one week and refused to call again until I returned to Pittsburgh. When my aunt asked about the sorority, if I had been calling the members against her previous advice, I lied and said no.

I wrote down numerous lists of who I thought would make the rumored Spring Line and became frustrated each time I looked at them. I knew that Renee, Candace, and Amber Jackson would make line for sure. I'd seen Teresa at most of their events and I assumed she would make the cut. Mya, a fellow English Writing major never talked with me much about interest things, but I had a feeling that she would be chosen. Vanessa was a nice girl, so I assumed that they would pick her as well. I prayed that I would make it, but there were still twenty other girls that I was competing against and each time I made a list I chose one of them over me.

Before returning to Pittsburgh, I changed my image a bit. I dyed my hair jet black and cut sharp bangs in the front. I tried to dress up at least once a week. I replaced my old phone and changed my ringtone to Gwen Stefani and Eve's "Rich Girl." I didn't know it then, but in a few weeks the "*If I was a rich girl—na-na-na-na-na-na*" sound of the chorus would almost always mean that I was about to do something for a TET.

X. Seaworthy

I went the first week of January without calling any TETs, and I planned to go for another until Tiffany pulled me to the side and said, "Whitney, I haven't heard from you in a while. Fix that."

Subject:	R.S.V.P. -- Pink Rose Tea
From:	wgw███████edu
Date:	Wed, January 9, 2008 6:37 pm
To:	█████1908@yahoo.com
Priority:	Normal
Options:	View Full Header	View Printable Version

```
Hello ladies of [Theta Eta Theta]Sorority,
Incorporated,
     I'm writing this email in response to the
email sent about receiving free admission to the
Pink Rose Tea event. I would like to reserve a spot
for this event.

Thank you all very much,
Whitney Gracia Williams
```

For the Pink Rose Tea event, I actually dressed up. I wore a black skirt with a black and beige blouse, pantyhose, and heels. The TETs were dressed in white skirt suits with the exception of Ivyana who chose to wear a colored tweed suit.

The event took place in a dining room in the athletic building on a Saturday morning. The room featured tables dressed in white table cloths and formal dishes with faux ivy centerpieces. Each table seated seven to eight interests, a current member from the Epsilon chapter, and a woman who had crossed in the chapter decades ago.

Sitting at my table was an older TET who held her PhD in biochemistry. She talked to our table about how determined she had to be to get through graduate school and how hard she had to work to have her career. She was proud to be a TET and she encouraged us all to pursue membership because, "There's nothing like having a soror."

We learned proper dining room etiquette, listened to an inspirational speaker, and applauded Kamille's rendition of "I Believe I Can Fly."

After the event I called Tiffany and three other TETs so that they could see that I was still interested. When the time of their centennial celebration event was made known to the public, I thanked god I had a night class. I nearly jumped for joy when it was announced that the new semester of book club conveniently fell on the other night that I had class.

Subject:	Missing Event-Founders Day
From:	wgw████edu
Date:	Tue, January 15, 2008 5:52 pm
To:	████1908@yahoo.com
Priority:	Normal
Options:	View Full Header	View Printable Version

```
Hello ladies of [Theta Eta Theta] Sorority,
Incorporated,
        I will be unable to attend tonight's event
that showcases the centennial mark of your
organization's founding due to a night class. I
hope that the event goes well, and I'm looking
forward to the other
events that are planned for this week--

Have an amazing day and an amazing event,
Whitney  Gracia
```

On the night of February 1, 2008, I was hanging in towers lobby with my friends discussing plans for a Super bowl party. I heard my phone, "*If I was a rich girl-na-na-na-na-na-na-na.*" It was Julia.

"Whitney where are you?" she asked.

"I'm in towers lobby."

"You have eight minutes to get to the lecture building. Room 5500," she hung up.

I told my friends that I would be right back and walked away. As soon as I was outside I raced across the crosswalk to the lecture building. The door was locked.

I ran back across the crosswalk, down two sets of steps, across the street, and towards the front entrance of the building. I ran to the elevators and punched "5." When the doors opened, I had two minutes left and I was on the wrong side of the floor. I dashed to the other side as fast as I could.

I found the room and knocked on the door. After hearing someone say, "Come in," I walked in and noticed that the TETs were all sitting around a rectangular shaped table. I heard them whispering, "What is that on her head?" and "Why is she wearing that?" as I made my way towards the empty chair that stood near the end of the table. I plopped down out of breath.

"Whoa, whoa, whoa. I need you to get up and leave," Tiffany said. "Go out there, get some water, take a few breaths, and then come back in the room *without* the attitude."

I went to the hallway water fountain, took a few sips of water, and re-entered the room.

TIFFANY: Much better.

IVYANA: Why are you here?

ME*: Because you called me.

IVYANA: What?

ME*: Because you called me.

IVYANA: Well, duh. We know that we called you, but *why* are you here?

ME*: Because…I want to be a member of your organization?

LATOYA: Why?

TIFFANY: You don't *sound* like you want to be a member of my organization. You don't seem excited or anything.

DEBORAH: Maybe it's her coat. Take off your coat, get comfortable.

SASHA: Do you plan on answering the question my number three just asked you?

ME*: (sliding out of my coat) I'm sorry. I mean, I want to be a member of your organization because I have a passion for community service, I want to be a part of a sisterhood, and I want to form a lifetime bond with a group of women and be able to inspire and help other young women through various programs.

JULIA: Boring!

TIFFANY: Yea, I need you to come harder. Come on, Whitney. You can do better than that. Did you even *mention* the sisterhood part, did you even—

ME*: I did mention the sisterhood part.

TIFFANY: Oh, well I didn't hear you, so you need to—

DEBORAH: Yo! She just put you in your place Tiffany! You didn't catch that? CHECKMAAAATE! She said, "I *did* mention the sisterhood part!"

ME*: I didn't mean—

DEBORAH: Wowwww!

SASHA: See? *Attitude.* I told y'all.

IVYANA: Wait, wait, wait. This isn't the Whitney I met over lunch weeks ago, because I actually *liked* that Whitney. I don't know who this hood chick is that you're tryna' be right now, but the old Whitney needs to come back. Quick.

TIFFANY: What's your GPA?

ME*: This past semester or overall?

TIFFANY: Both.

ME*: It's a 3.0 for overall and a 3.2 for the last semester.

BRITNEY: (writing on a notepad) How many credits are you taking this semester?

ME*: Fifteen.

BRITNEY: What activities are you going to be involved in?

ME*: The newspaper staff, freshman peer mentor group, and community service.

BRITNEY: Okay, thank you.

REGINA: Why do you want to be a member of the Epsilon chapter?

DEBORAH: Better yet, what do you feel that you would contribute to my chapter?

ME*: I'm very creative—

DEBORAH: So am I.

ME*: I'm good at writing, so if there was ever a need to write up an event I could—

SASHA: So you can create *arts and crafts*?

ME*: I mean, not literally arts and crafts, but I'm really good at designing things.

SASHA: Righhhhttt.

REGINA: Could you answer my question please? The one about why you want to be a member of *this* chapter. Why not grad school? Why not at another chapter?

ME*: I mean, I really want to have the undergrad experience, and I feel that there's more bonding and abilities to have a presence on campus at this level. I also want to be able to experience bonds with the people who are currently in the chapter.

REGINA: Okay, thanks.

TIFFANY: That sounded *rehearsed*. But anyway, what do you know about the Epsilon process?

ME*: I—

IVYANA: And tone down the attitude please.

SASHA: *Please.*

ME*: Um…

IVYANA: What do you know about the Epsilon process?! It's not a trick question!

ME*: Um, there are wood beatings.

IVYANA: Wood beatings! Do we look like *barbarians?*

DEBORAH: Whitney just wants a process! She doesn't care which organization she joins, she just wants a process!

TIFFANY: You're a mess Whitney. Speaking of *mess*, what is that thing on your head?

ME*: It's a hat.

IVYANA: We know it's a hat. *Why* is it on your head?

ME*: I had an EEG scan earlier this week and I didn't get the chance to wash out my hair.

TIFFANY: Please, her hair always looks like it belongs under a hat.

IVYANA: Just leave Whitney.

SASHA: And please work on this word called humility. Wait. Before you leave, what's the definition of humility?

ME*: It means humbling yourself and being modest...um—

LATOYA: You're just saying the same thing over and over! You're wasting our time. Just leave.

TIFFANY: Yea, we're not impressed with you.

> *I put on my coat and headed towards the door.*

JULIA: And you need to leave better than the way you came in!

*I looked back and said, "Thank you ladies very much"
before closing the door and leaving the lecture hall.*

Knowing that Vanessa and Mya had already been called by
the TETs, I met with them in the basement of a dorm.
VANESSA: So, I'm pretty sure that my chances of being a TET
here are shot.
ME: Why?
VANESSA: Because I laughed during the interview, and they kept
making fun of me.
MYA: They told me that I had no personality and that I didn't
know how to think for myself. Like, Vanessa's interview was first
and mine was right after. They asked me what I would do if my
roommates started asking questions about where I was late at night
and I said, "I'll just tell them I have a boyfriend at Duquesne."
They said that Vanessa had given the same answer and they
immediately told me to leave...I swear it was a coincidence.
VANESSA: They made me run out of the room at the end and they
kept telling me to stop laughing. I was really nervous, but they
probably think they can't take me seriously now.
ME: They just told me that I had an attitude and played my life.
Did anybody else get an interview?
MYA: I don't know.
VANESSA: No clue.
ME: They're probably going to call more people. They've got to
give Candace an interview.

We'd been talking for about an hour when Renee called me
crying. "They really don't like me. They were all yelling at me!"
"We all got yelled at Renee! What are you talking about?
You should just come and meet with us. We're across from
Vanessa's dorm in the workout room. Where are you?"
"I'm close by too, I'm about to come down," she said, and
minutes later she found a spot on the floor.
MYA: What kind of stuff were they saying to you Renee?
RENEE: They said that I talked too much and that I was a liar.
They kept saying that I was a liar over and over again. Anytime I
answered a question they would just say it was a lie.

ME: They talked about our flaws too.

RENEE: They were *attacking* me. They said I would never get in. They weren't joking at all.

ME: Are you sure Renee? You sure you aren't exaggerating?

RENEE: No. I'm sure. They don't like me.

ME: Regina's your friend, she likes you.

MYA: Was Regina was yelling?

RENEE: No...Regina wasn't saying anything. She just sat there. She didn't stand up for me or anything. She just sat there.

VANESSA: Don't worry about it. They gave you an interview for a reason.

The next night Mya and I met in the cathedral to hear about Candace's interview.

CANDACE: Okay, so I was in the bathroom when Sasha called me and when she asked me where I was I said, "I'm in my room...actually I'm in the bathroom," and she said "What? That's too much information! You've got eight minutes to be in room 55 in the lecture hall." I got to the building but I couldn't find the room. I called Sasha and told her that I had been walking around and didn't see room 55. Then she yelled, "You want to know why you can't find room 5500?! It's because it's on the *fifth* floor!"

ME: Wow, really Candace? That should have been common sense.

MYA: Yea.

CANDACE: Wait, I'm not even finished yet. I got to the room and they were all sitting around this long table and there was an empty chair at the front so I sat down. I said "Hello ladies" and Tiffany mocked me. They got on me about wearing a blue coat and said that I didn't want to be a TET, that I really wanted to be a Beta deep down inside. They kept throwin' up the Beta hand sign and sayin' "Beta! Beta!" Then, they asked me to re-tell the story about the "Deborah's scary" text because they're still under the impression that *I* was talking bad about her that day.

ME: Sorry, homie.

CANDACE: Yea, whatever. When I was done telling that story, Julia looked at me and said, "Well since you like to text your thoughts about us, why don't you pull out your phone and text Deborah what you thought about me when I met with you?" I started to pull out my phone, but Sasha looked at me like, "Don't even try it." And then they continued to make fun of me for about twenty minutes. Britney kept falling asleep because they said I was boring.

MYA: What do these interviews mean? Are they doing this just to be doing it?

CANDACE: Well I think that—Oh wait, Kamille is callin' me!

We separated and ran down different stairwells. I ran towards the student union and sat on a bench. My phone vibrated. It was Kamille. "Call me back in two minutes and eight seconds and give me the definition of discretion."

I couldn't think. I knew what it meant but I was too nervous, too scared to fuck up. I started counting the seconds out loud and when I got to 128 I called. It went to voicemail.

I called again. It rang and went to voicemail. When I heard the beep I blurted out, "Hi, this is Whitney and I was just calling to give you the definition of discretion. It means being careful and using one's judgment in binding situations."

Ten minutes passed and I got another call. It was Sasha.

"Whitney, what did we just tell you to do?"

"Um, give the definition of discretion?"

"Do you think it was very *discreet* to leave the definition on my LS's *voicemail?*"

"No, I'm sorry. I didn't know, I—"

"Whatever. Next time pay attention. Think smart! Tomorrow you need to report to the engineering building, room 722, at 8:00. Bring your books and be prepared to study."

She hung up.

Candace received the same instructions for the next night and so did Mya. Vanessa called me and let me know that she received a phone call as well, but she wasn't sure if Sasha meant 8:00 am or 8:00 pm.

I didn't hear from Renee.

XI. Navigation Rules

RENEE: I wasn't invited to the study session tonight.
ME: Don't worry about it. You'll probably get a phone call later today.

She didn't.

I arrived at the classroom in the engineering hall and there were four interests already there: Candace, Mya, Vanessa, and Teresa. I took a seat in a row by the window and pulled out my books. Amber walked in next and sat two rows over from me. A girl that I had never seen before walked in next. After she took her seat, two other girls that I had never seen walked in. At 7:50 another girl, a freshman I'd seen a few times around campus, walked in and sat at the front. Amber and I looked at each other in confusion.

There were ten of us, but none of us spoke to each other. We'd been sitting in silence for half an hour when Latoya came into the room, looked around, and walked back out. Seconds later, all of the TETs came into the room yelling: "Look at them!" "They look scared!" "Why aren't y'all sitting next to each other?" "Y'all don't like each other!" "Get up and move your desks into a circle!"

We moved our desks into a circle and the TETs surrounded us.

TIFFANY: Take a look around the circle. You'll probably notice that some of your friends aren't here. Some of the people you thought would have been here aren't here.
SASHA: They didn't make it.

Candace and I exchanged glances.

JULIA: Take everything out of your bags and purses and put it on the desk.
TIFFANY: Everybody go around and introduce yourself—name, year, major, whatever.
AMBER*: I'm Amber Jackson.
TIFFANY: Why does Amber Jackson *always* have to go first! She thinks she's *priority*! (sighed) Keep going.
AMBER*: I'm a sophomore and a Communications Science major.

TIFFANY: I still don't understand how you plan to teach other people how to talk when you have problems talking yourself.

SASHA: Next!

JULIA: Is that a *green* folder? Get rid of that. And get rid of that highlighter too!

SHELBY*: I'm...Shelby Layton...and I am a junior...and I am a Sociology major.

IVYANA: Shelby, I feel like you look stressed, very stressed.

SHELBY*: I'm...sorry.

IVYANA: Get up. GET UP!

Shelby stood up and Britney Lynn began walking around the circle asking each of us what we were studying.

IVYANA: Stretch yourself out, Shelby.

TIFFANY: Wave your arms in the air and go, "Brrrrrrrrrrrr!"

SHELBY*: (awkwardly moving) Brr.

IVYANA: MORE!

SHELBY*: Brrrr.

IVYANA: MORE! You're not doing it right! Do it with confidence!

SHELBY*: Brrrrrr!

IVYANA: Ugh, sit down Shelby. Next!

VANESSA*: My name's Vanessa Brown. I'm a sophomore and I'm a Business major.

DEBORAH: You look different today, Vanessa. What is it?

JULIA: It's her eyes!

TIFFANY: (looking at Vanessa's face) Your eyes are *brown*?

SASHA: I thought her eyes were *green*!

JULIA: I thought they were blue!

DEBORAH: She's trying to imitate that book we're reading in book club—*The Bluest Eye*!

TIFFANY: Okay, look. Colored contacts are not *cute*. You don't need to wear those anymore. You don't need to wear that big ass flower in your hair anymore either!

JULIA: Whitney used to wear a flower too!

TIFFANY: Yea, we don't need to see those ever again. Next.

TERESA*: I'm Teresa Lane, I'm a sophomore, and I'm a Political Science –

SASHA: Time out, time out. Teresa why the hell were you runnin' to your interview wearin' business casual? You don't think that looks suspect? You think somebody runnin' across the crosswalk late at night in a suit looks *normal*?

JULIA: No LS, my favorite part about Teresa's interview was that when we called her and asked where she was, she said she was eating dinner with her aunt, the one that's *a TET*! Like, why would you just leave dinner? What did you say?

TERESA*: I said that my roommate got robbed.

DEBORAH: And you just jumped up and left?

TERESA*: No I—

SASHA: Teresa is gonna get us sent to jail!

DEBORAH: You're such a liability!

IVYANA: She's always been a liability!

DEBORAH: At least she didn't show up to her interview drunk like Miss Eva over there! Go ahead and introduce yourself to the group Eva, so the rest of the girls know how responsible you are.

EVA*: I'm Eva Downs. I'm a junior and I'm—

TIFFANY: An alcoholic!

EVA*: A Journalism and Communications major.

DEBORAH: Why are you wearing that *blue* sweater Eva?

JULIA: She wants to be a *Beta*!

DEBORAH: Take it off!

SASHA: She's stripping!

IVYANA: (looking at Eva) Why don't you have your sweater on?

EVA*: Because they said—

IVYANA: Put your sweater back *on*.

Eva clipped her sweater back on and looked down at the floor.

IVYANA: Eva!

Eva looked up at Ivyana and looked back down again.

IVYANA: Eva! What's my line name and what's my ship name?

Silence.

IVYANA: What. Is. My. Line. Name. And. What. Is. My. Ship. Name? So you're not going to answer me? Does anyone know?

The freshman girl raised her hand.

JAMIE*: Your line name is Floetry and your ship name is "Violet R.E.E.G.N.: Seven the Right Way."

IVYANA: Eva, I'm gonna need you to wake me up at 6 am and tell me my line name and ship name. And I *better* hear from you. While we're on the subject, why do you think I would have you call me at six?

EVA*: (looking down) I don't know.

IVYANA: Look up! What did you say? It's the same reason why you would call Sasha at *two* and Tiffany at *nine*.

EVA*: (looking up) I don't know.

LATOYA: I'm not surprised!

IVYANA: Oh my God! Somebody please tell her!

JAMIE*: (raising her hand) It's because six is your line number.

IVYANA: Thank you, Jamie!

SASHA: Introduce yourself to the rest of these *coons*, Jamie.

JAMIE*: I'm Jamie Henderson, I'm a freshman, and I'm a Biology major.

DEBORAH: She was the only one who was respectable in her interview!

JULIA: Yea, the rest of y'all just knew y'all were gonna make it huh? All the sophomores already knew each other! They were already throwin' up the pinky and puttin' up line photos on Face Book!

LATOYA: Well, if that's the case Brooke and Eva thought they were going to be sorors by association because they were already cool with Nicole and Julia! Please!

TIFFANY: Whitney hasn't gone yet. Go.

ME*: I'm Whitney Will—

TIFFANY: I thought it was Whitney *Gracia, Garcia*, whatever your name is.

ME*: It's both.

TIFFANY: Then say *both*.

ME*: I'm Whitney Gracia Williams. I'm a sophomore, and I'm an English Writing major.

IVYANA: (placing her hand on my shoulder) Whitney, I am so glad you got your hair done because if I *ever* see you walkin' around campus looking like "who shot john"—are you laughing?

ME*: No.

IVYANA: I see teeth! You think this is a *joke*?

ME*: No.

IVYANA: I can already tell that you're not going to last long. Brooke, introduce yourself.

BROOKE*: I'm Brooke Teal, I'm a junior, and I'm a communications major.

SASHA: You left out the part where you're a professional at throwing people under the bus!

TIFFANY: Yea Eva, your own best friend wasn't even tryna' claim you! She was like, "That is not my sister!" Shame. Your eyebrows look good though. Maybe you can help Candace out over there because hers look jacked!

JULIA: You need to get an eyebrow pencil, Candace. Introduce yourself.

CANDACE*: I'm Candace Blake, I'm a sophomore, and I'm a Communications Science major.

IVYANA: BORING! Next!

MYA*: I'm Mya Harris, I'm a sophomore, and I'm an English Writing major.

IVYANA: And you're BORING! As a matter of fact, you AND Candace bore the hell out of me! Have you ever noticed that when I'm on the phone with one of y'all I always conveniently have something else to do? I don't really have anything else to do, I just don't want to talk on the phone with you because you put me to sleep!

JULIA: At least Candace can think for herself! Mya doesn't even have a brain of her own!

TIFFANY: Yea, LS—I know exactly what you're talking about! Mya gave the same answer as Vanessa at her interview! Saying that if she was on line she would just say that she had a boyfriend at Duquesne! No original thoughts, whatsoever!

JULIA: Four of you have moms who are sorors and a lot of y'all have sorors in your families. Tell me who my founders are. Shelby, you start!

SHELBY*: Heather Kyle, Lacey Stone, Nila Jones—

JULIA: Too slow! Amber go!

AMBER*: Heather Kyle, Dorian Smith, Tracy—

JULIA: Ugh, Candace you go.

CANDACE*: Um, Ester Reynolds, Dorian—

JULIA: Why wouldn't you start with Heather Reynolds like Amber and Shelby? Why would you just start in the middle? Just forget it!

SASHA: You're interested in my organization but you can't tell me my founders? Lame! Y'all are so LAME!

JULIA: Neutrals are going to be your new best friends. Black.

DEBORAH: Brown.

SASHA: Beige.

IVYANA: Cream. Actually, *no* cream.

JULIA: Brown, White, Gray.

BRITNEY: Navy Blue.

JULIA: Yea, navy blue—not *Beta* blue! And you can wear university gear. You are to report to this building every Tuesday, Thursday, Friday, and Saturday. You need to call Britney Lynn at 9:00 letting her know that you all are here. On Tuesday and Thursday you will call Britney at 12:00 and—Candace, are you writing this down in your *planner*? Does the word *discretion* mean anything to you?

CANDACE*: I'm sorry.

JULIA: Anyway, you need to call Britney at 12:00 and ask if it is okay for you to leave. You are not to leave the room under any circumstances.

TIFFANY: If you need to use the bathroom call Britney and *ask*.

SASHA: You all are still interests. You still need to be calling and getting to know us.

DEBORAH: I'm glad you brought that up Sasha. This does not mean anything. Nothing is guaranteed.

JULIA: Exactly. On Friday and Saturday the same rules apply but we'll call you and let you know when we *feel* like you can leave. From here on out, you all need to be tryin' to get your grades as high as possible, so you all are on social probation.

DEBORAH: Social probation.

IVYANA: That means no parties, no get-togethers, no events, nothing, unless we say otherwise.

SASHA: And from now on, what *one* of y'all know, the *rest of y'all* know. Get to know each other, because this is it.

BRITNEY: Can I say something? On Tuesday could each of you bring your transcript, and five copies of your class schedule with the activities written on the back?

TIFFANY: You don't have to *ask* them anything. *Do* what my LS just told y'all to do for Tuesday.

SASHA: Y'all really need to get to know each other as best you can real quick. And Shelby, you're going to be my project. You need to call me at the beginning of every study session. And somebody needs to bring me two crunchy tacos with no cheese and a Pepsi to the next study session. Who's going to do that?

Jamie raised her hand.

SASHA: Thank you, Jamie. No *cheese*.

JULIA: Candace, you need to call me after you all are allowed to leave tonight and tell me why Shelby is so passionate about joining Theta Eta Theta.

LATOYA: Brooke, I don't know you and I feel like you don't know me. You need to call me within the next three days and give me a list of interesting facts about myself.

IVYANA: And y'all need to find somewhere else to study on the weekdays. Call us and let us know where that is. Only come here on the weekends so there's less chance of random people walking by. And don't you all leave at the same time either. Leave in pairs and with people that you knew before.

DEBORAH: Are we done? I'm tired.

TIFFANY: Candace isn't coming back, look at her.

DEBORAH: Eva isn't coming back.

LATOYA: I hope Eva doesn't come back.

JULIA: I'm bored with them.

IVYANA: Let's go.

The TETS left the room, with the exception of Sasha and Kamille who lingered for a while more as we exchanged numbers and re-introduced ourselves. When they left, we sat in silence before Amber spoke up, "Okay, so does everyone have all of the TET numbers?"

The four new girls shook their heads. I watched as those four girls that I had never met or seen at a single TET event copied down all of the information that had taken me months to get.

AMBER: So, if you don't know their line names and numbers, you've got to memorize those quick.

TERESA: Can I say something? I just want you all to know that the whole thing about me being at dinner with my aunt was a lie. I was at the movies with two of my friends and I wasn't trying to leave—just wanted to put that out there.

BROOKE: Wow that was a good lie.

JAMIE: You just made that up?

TERESA: Yea, I didn't even wanna answer my phone because I thought they were gonna ask me to do something. I'm tired of driving Ivyana to the mall and getting her food.

ME: What? I thought she only had Amber running errands.

TERESA: No, ever since she found out I had a car I've been her personal chauffeur. Do you know how high gas is right now? It's almost four dollars a gallon and she thinks my car runs on water!

We laughed.

CANDACE: Damn. Shelby?

SHELBY: Yes?

CANDACE: I need you to tell me your story about why you want to be a TET because I have to call Julia later.

SHELBY: Oh okay, here's what I told them: When I first got to college I wasn't really that outgoing. I was always studying and although I was in the elite university organizations, I never had too many social things to do. So, my friends convinced me to join a white sorority and I got a bid for Gamma Gamma Gamma. I was never really into it, but one day while I was at an event—actually I was leaving an event—I overheard one of the Gammas say that she didn't want any more niggers in the sorority.

AMBER: Really?

SHELBY: Yea. I was a little hurt by it, but I decided that I didn't want to be around people who didn't want me in their organization. I denounced my letters and sent all of my things back to nationals. Then, I started talking to one of my friends who is a TET and she told me to do research and I became intrigued. Like, everything about the organization is so positive, especially since it was founded by black women and is still around today. So, that's kind of how I ended up becoming so passionate about joining.

TERESA: Deep. So you never said anything to the girl who said that stuff?

SHELBY: No, I just brushed it off.

CANDACE: Okay, thanks. What else do we need to do tonight?

MYA: We need to go around and get interesting facts on each other. They said we need to know each other well, so that's a start.

AMBER: We'll be here all night if we do that now.

VANESSA: Yea, I'm not trying to stay here after midnight.

MYA: Are there any suggestions then?

SHELBY: We could all meet up somewhere tomorrow night since we won't have study session on Mondays.

JAMIE: Nowhere on campus though.

BROOKE: I can't come tomorrow night because I have a meeting but I'll give you my info at the next study session.

MYA: That's fine. We'll get the lists of facts about Latoya to you too.

SHELBY: How about my house? I live down the block from CVS.

AMBER: That works.

For the rest of the night, we went over each other's majors, talked about why we wanted to be TETs, and wondered when we were going to go on line.

The next day at noon, I got a mass text.

SASHA: One of you needs to bring me a pep pizza and a sweet tea by 1:00.

I immediately received texts from all the girls in the study group: "Who can do this?" "Who's free right now?" "Is anybody gonna be able to get it there in time?" After about twenty minutes of going back and forth, it was settled that Mya would get the pizza and the sweet tea from the student union, Teresa would pick me up from my dorm and take me to pick up the food from Mya, and then Teresa would drive me to take the food to Sasha.

I called Sasha. "Hello may I speak to Sasha?"

"This is me."

"Hi, this is Whitney. I was wondering what your address was?"

"Brooke knows where I live."

Click.

I called Brooke, asked for Sasha's address, and Teresa dropped me off five houses away. I walked towards her home, a small brick front with a small porch, and knocked on the door.

She didn't answer.

I called her phone and within seconds she came to the door. "Hey Whitney, come on in. Go on to the back, that's where my room is."

I placed her food on the bed and sat on the edge. Her room was filled with TET paraphernalia—violet and green collectibles, photo books, and picture frames.

"How are you today?" she asked.

"I'm fine."

"I couldn't give you my address because we told y'all last night, 'What *one* knows, *you all know*.' Got it?"

"Yea."

"Good. I was really about to strangle you at your interview the other day. I was like, if this girl says *I mean* one more time!" she laughed.

"Sorry, that's just how I talk."

"Clearly. I feel like I don't know anything about you though. What do you want to do after college?"

"I want to be a screenplay writer."

"You want to write movies? Wow, I've never met someone who actually wanted to write a film. You really like writing?"

"Yea, I love it."

"Okay, that's cool. How did you feel about last night?"

"It was…intense."

"I remember my first study session. My prophytes were definitely about the business. You'll meet them later though. You know this is it right?"

"No, what do you mean?"

"This is pre-pledging. Y'all are the lucky ones. If we decide to have a line, we might pick some of the people from this group, trimming the fat if we have to. Are you excited?"

"Yea, I am."

"That won't last long, trust me. Right now, everyone is going to be hype and happy to be getting a call to do something, but y'all are going to get sick of doing errands because we definitely did."

At that moment, Renee texted me. I turned my phone on silent.

"How do you feel about Shelby, Whitney?"

"I like her, she seems nice."

"She's really sweet, but she's really shy. I'm going to give her more self esteem. Have you talked to Renee?"

"I haven't talked to her since yesterday afternoon."

"I know that you two are friends, but we chose not to pick Renee for one reason or another and that's just how it is unfortunately. Did she know you had an interview?"

"Yea."

"And did she tell you or anyone else that she got an interview?"

"Yea. Me, her, Mya, and Vanessa all met up to talk about them afterwards."

"Figures. Ugh, interests. Anyway, don't feel like you have to act different towards Renee or anything. You don't have to be like, 'Oh I can't tell you' if she asks where you are or what you're doing. Just make up something believable, and if it gets to be too crazy just let one of us know."

"Um, okay…"

"So, your dad was a Theta?"

"Yea, he pledged at Tennessee State."

"How did he die?"

"He was shot to death."

"Oh, I'm sorry to hear that."

"It's alright. I'm over it for the most part."

"Do you like my shrine?" she pointed to a caddy-cornered shelf that was stuffed with TET trinkets.

"Um…yes."

"Maybe one day if you're lucky enough you'll be able to create a shrine of your own. I'm so grateful I had my prophytes harassing me last spring. They made me appreciate this so much more. I don't understand how my paper sorors can feel the bond I feel with my LSs. They crossed in three days and that was it. Especially on those big lines, I'll never understand how you can cross with forty or more girls and consider them all your sisters. How well can number forty three know number twelve?"

I nodded my head.

"Do you not have class today?" she asked.

"No, I don't."

"So you have a three day weekend?"

"Technically, it's like four."

"You don't have classes on Friday either? So all your classes are on Tuesday, Wednesday, and Thursday?"

"No, they're just all day on Tuesday and Thursday."

"Are you sure you're a full time student?"

"Yes."

"Well, that's nice. I don't want to hold you up from anything you need to do today. You're free to leave. I'll see you tomorrow night."

"Okay, bye."

I left her house and trekked down to lower campus. I texted Renee back and agreed to meet in her dorm.

"Okay," she sighed. "So I just called Sasha and apologized."

"Apologized for what?"

"Well, not *apologized*. I just wanted her to know that I wasn't a liar and that I honestly didn't know much about their process and that I didn't talk to other people about theirs."

"Oh, okay. What did she say?"

"She was actually nice about it. Oh, and if she asks you, I haven't talked to you since the day before interviews because I told her that we haven't talked in a few days, okay?"

I sighed. "Renee, I was just at Sasha's house and I told her that me, you, Vanessa, and Mya talked after our interviews...I didn't know that you were gonna call and say that. I wouldn't have done that if I knew."

"So, *I am* a liar."

"You're not a liar. You were just trying to make things right."

"I just wasn't meant to be a TET...It's cool, it's cool. I'll still be at your probate, okay?"

"Renee—"

"Let's talk about something else."

The study group met at Shelby's house Monday night to go over information. We created a document that listed our full names, birthdays, majors, hobbies, favorite colors, favorite foods, and talents. We also made a separate document for the information we knew about each of the TETs.

Subject: [Fwd: RE:]
From: [Teresa]
Date: Tue, February 5, 2008 9:35 pm
To: ███████.edu (more)
Priority: Normal
Options: View Full Header | View Printable Version

```
-----------Original Message -----------
Subject: Re:
From:    "[Teresa]" <███████edu>
Date:    Tue, February 5, 2008 10:09 am
To:      ███████.edu
-----------------------------------------------
--------okay i'll send it again to everyone...sorry
about that....im gonna just copy and paste it into
here for you right now:

[Latoya]:
-played softball in high school
-from Roanoke, VA
-Went to William Flemming High School
-She went to high school with [Jamie's] cousin
-Spec is [Tamera from fall 2004]
-She used to be a [Nu Pi] Sweetheart
-She is a nanny
Aunt was a major influence on her ([a TET])

[Ivyana]:
        -lactose intolerant
        -penne   with   blush   (all   vegetables/no
onion/no mushroom/no broccoli)
-number 13 nationally and number 6 after being
"made"

[Mya Whitney Harris]:      ███████.edu
        -Born: November ███, 1988 (Scorpio)
```

             -2 brothers
             -dog: max (German shepherd)
             -favorite food: Lasagna
             -Rochester, NY
             -Favorite artist: [Mya] bangs with Jay-z
SOOO hard
             -Major: English Writing and psychology
             -wants to be a journalist or a teacher

[Shelby Elaine Layton] : ▮▮▮▮▮gmail.com
             -Born: September ▮▮, 1987 (libra)
             -sister
             -Major: Sociology; Minor: Statistics and
Chemistry
             -3 cats (Cappy, Cosmo, Casper)
             -From Paterson, NJ
             -Favorite Food: Fuel and Fuddle Garlic
Portabello Pizza with avocado
-Favorite color: Brown
             -Favorite Music: R&B and Rap
             -Talent: Butterfly stroke
             A Pharmaceutical Brand marketer

Whitney Gracia Williams wgw▮▮▮▮▮.edu
Oct 16, 1988
Younger sister Jennifer 16, 2 younger brothers Jay
13, Ray 7
Memphis, TN
Hot wings (Quaker Steak)
Color: Orange
Beyonce and Jay-Z
English Writing and Communications
Screenplay Writer
Talent: writes

[Vanessa Charlotte Brown] ▮▮▮▮▮▮▮.edu
Febuary ▮▮, 1988
2 younger sisters, older brother (raised as an only
child)
Don't like animals
Philadephia, PA
*White chocolate bread pudding Joe Mama's
Purple (fav color)
Music: Abhor—neosoul. // Likes: old school. Minnie
Ripperton (70's throwback old)// Mainstream music
Major: Finance and Accounting (dual)

Future: Law school (foreign politics// int'l relations)
Talent: Undefined

[Teresa Janet Lane] ██████████.edu
Oct ██, 1987
3 siblings
Animals: indifferent
Hometown: everywhere (born in Hampton, VA) (home now is Harrisburg) lived in VA, MD, PA, SC, TX
Food: Seafood
Color: Orange
Music: Mariah Carey (listen to everything)
Major: Political Science and Communications
Minor: Legal Studies (and a writing certificate— Public and Professional Writing)
Career Path: Lawyer
Talent: Nothing

[Eva Aaliyah Downs]: ██████████.edu
-January ██, 1987
-siblings: two older sisters
-no pets
-born in Brooklyn
-likes shrimp and likes NY style pizza
-favorite color is purple
-music: loves beyonce & Jay Z
-major: political science and journalism
-career path: law school
-talent: sings

[Jamie Selena Jones]: ██████████.edu
-born December ████ 1988
2 siblings
Pets: dog named rex that died from cancer
Born and raised in Monroeville, pa
Favorite food: chicken fetuccini alfredo
Favorite color: black
Favorite music: r&b, rap, in love with lauren hill
Major: Biology and Pre-med
Family Practice
Talent: lifeguarding

[Amber Destiny Jackson] ██████████.edu
Born October ████, 1988
Only child

```
Dad is a [Nu Pi] and mom [TET]
Never had a pet
From Burlington, nj
Food: olives and pasta
Color: purple
Music: everything except country
Major: Communication Science & Disorders
Career Path: Speech Language Pathology
Talent: Sings

[Candace Helena Blake]: ███████.edu
Born: April ████ 1988
From Montgomery County Maryland
Siblings: [two brothers]
Fish died while she was at her interview and it's
still in the bowl
Food: Ms. Field's Cinnamon Sugar Cookies
Color: Orange
Music: Alicia Keys
Major: Communications Science and Disorders
Career Path: Speech Language Pathologist
```

For the first study session, we decided to meet in the nursing hall since it was tucked away from the rest of campus. We were ten minutes early, except for Jamie, who had forgotten to get Sasha's Taco Bell. Upon remembering it at 8:50, she stumbled into the room at 8:59.

Vanessa called Britney Lynn at 9:00 and Shelby called Sasha at 9:02. Both of them came to the room an hour later. While Britney Lynn called us over to her chair one by one to go over our transcripts and class schedules, Sasha asked random questions aloud.

I was excited. I couldn't believe that I was about to be a TET. All of my work as an interest had paid off. I couldn't wait to go on line. I couldn't wait to cross.

The next day while Candace, Amber, and I were quizzing each other on the study group's information, my phone went off, "*If I was a rich girl-na-na-na-na-na-na-nah.*" Tiffany.

"Hello?" I answered.

"Are you alone, Whitney?"

"No."

"Call me back when you are."

Click.

"What did she want?" Candace asked.

"I don't know. I'll be right back."

I went down a few floors and called Tiffany back. She didn't pick up. In two seconds she returned the call. "Whitney, do you think you're *on line*?"

"Um...no."

"Do you think you have *line sisters*?"

"No..."

"Well, your little friend Brooke seems to think that you all are pledging. Since you already have LSs and know everything, there's really no need for *us* is there? Y'all are dropped. Study sessions are over. Return to your normal life."

Click.

I ran upstairs to Candace's room. "Yo, Tiffany just called me and—"

"Yea, she called me too. What happened?"

"I don't know—something about Brooke. Send out a mass text."

"I'll just call Teresa...Hey Teresa...Yea, me and Whitney got a phone call too...So did Mya and Vanessa? Tell me what happened... WHAT! You're joking right? Are we still going to show up for study session Thursday? Alright," she hung up her phone.

"So?"

"Brooke was talking to Latoya and apparently she referred to us as her line sisters."

"We're screwed."

We all showed up to study session Thursday night. Britney Lynn hit ignore when Amber called, and Sasha instructed for Shelby to put her on speaker phone.

"Am I on speaker?" Sasha asked. "Okay, well...GO HOME! STUDY SESSIONS ARE OVER! WE ARE NOT PUTTIN' OUR CHAPTER ON THE LINE FOR ANY OF YOU! GO HOME! IT'S OVER!"

SHELBY: She hung up. What if this is it? What if they're really done with us!

AMBER: They're not going to—

SHELBY: No Amber! What if we're really done?

Silence.

ME: Okay Brooke, what happened?

BROOKE: I'm so sorry, I'm so sorry. I was talking with Latoya and giving her those facts and she asked me where I got them from and I said my LSs. I didn't mean to say that, I swear I didn't, but then she asked me again and I just repeated what I had already said. We talked for like an hour after that. I didn't know that it would get everyone in trouble.

AMBER: It's alright, we're all gonna make mistakes. Just don't say "LS" ever again.

JAMIE: Yea, like, *ever*. If you want to call us something you could call us your study buddies—

VANESSA: Study friends?

JAMIE: Study homies! (laughing)Your *SHs*!

EVA: I like that!

CANDACE: Me too!

MYA: That…makes me kind of uncomfortable, but I like it.

TERESA: Okay *SHs*, what we need to do is start calling them all tomorrow and apologize.

BROOKE: I don't think I'm gonna do that. I think I'm done.

VANESSA, MYA, ME: Done with what?

JAMIE: Yea, what are you saying?

BROOKE: I can't do this anymore guys.

CANDACE: Brooke, it's like the *third* day.

BROOKE: I know! And look at how messed up I'm getting over something like this!

AMBER: It's not that big of a deal. We're just going to call all of them tomorrow and apologize. They'll take us back. We just need to figure out what to do.

VANESSA: What can we do?

TERESA: Kamille texted me, "Idk gift?" earlier today. I don't know what that means though.

ME: Gift?

AMBER: Yea, when people are on line and they get dropped they make a gift to get back on line.

ME: Whoa. The whole idea of them dropping us in the first place was because Brooke was acting like we were on line and we're not. Now you want us to act like we're on line for real and make a gift?

CANDACE: It doesn't have to be anything expensive. It can just be candy or something.

VANESSA: How about CDs? We have their favorite artists listed on that document we made.

AMBER: Okay that works. Who is gonna make the CDs?

TERESA: I got it.

VANESSA: I'll help.

JAMIE: Me too.

ME: I'll buy the candy.

After a few days of being ignored and delivering a cup of candy and a CD to each TET, Sasha said that study sessions could begin again.

At a study session:

VANESSA*: Hello may I speak to Britney Lynn? Hi Britney, are you available to speak? This is Vanessa. I was just calling to let you know that we are all here. We're on the seventh floor....Okay.

SHELBY*: Hel-lo? He-he-hello? Can I speak to Sa-sa-sa-sha? Hi, this is Shelby. I was calling to let you know that we're all here. Okay. Goodbye.

Minutes later the TETS came into the room.

LATOYA: Why are y'all sitting in the front of the room where people can walk by and see y'all? Does that seem *discreet*? Let me guess whose idea that was (looked at Eva and Brooke) Tweedle-dee and Tweedle *dummbb*!

TIFFANY: Whitney, why are you wearing that hood over your head?

ME*: I don't—

TIFFANY: Take it off!

I pulled my hood off.

TIFFANY: Oh my god, put it back on *now*!

IVYANA: Don't ever take it off again!

JULIA: Are y'all sure y'all want to be TETs? I feel like y'all think this is going to be a walk in the park!

SASHA: The road to Epsilon is long and hard, I hope you know that!

JULIA: Yea, because if you're trying to graduate summa cum laude you might as well get up and leave the room now!

SASHA: When y'all make gifts, y'all know that y'all can use violet and green right? It seems like y'all didn't know that.

TIFFANY: They couldn't have known that. That's why we got the cups of candy with black and white checkerboard paper and *RED* writing on the CDs!

LATOYA: I have yet to hear from *Eva*! It's not going to be a good thing later on if I don't know you, Eva!

JULIA: LS, I don't even think they know each other! Mya, give me an interesting fact about Amber Jackson.

MYA*: Amber Jackson has never had a pet ever, a day in her life.

TIFFANY: She's trying make the fact extra long! "Ever? A day in her life?" Did you really think that was *adding* something to that wack fact? Whitney, give me a fact about Candace.

ME*: Her father is a computer engineer.

TIFFANY: That doesn't count. Y'all were homies before. Brooke, give me an interesting fact about Teresa.

BROOKE*: Teresa's favorite teacher is her teacher from the third grade.

SASHA: Oh my god these facts are so LAMMMEEEE! They're called interesting facts because they're supposed to be *interesting*! Why are you looking like that, Shelby? Are you scared?

SHELBY*: No, actually—

TIFFANY: *Actually*, don't say "actually." That makes it seem like you're getting an attitude. Nobody else needs to say that word to us either.

IVYANA: This is a mess. I think we need to look at new girls. I think we made the wrong decision. Brooke and Eva, we don't need *both* of y'all. You two are pretty much the same person. Get in the center of the circle.

They got up and stood in the center of the circle.

TIFFANY: Play rock paper scissors! Whoever loses has to leave! I'm sure we won't notice who's missing after awhile.

Brooke and Eva played. Eva erupted in nervous laughter.

TIFFANY: I hope you lose Eva since you think this is so funny!

IVYANA: Nope, Brooke lost! Get your stuff and leave Brooke! See ya!

Brooke went back to her desk and closed her folder. She put on her coat and began to button it.

JULIA: Sit down, Brooke! You're not going anywhere!

DEBORAH: Maybe she should go if she's that excited to leave!

LATOYA: I really wish she would!

JULIA: Candace, stand up.

Candace stood up.

JULIA: I think you should just tell us all now that you want to be a Beta. You look just like a Beta!

TIFFANY: Throw up the kitty sign!

JULIA: (throwing up the Beta hand sign) Say, BETA! BETA! BETA! Why aren't you doing it?

CANDACE*: I'd rather not.

JULIA: I didn't ask you what you would *rather* do, just do it! Throw your sign up and say BETA!

IVYANA: No, just sit down Candace. I'm glad you didn't do it. You don't need to disrespect yourself like that.

Candace took a seat.

For the remainder of the study session we sat and listened as the TETs made fun of us, and tried to remember any interesting fact or bit of advice that they offered.

In the fell clutch of circumstance
I have not winced nor cried aloud.
Under the bludgeonings of chance
My head is bloody, but unbowed...

XII. Afloat

There were three ways to get around Pittsburgh and the university. There was the city bus, which any university student could ride for free with his or her school ID, the campus shuttle which rode to specific places on a designated schedule, and then there was Safe rider, an ingenious tool for students who didn't want to walk the streets of Oakland late at night. Each university student received twenty Safe rider passes a semester. All a student had to do was call, give a location and a destination, and a Safe rider shuttle would arrive within half an hour.

A few of the TETs lived within walking distance in on-campus apartments and dorms: Julia, Regina, Cari, Nicole, and Britney. The other TETs lived off campus, and it would be necessary to take a campus shuttle to get their houses: Deborah, Ivyana, Felicia, Kamille and Sasha. Tiffany's house was a fifteen-minute bus ride away to the North side, and Latoya's house was a thirty-minute bus ride away to Brownsville Road.

Each of us familiarized ourselves with the campus shuttle stops and times, and kept track of the 500, 71A, and 54C city bus schedules. Anytime we ran an errand for one of the TETs, we sent a mass text to each other and elaborated on the errand at the next night's study session.

If I was a rich girl—na-na-na-na-na-na-na-na-na-nah. Sasha.
"Hello?"
"Do you know how to cook?"
"Yea."
"Okay, well you can teach Brooke because she claims she doesn't know how. Me and Latoya want breakfast. We already have eggs. You need to get pancake mix, bacon, and grits. Call me when y'all are outside."
Click.
I called Brooke. "Yo, where are you?"
"I'm leaving my apartment."
"Okay, Sasha just called me and said me and you have to go cook breakfast. I think CVS sells bacon and shit. Do you wanna meet me there?"

"Yea that's cool. See you in a minute."

I bought the bacon and Brooke bought the pancake mix and the grits. As we were walking to the campus shuttle stop she sighed. "Whit, I don't know if I can do this."

"Why? What's wrong?"

"This isn't what I thought it would be. That was my parent's money I just spent. It wasn't mine. I don't have a big meal plan either. I know we've only been doing this for a couple of days, but I'm not going to be able to spend a lot more money on them."

"Oh, I feel you. If you ever need to use my meal plan or anything just let me know and I'll give you my card."

"Okay."

When we arrived to Sasha's house, she ushered the two of us into the kitchen. She pulled out a few drawers, "Ivyana may be coming up here later but I'm not sure. I like my bacon slightly crispy but not too crispy and Latoya likes her soft with a little crisp in it. Make sure you scramble the eggs good. All the pots and pans are in the bottom cabinets. If you need to know where anything is, just ask. Oh, and since you said you were kind of sick Whitney, you can have my Mucinex if you need it. We'll be in the back or in the dining room when you get done."

Brooke scrambled the eggs and made the grits, and I fried the bacon and made the pancakes. We made plates with equal proportions and set them out in Sasha's dining room.

Ivyana entered the kitchen and looked around. "Y'all didn't make me a plate?"

"Y'all didn't make my prophyte a plate? Didn't I tell y'all she was coming?" Sasha yelled.

Brooke and I exchanged glances.

"Well, just set aside two eggs for me," Ivyana sighed. "I'm particular about my eggs anyway so I'll just show you how to make them and next time you'll know how."

She left the kitchen and Brooke and I continued to clean.

AMBER: On my way to Sasha's house.

Minutes later, Ivyana tapped me on my shoulder. "Whitney where are my eggs?"

"I put them by the stove."

"You set them aside and you weren't going to tell me? Don't you think it would *behoove* you to let me know when you have completed something that I asked you to do?"

"Yes."

"Ugh, come over here—you too Brooke. I'm going to show you how I like my eggs. You need to pay special attention because in the future you're going to have to make them. And if they're not made right, I will have you remake them *over and over* until you get it right. I use cheese and granulated garlic. First, I scramble the eggs," she poured the eggs into the skillet.

I tried not to roll my eyes, tried to remain as still as possible.

"Yes...There it is...Watch. See how I'm adding the cheese onto the eggs as they scramble? See how I add the garlic and it gets into the cheese *and* the eggs?"

She pushed her eggs onto a plate and went out into the dining room.

"Wow. She's wild," Brooke whispered.

"I hope I never have to make her eggs. Make sure we tell everyone how she likes them made tonight."

"Okay, I will. Did you get that text from Amber?"

"Yea, she needs to hurry up and get here so they can leave me alone."

"I'm leaving too. I have a group meeting."

"Whitney!" Sasha called.

I went out to the table.

"Do you have somewhere to be soon?"

"Yea. I have a meeting with the newspaper," I lied.

"Oh, well never mind. You can leave when you get done cleaning up."

The university meal plan consisted of two things: swipes and dining dollars. Swipes could only be used at Market Central, an all you can eat center with six different restaurants. Dining dollars could be used at any university sponsored snack shop or restaurant—Taco Bell, Burger King, Quick Zone, Pasta Plus, Sub Connections, Pizza Hut, Jazzman's Café, Einstein's Bagel Co., Sutherland dining, and Common Grounds.

I sat down with the book for my Literature and Race class. I was three chapters behind. I read to page four and got a mass text.

IVYANA: Do any of you know how to braid or twist hair?
ME: Nope.
IVYANA: What are you doing?
ME: Studying at the ARC.
IVYANA: I want food before your next study session.

I put my books in my backpack, slipped on my coat, and left the study center. When I got outside I called Ivyana. "Hello, may I speak to Ivyana?"

"Hi, Whitney. I want food from the Pete. Call me when you get there."

It took me ten minutes to get up the hill. It was snowing heavily and I had to stop to take a breath every two minutes.

"Hello, may I speak to Ivyana?"

"Are you at the Pete?"

"Yes."

"Okay. Go to Pasta Plus and call me back when you have an order form in your hand."

I hated when she treated me as if I was an idiot child, like she couldn't tell me what she wanted all at once instead of using my daytime minutes so she could feel like her phone was some type of hotline. I picked up an order sheet and called her again.

"Do you have the order sheet?" she sighed.

"Yes."

"Could you read out the menu please? Start with the noodles."

"There's penne—"

"What?"

"Pee-nay, like p-e-n-n-e."

"It's *penne*."

"Yea, there's that and there's—"

"No, no, no, could you pronounce it properly please? Say *penne*."

"Penne."

"Good. Continue."

She had me read out the entire menu twice, correcting my pronunciation of every word. After going back and forth about what she wanted aloud, she settled and said, "Get me a pasta with penne, blush, tomato, green peppers, absolutely no onions, only a tad bit of garlic, just a tad bit, chicken, parmesan cheese, and a roll on the side. Oh, and I want a bottle of water. Got it?"

Before I could respond she hung up. I filled out the order sheet and handed it to the cashier.

"Will this be all?"

"Can I get a bottle of water?"

"You'll have to get that from another restaurant, we only have cups."

"Oh okay."

"Your total is $9.09. Does this order say no garlic?"

"Um, no. I'm sorry. I meant *extra* garlic, lots of it."

"Extra garlic on order 77!" she shouted behind her shoulder as she swiped my card.

A few days later I paid for Felicia's lunch in Market Central. Since we passed Ivyana on the way, she tagged along. While Felicia was in the middle of explaining the concept of a new song she was producing, Ivyana interrupted, "Whitney, when you bought my pasta the other day did you tell them that I only wanted a little bit of garlic?"

"Yea. I'm pretty sure I did," I lied.

"Well, there was way too much garlic on my order for some reason."

"Oh, well it's probably because they were super busy. There were a lot of people in line so they probably added too much by accident."

"Oh, that makes sense. They did that to me once last year."

TERESA: WAKE UP WHITNEY! PICK UP THE PHONE!!!

I rolled over and opened my phone. There were four missed calls from Teresa. I looked at the time: 4:49 a.m.

ME: My bad, what's up?

TERESA: Tanya is driving on the highway and she wants to speak to each SH since she's not going to be around this semester. Someone should be calling you when it's your turn to talk to her. Stay up.

If I was a rich girl—na-na-na-na-na-na-na-na-na-nah. Julia.

"Hello?"

"Hi, Whitney. What are you doing?"

"I'm turning in a paper at the cathedral."

"When's your next class?"

"I don't have class today."

"Okay. Well when you get done with that I need you to come get my card, withdraw twenty dollars, and get two rolls of quarters from the bank."

JAMIE: Going to Station Square with Teresa to get Ivyana.

"Okay, I'll be—"

"And on your way could you grab me a bottle of water and a cinnamon raisin bagel with strawberry cream cheese from Einstein's?"

If I was a rich girl—na-na-na-na-na-na-na-na-na-nah. Ivyana.

"Hello?"

"I need a ride from Melwood to Chesterfield. Call Safe rider."

If I was a rich girl—na-na-na-na-na-na-na-na-na-nah. Tiffany.

"Hello?"

"Whitney, what did I tell you to do? What CDs did I tell you to make?"

"Common, SWV—"

"And yet, you did them wrong! I told you I wanted the CDs to be *in order*."

"I did put—"

"No you didn't. I'm looking at iTunes right now for SWV and the songs are out of order. The Kanye mix-tape you made for Ivyana is missing a few tracks so you need to do them all over and have them to me by tomorrow."

At a study session:

CANDACE: Today I was with Ivyana and she was telling me about her dreams of being a superhero. She said that if she could have a superpower she would want to have the power to be invisible, something about a Harry Potter cloak.

ME: Does that count as an interesting fact?

CANDACE: I guess. She also gave me a hug in the middle of Quick Zone.

ME: Eew.

JAMIE: The other day when I was in the trunk of Teresa's car—

EVA: Time out, *what*?

JAMIE: I was in the trunk of Teresa's car when I sent y'all that text about me and Teresa going to Station Square to get Ivyana.

EVA: Why?

TERESA: (sighing) Ivyana told me to drive to Station Square to get her house keys. Then she told me to take the keys back to her house to get her a black bra, and then I had to bring the bra back to Station Square and then take her from Station Square to the Southside.

JAMIE: I was hiding in the trunk when Ivyana got in the car, and I was just typing everything she into my cell phone.

EVA: Wow, how long did it take you to do that?

TERESA: According to Ivyana, it should have taken me twenty minutes, but we got it done in almost an hour.

BROOKE: She's wild! When I had to go do something for her the other day she was acting like I could teleport!

For the rest of the study session we went around the room filling in details of errands we ran over the weekend. The next few study sessions went the same way: calling Britney Lynn at 9:00, calling Sasha at 9:02, possibly listening to the TETs come and talk about us, and going around the room one by one to discuss errands—reiterating any interesting fact we learned and placing it into the "info on them" document. But after awhile, it became too time consuming. By the time each of us had gone around and given a recap of our day, study session would be over and we would have to stay up additional hours to do schoolwork.

While we were discussing our errands at another study session, Amber shook her head. "Okay, stop. This is getting ridiculous. We can't keep using up all our time. There's gotta be a better way to keep up with all the errands and interesting facts."

CANDACE: Yea, and I don't think walking around with all the facts on a paper document is very discreet.

VANESSA: Well, what do y'all suggest then?

EVA: Maybe more detailed texting throughout the day?

MYA: Isn't that what we do now?

BROOKE: No, we don't need to do that. Y'all know my phone is late. That wouldn't work for me.

ME: Yea, that's not going to work. We'd still have to talk about them later.

TERESA: We could email stuff to each other.

AMBER: Every single time we do an errand or find out something interesting though? Do you know how much time that would take?

TERESA: It was just a thought.

JAMIE: No wait, that's a good idea actually. How about a Gmail account that we could all share? Gmail has documents and chats and we could all have the password and just update it every week with stuff and make sure that we all read it and know it.

CANDACE: Good idea, I like that.

SHELBY: Okay, I see you *SH*!

TERESA: So if Jamie says it, it's a good idea. But if I say it—

EVA: Let's just start doing that account soon. We can still talk about errands, but only for the first few minutes since we never know if they're going to show up or not. And we can finish passing around the "info on them" document and doing the mass emails for important stuff. But after that, this Gmail thing needs to be our main source of info.

A few days later, Jamie created our email account: studybuddies040507@gmail.com. Our account user name was Victoria Benedum and the password was *Victoria451*.

If I was a rich girl—na-na-na-na-na-na-na-na-na-nah. Sasha.

"Hello?"

"Are you by my house yet?"

"Yes."

"The door is unlocked. Just come in and shut the door behind you. When you leave lock it back."

I walked into her house and closed the door.

"Hi Sasha, I have your food," I said when I reached her room.

She rolled across the bed, wrapped in her blankets like a human burrito. "Just put the food over there. I'm so depressed right now."

"Sorry to hear that…"

"Sure you are. Could you take that basket of clothes to the basement and put them in the washing machine? And bring the clothes that are in the dryer back up here. Amber's coming over later and she's going to fold them for me."

After I finished hauling her clothes, I stood by her door.

"Can I go now?" I asked.

"Ugh, just go Whitney."

AMBER: Hey SHs, I just want to let y'all know that I was doing Sasha's laundry today & I knocked her pearls of service book off her shrine. She said that I have to give her $60 to replace it so could you each bring 3 or 5 dollars to SS tonight? Thanks.

We started to become more efficient with communication. We began to memorize each other's class and work schedules. We went over our interesting facts and quizzed each other incessantly.

Whenever I wasn't talking with an SH or running an errand, I was in my friend Tiara's room. Since she lived in the tower dorms, I could get to anywhere else on campus quickly if I needed to run an errand.

"Son, I'm so happy for you!" she said to me one day.

"Thanks, I'm excited. I like everybody in the group."

"That's good. When are y'all supposed to start pledging?"

"I don't know maybe in a couple of—Wait a second, Candace is calling me. Hello?"

"Whitney, could you come to Quick Zone and help me get some stuff for Tiffany and Ivyana? When we get done could you ride with me to the North side?"

"Yea, sure."

It took four shopping bags to contain everything that Ivyana and Tiffany requested. When we arrived to the North side,

Ivyana let us inside Tiffany's apartment and said that the kitchen needed to be cleaned. While she and Tiffany rummaged through the groceries, Candace and I washed the dishes.

IVYANA: (holding up an orange) Candace! What is *this*?

CANDACE: Fresh fruit.

IVYANA: I meant fresh fruit in a *cup*. You know, like sliced peaches and pears, things like that.

CANDACE: I'm sorry.

IVYANA: It's okay. You didn't know. Whitney, (rubbing my arm) why do you look so tense?

I flinched.

ME: I'm not tense.

IVYANA: Whatever. This new diet I'm on is all fruit cups, water, yogurt, hummus here or there, and the occasional snack. Do you think I'll get in shape by Spring Break if I stick to it?

ME: Um...yea...

TIFFANY: Whitney doesn't care!

IVYANA: You're right, Tiffany. Do you think I'll get in shape by then Candace?

CANDACE: Yes.

IVYANA: You know what would be great? If I made you two my pointer people! Like, I could just text you two when I wanted food and you could just figure out who in your group could get it! That'd be great! Hmmm (laughing) if I texted you a sad face like this (frowned her face) you could bring me a fruit cup and green tea, and if I texted you a surprise face, you could get me a fruit cup and water. Go ahead and finish cleaning up though.

We wiped off the counters, finished washing the dishes, swept the floor, and asked if it was okay for us to leave.

IVYANA: Tiffany, do you need anything else to be done?

TIFFANY: No, I'm good.

IVYANA: Okay well, I guess you can go. The next bus is supposed to come in a few minutes but sometimes it's early. If you miss it just come back here. I'm sure I can find something else for you to do.

As soon as I shut the door to the apartment, I bolted down the steps and ran as fast as I could to the bus stop. I nearly forgot about Candace, and when I reached the bus stop I realized that she was ten seconds behind me.

"Whitney," she caught her breath. "Why did you run like that?"

"I was trying to make sure I caught this bus. I don't want to go back up there and do anything. I think I'm getting sick."

"I've got medicine if you need it. Isn't Ivyana hilarious?"

"Hell no!"

"I think she's so funny!"

"Why?"

"You don't think the smiley face thing was funny?"

"I'll give it to her. That was funny. She wasn't serious though, right?"

"No, definitely not."

At eight the next morning I found myself at the library attempting to catch up on my homework. I was still chapters behind in my Literature and Race class and I needed to write five pages for Nonfiction 2. I read one chapter and felt my phone vibrate.

IVYANA: :-(
CANDACE: Who can get a fruit cup and green tea for Ivyana? I can't, I'm in class.
ME: Is she serious?! I'll get it this time...

I bought the fruit cup and tea and called Ivyana. "Hello may I speak to Ivyana?"

"This is she."

"I have your fruit cup and tea."

"I'm in the union so just bring it here."

After I dropped off her food, I returned to the library. I read three more chapters and felt my phone vibrate.

IVYANA: :-o

If I was a rich girl—na-na-na-na-na-na-na-na-na-nah. Nicole.

"Hello?"

"Hey sweets, how are you?"

"I'm fine, how are you?"

"I'm good. I'm calling to ask you for a favor. I need change for a ten and then I need quarters for laundry. You don't have to do it in eight minutes or anything like that. Just let me know when you get to my apartment."

I was leaving Sasha's house, headed to towers to table for the freshman peer leader group. I stood at the campus shuttle stop for twenty minutes. The shuttle didn't come. I started walking.

BROOKE: Hey Guys, I just packed Ivyana's clothes. I need someone to take her suitcase to the North side by 5. Can someone do it?
ME: I'm about to go table.

I continued walking towards lower campus and made it to the student union. My phone rang. Jamie.

"Whit, what are you doing?"

"I'm about to go table, what's up?"

"Well, I'm doing some last minute work for lab and everyone else is doing something else or not picking up. Brooke just called me flippin' out, could you help her please?"

EVA: Taking food to Latoya.

"Ugh, fine."

I called Brooke. "Hey, where are you?"

"I'm still at Melwood. I need to find her black tie before I zip her bag. I'll just bring the suitcase to my group meeting at the cathedral and you can just pick it up from there."

"Brooke, that doesn't make any sense—I'm just gonna come to Melwood. Be right there."

ME: On my way to Melwood for Ivyana's crap. Can someone ride with me to the North side in the next twenty min.?
MYA: I'll go.

Brooke let me into Ivyana's apartment and we searched the dressers and drawers for the black tie.

"Oh, here it is," Brooke said. "She made a list of stuff for me to pack and I was here all day cleaning up."

"She left you here all day?"

"Yea, I guess she trusts me," she placed the tie in the suitcase and zipped it.

When Mya and I made it to the North side, Ivyana had us sit on the floor of Tiffany's bedroom.

IVYANA: Whitney, call Teresa. Tell her that she needs to drive here and take me to the airport.

ME: Okay...Hey Teresa, Ivyana says that you need to come to Tiffany's place to pick her up and take her to the airport...Oh...Oh okay...(I closed my phone) Ivyana, Teresa said that her brother has her car for the weekend.

IVYANA: Ugh! My plane leaves in fifty minutes! This is all Teresa's fault!

If I was a rich girl—na-na-na-na-na-na-na-na-na-nah. Latoya.

"Hello?"

"Hey, I need you to get me a Cherry Pepsi from Seven Eleven and bring it up to Sasha's house in the next eighteen minutes. Keep the receipt. I'll pay you back."

I bought her soda and boarded the campus shuttle. I'd been sitting for ten minutes when the bus driver decided to step off to take a smoke break. I got off and started power walking to Sasha's house. I was ten minutes late.

"How long does it normally take you to get up here Whitney?" Sasha asked as I handed Latoya her Pepsi.

"Twenty minutes."

"And it took you half an hour this time, because?"

"The bus wasn't running."

"Right."

I stood awkwardly in the corner and watched Vanessa and Mya take down Sasha's hair while Latoya and Tiffany lounged on the floor. Realizing how insignificant my presence was, I prepared to ask to leave.

TIFFANY: Whitney, what was my interesting fact at my probate?

ME: I don't know.

TIFFANY: Were you at my probate?

ME: Yes.

TIFFANY: And you don't remember? Mya or Vanessa do y'all know?

MYA: No.

VANESSA: No, but I can—

TIFFANY: I don't want you to look it up later. If you don't know it, then you don't know it.

LATOYA: Do y'all remember my interesting fact?

SASHA: Do y'all remember mine?

US: No.

LATOYA: (sighing) These are the girls who *desperately* want to be TETs?

SASHA: (singing) *Beat it, just beat it.*

TIFFANY: Why are you singing that Sasha?

SASHA: Because I want Whitney to leave.

I picked up my bag and headed towards the door.

TIFFANY: Whoa, wait a minute! Whitney's just ready to leave! She's like, "Okay peace!"

SASHA: You know what, don't leave yet—since you *claim* it takes you twenty minutes to get down and back up, I need you to go get me a rat tail comb. *Twenty* minutes. Bye.

I left her house and started running towards my dorm. I stopped. It was impossible to get to my dorm and back in twenty minutes. I called Teresa. No Answer. I called Jamie. No answer. I called Candace. "Candace! Hey! Do you have a rat-tail comb? If you do could you meet me—"

"I can't...I'm running...getting bread for Ivyana."

"What?"

"Bread! I'm getting *bread* for Ivyana...Rite Aid didn't have any so I'm going to...Exxon."

"The gas station?"

"Yea! Gotta go, I'll call you back!"

I called Eva. "Eva where are you?"

"I'm in a meeting Whit, I'll call you—"

TERESA: I'm getting food for Felicia. What's up?

I called Amber. "Hey Amber, are you busy?"

"No, what's up?"

"I'm running towards lower campus from Sasha's house. Are you in your room?"

"Yea."

"Do you have a rat-tail comb?"

"Yea."

"Okay, could you bring the comb and meet me halfway?"

"Coming."

I ran down past Centre Street and called Amber again. "Hey where are you?"

"I'm near Chevron, the chemistry building. Do you know where that is?"

"No...Could you come to Centre Street?"

"Just run towards the center of campus, we should meet up."

"Okay, bye."

I had two minutes left to get back to Sasha's house when Amber and I met up. When I was seven houses away, I called Mya. "Hi Mya, could you come get the comb from me?"

I stopped running. I waited for Mya to come out, but I didn't see her.

If I was a rich girl—na-na-na-na-na-na-na-nah. Tiffany.
"Hello?"

"Whitney where are you? You lied! Mya said you weren't outside!"

"I'm outside the door."

"Well, you weren't there before! Mya's coming back out again."

Mya came outside and I handed her the comb. "Mya, I'm not trying to come at you or anything, but don't you think you could have called me when you were outside if you didn't see me, instead of going back in and telling them I wasn't there?"

"I'm sorry, I really didn't see you."

"I stopped running. I was back by that house with the weeds."

"Oh, I'm sorry Whit. Are you coming inside with me?"

"No. Just tell them I have asthma and needed to go home and get my pump or something."

"Okay, see you later."

If I was a rich girl—na-na-na-na-na-na-na-na-na-nah. Britney.
"Hello?"

"Hi, Whitney. How's your day going?"

"It's going good, how's yours?"

"It's okay so far. Are you busy?"

"No."

"Could you bring me a pepperoni pizza with ranch dressing and a brisk tea or pink lemonade to tower C?"

Teresa put her car in drive. "My car does not run on *water*. What don't they understand Whitney?"

"I don't know. I really don't," I fastened the seatbelt.

CANDACE: I have to make a wake-up call for Deborah tomorrow morning. I might need a reminder.

"I've taken Sasha to the mall, to her mom's house and everywhere else. I've taken Ivyana all over the world and neither of them has ever offered a dollar for gas! As a matter of fact, remember when I had to take Ivyana to the airport last week for her other flight?"

"Yea."

"Tiffany was supposed to take her, but she said she couldn't because gas was too high! They really think my gas is *free!*"

"I guess we'll have to start giving you gas money."

"Yea. I hate to ask y'all, but my parents are starting to ask questions and I can't keep hitting them up for money. Hold on," she opened her phone. "Alright Amber, we're outside."

Amber got in the car and called Sasha.

AMBER: Yea, I'm on my way to the Pete now...No, I'm with Teresa and—yea I'm in her car...Oh...Oh okay.

TERESA: What does she want from the Pete?

AMBER: She wanted pasta, but when I told her I was in your car she said that she wanted Eatn' Park.

TERESA: That's at the waterfront. That's *too* far.

ME: There's one in Squirrel Hill too, it's a lot closer.

TERESA: Is it open though?

AMBER: It should be.

TERESA: (sighing) Alright, I'll turn around after the next light.

If I was a rich girl—na-na-na-na-na-na-na-na-na-nah. Tiffany.

"Hello?"

"Where are you?"

"I'm in the ARC."

"You're at a study session?"

"Yea."

"Okay good, come outside."

I stuffed my things in my bag and left the building. Her car was parked on the other side of the street. I walked over to her window.

"Get in the car, Whitney!"

"Oh."

I walked to the other side and got in. She put the car in drive and sighed. "This is what we're going to do. This diet Ivyana has me on is killing me. I need some real food. Fruit cups and yogurt are for *birds*. Here's my debit card. I'm going to drop you off at Panera and you're going to get me a BLT. Call me when you have it and I'll come take you back to your study session. Bring me the receipt."

If I was a rich girl—na-na-na-na-na-na-na-na-na-nah. Kamille.

"Hello?"

"Hi Whitney, how are you?"

"I'm fine, how are you?"

"I'm well. Sasha wants you to go to the Pete and get her Burger King. She says don't forget to tell them no cheese."

"Okay, do I need to get you anything?"

"Um, just call me when you get to the Pete and I'll let you know."

"Okay."

I made it to the Pete, called Kamille back, submitted her pasta order, and went to Burger King.

"You want cheese on this?" the cashier asked.

"Yes, please."

When I arrived to Sasha's place she laughed. "You look like Frosty the Snowman, Whitney! Come in!"

I closed the door behind me and handed her the food. She went back to her room and told me to bring Kamille a fork from the kitchen.

"Whitney! There's *cheese* on my burger!"

"I'm sorry. I definitely told them no cheese twice."

"It's okay. I guess since you look like Frosty I'll just deal with it, but don't do it again."

XIII. Sway

I realized what pre-pledging meant: going to late night study sessions and running errands all day.

At a study session:

TIFFANY: Vanessa comes to every study session looking nice, rockin' the silky tresses, but lets her own roommate, her own homie Mya, come in here lookin' like *Crack head Tina*!

IVYANA: She does look like Crack head Tina! Scratch yourself Mya! Be a *crack head*!

Mya sat still.

TIFFANY: Go on, you gotta get the tick and the scratch together so it looks like you're crazy.

Mya started to scratch herself.

IVYANA: Oh, Crack head Tina, you can stop now. Wait, while we're on the subject of Crack head Tina, can we discuss the way she talks?

TIFFANY: How does she talk?

IVYANA: She talks in mystical tones! She leaves voicemails that are like, *"Hi...This is...Mya...I have a tarot reading...in three days you will..."*

TIFFANY: (laughing) I think we should try to find Mya's personality. Hold on, let me get my bag (pretended as if she was searching in an invisible bag). Ivyana I don't see it...There's some cards, some bones... Is this it? Is *this* her personality?

IVYANA: No, that's not it Tiffany. It doesn't exist.

TIFFANY: That's so unfortunate. Whitney, what did I tell you about that hoodie?

ME*: Not to wear it.

TIFFANY: Then why are you still wearing it?

ME*: Because it's cold and I'm kind of sick.

TIFFANY: Excuses. Let me tell you what Whitney does when she calls me. In the event that I actually pick up she'll say, "Hi Tiffany, how are you?" I'll say something like "Fine," and then she'll say, "So, do you wanna go out to lunch?" She already knows the deal. She doesn't want to stay on the phone with me either!

IVYANA: Teresa, does your brother have the car this weekend too? Is that the *excuse* you're going to give me whenever I ask you to do something?

TERESA*: No.

IVYANA: "No" to your brother having the car or "no" that's not going to be your excuse?

TERESA*: Both.

IVYANA: Good.

TIFFANY: Candace, stop looking like you don't want to be here!

IVYANA: Wow, she even looks *boring*!

TIFFANY: I'll take "boring" over "unsisterly." I still have no idea why we said "yes" to Amber Jackson! She's going to be the unsisterly one of the group y'all. I'm warning all of you in advance...

If I was a rich girl—na-na-na-na-na-na-na-na-na-nah. Deborah.

"Hello?"

"Hi Whitney, are you available?"

"No, I'm about to go to class."

"Okay. Well someone needs to bring me three Supreme tacos from Taco Bell with mild sauce and a raspberry sweet tea in the next fifteen minutes."

ME: Who can get Taco Bell for Deborah?

If I was a rich girl—na-na-na-na-na-na-na-na-na-nah. Latoya.

"Hello?"

"Hi, what are you doing?"

"I'm studying."

"Good. Come study with me. Get on the next 54C."

IVYANA: :-(
ME: Who can get shyt for Ivyana?
JAMIE: It might take me awhile....
AMBER: I'm in class.
VANESSA: I'll do it.

The TETs never mentioned anything about us going on line. I didn't care though, I was going to be a TET. That was all that mattered.

At a study session:
Brooke gathered her things and began putting on her coat. She
pushed her chair up to the table and looked around.

BROOKE: Goodbye guys. I'm going now.

MYA: Going where?

CANDACE: To the bathroom?

JAMIE: Why do you need your coat to go to the bathroom?

BROOKE: I'm not going to the bathroom. I'm leaving. I can't do this stuff anymore guys. I just can't.

ME: We haven't really done anything yet.

BROOKE: I'm just...I'm already stressed out about my school work and then y'all text me and call me all day everyday and I don't know if this is for me.

MYA: Eva, did Brooke tell you that she wanted to quit?

EVA: Yea.

MYA: And you didn't try to stop her?

EVA: It's her decision. I told her that she shouldn't, but I can't force her.

BROOKE: Mya, I just don't think this is right. Why do we have to buy them stuff, for them to get to know us? Why can't they be nice to us now and pledge us later?

VANESSA: (putting on her Ipod) Well, I'm not going to try and convince someone why she should want to be a TET. I have homework. I'll be your friend if you decide to stay or leave but I'm sorry, I can't force you to stay.

SHELBY: Yea, let me tell you something Brooke. We are all going to be on line together hopefully. But if you're having doubts now, and you're the shortest one and the potential ace, then you should do us all a favor and leave now. All of our asses are gonna be on the line and I don't need a wishy washy ace. So if you're gonna leave, leave.

With the exception of Vanessa, we talked to Brooke for the rest of study session and persuaded her to stay. I thought that Brooke had lost her mind. She wasn't thinking straight, she wasn't making any sense. I hoped that she wouldn't be tempted to drop again, and that she would continue to think like the rest of us.

IVYANA: :-(

CANDACE: Who can get a tea and fruit cup for Ivyana?
ME: I'm with Deborah.
CANDACE: Shelby is going to do it.

If I was a rich girl—na-na-na-na-na-na-na-na-na-nah. Julia.

"Hello?"

"Hi Whitney, how are you doing today?"

"I'm good, how are you?"

"I'm fine. You don't have class today, correct?"

"Correct."

"Well, could you come over right now? I want to talk to you about something."

"Okay."

When I arrived, she led me into her room and closed the door. TET memorabilia adorned her dresser, desk, and shelf—paddles, photos, pearls.

"Have a seat," she sat on her bed. She took a sip of water and sighed. "My sorors have been telling me that you have an attitude. Britney Lynn said that she asked you how your day was going at a study session and you were like, 'It was aight' and shrugged your shoulders. If you continue to come across like that, the basement is going to be a big problem for you."

JAMIE: SHs, I have to make a slideshow for Sasha at SS tonight and I might need help. Thanks! <3

"I apologize. I didn't mean anything by the 'aight' comment. I just really had an average day."

"And whenever we all come to study session to talk to y'all you just...I don't know what it is but it just looks like you're getting an attitude. Can you explain that?"

AMBER: Going to clean Deborah's place.

"I just don't show emotion. I never really have unless it's something deeply personal, but I'll try to work on it."

"Please do that. I'm trying to help you out. Speaking of helping you out, let me give you some advice to take back to your little study friends. You all really need to be trying to get to know us. Bottom line. You need to be calling us and trying to build relationships with us. We have something that y'all want. If I don't pick up the first time, call me again. If I don't pick up that time, call me again. I am a number four. Don't you think you should try to reach me *four* times?"

VANESSA: Getting stuff for Kamille.

"Yes."

"Okay, good. Because I don't think you all are getting it. Y'all are being lax and getting comfortable. You have no idea how hard getting into Epsilon is going to be. It doesn't hurt to build trust because if you're lucky enough to get chosen for pledging, you won't be angry at us for whatever happens during the process. For example, your little friend Mya—she doesn't call me, she doesn't acknowledge me. And to think I voted "yes" for her...I don't like Mya, so you can bet if she gets into the basement I'll," she didn't finish her sentence. She just looked away and shook her head.

At a study session:
Latoya and Sasha came inside the room and took seats.

SASHA: I feel like y'all don't communicate enough. That's going to be a HUGE problem in the future. Have y'all been working on that?

US: Yes.

SASHA: Good, because y'all were a mess last weekend. Does anybody have a test or a quiz soon?

No one raised their hand.

SASHA: Okay cool. I don't like this room. It's hot and y'all can't sit in a circle.

LATOYA: The nursing hall *is* tucked away though, I'll give y'all that. Eva!

Eva slumped and looked down at the floor.

LATOYA: Eva stop looking down at the floor! Why do you do that? Move your chair away from the rest of the group. NOW!

Eva moved her chair away.

LATOYA: Further!

She moved a few more feet away.

LATOYA: Good! Stay there!

SASHA: Brooke you're *unsisterly*! Don't you think that you should move closer to fill in the gap so Eva won't be by herself?

BROOKE*: I—

SASHA: Whatever, Eva you can move back over. I can't picture any of y'all on line. I really can't, y'all aren't ready.
LATOYA: I can't picture any of them on line either, especially *Eva*.

I attempted to call the TETs to ask about their days or ask them out to lunch, but they didn't answer often. If they did answer, they would ask me to run an errand or say they were busy.

One Tuesday I got out of my night class early. I decided to call Britney Lynn and apologize about making the "aight" comment. I called her and it went to voicemail. I called again and it went to voicemail. I left a message and prepared to take a nap.
BRITNEY LYNN: Hey what's up?
ME: I was just calling to speak with you.
BRITNEY LYNN: Oh okay, you're not in class?
ME: No, I got out early tonight.
BRITNEY LYNN: Are you busy?
ME: No.
BRITNEY LYNN: Could you bring me a pink lemonade to towers?

If I was a rich girl—na-na-na-na-na-na-na-na-na-nah. Mommy.

"Hello?"

"How's it goin Whit? I haven't heard from you this week."

"It's going good. I've just been really busy with the school newspaper and my writing class."
CANDACE: Giving Tiffany my charger.

"Oh okay. What's going on with TET?"

"They're just having a whole lot of events."

"They haven't had an interest meeting or a rush yet?"

"No, I don't think so. I haven't seen or heard anything about one."

"Oh alright. Your aunt and I just wanted to know if you'd heard anything."

"Nope, but I'll let you know if I do."

XIV. Full and By

IVYANA: :-O
CANDACE: Who can get a fruit cup and water for Ivyana?
ME: I'm in class.
CANDACE: Mya is going to do it.

Subject:	Info on THEM [Fwd: directions and an attachment]
From:	"[Candace]" ███████edu
Date:	Wed, February 20, 2008 4:22 am
To:	wgw████edu
Priority:	Normal
Options:	View Full Header	View Printable Version

------------------Original Message -------------
    Subject: directions and an attachment
From: "[Teresa]" ███████████edu>
Date: Mon, February 18, 2008 8:05 pm
    To: ██████.edu
----

hey guys, when you get this, can you guys fill in
what you know and then email it or forward it to the
next person in this order (no particular
order)...also, can the last person ([Amber]) email it
back to me (██████████.edu) and i will fix it up and
email it out to everyone:

[Candace] (███████████edu)

Whitney (wgw█████.edu)

[Brooke] (████████████.edu)

[Eva] (███████edu)

[Shelby] (███████gmail.com)

[Jamie] (███████████.edu)

[Mya] (███████████.edu)

[Vanessa] (████████████.edu)

[Amber] (████████.edu)

[Teresa] (████████.edu)

On Friday, Julia told Amber that we needed to come up with a list of programs that addressed each of the sorority's platforms. We met at Shelby's house to come up with ideas. By the time we finished completing the program list it was 8:40.

AMBER: It's late! I gotta go! I'll see y'all at study session.

JAMIE: Me too. I have to run to my room real quick.

TERESA: Whitney, are you going back to your room?

ME: No, just straight to study session I guess.

TERESA: Let's go to Five Guys first.

ME: Okay.

Teresa ordered the food while we were on the way. The cashier took his time cashing our orders and as soon as we received our food we ran towards the engineering building. We arrived at 8:58 and saw the other SHs standing around in the lobby.

ME: Why is everyone standing around? Did y'all find a room?

VANESSA: Yea, we're on the eighth floor. Amber's not here yet.

MYA: She said she was on her way when I called her a minute ago.

SHELBY: Can we call Britney Lynn a few minutes late?

TERESA: No, that'll just add to our list of mistakes.

MYA: Somebody can just fake Amber's voice if she asks us to pass around the phone.

VANESSA: Yea, who can do it?

CANDACE: (imitating Amber's voice) Hi this is Amber.

SHELBY: Perfect!

VANESSA: Okay I'm calling. Hello, may I speak to Britney Lynn? This is Vanessa, are you available to speak? I was just calling to let you know that we're all here…Okay. (handed the phone to Candace) Pass it around.

CANDACE: Hi Britney, this is Candace.

SHELBY: Hi Britney, this is Shelby.

ME: Hi Britney, this is Whitney.

TERESA: Hi Britney, this is Teresa.

BROOKE: Hi Britney, this is Brooke.

MYA: Hi Britney, this is Mya.

EVA: Hi Britney, this is Eva.

JAMIE: Hi Britney, this is Jamie.

CANDACE: (imitating Amber's voice) Hi Britney, this is Amber.

VANESSA: Okay. Alright, bye.

ME: Amber's calling me. Hello? Where are you? Oh, okay. (I closed my phone) She says she's outside. Somebody open the side door.

Amber stood with us in the lobby and explained why she was late. A group of five SHS got on the elevator and five of us stayed behind. While we were talking about how Candace faked Amber's voice, Deborah walked into the lobby. She stopped, shook her head, and got on the elevator.

AMBER: Oh my god. Was that really Deborah?

ME: (sighing) Yea.

We boarded the elevator and went to the eighth floor. We found the room and saw that Deborah had already made it there. We sat down in the circle with the other SHs and took off our coats. We placed our books on the desks and started to study.

DEBORAH: Put your coats back on! Put the desks back in rows! You have ten seconds! LINE UP!

We pulled the desks out of the circle and lined up in the center of the room facing the windows.

DEBORAH: YOU ALL ARE NOT GETTING IT ARE YOU? WHAT DON'T YOU UNDERSTAND? ARE YOU TRYING TO GET MY CHAPTER SNATCHED?

She stood in front of us.

DEBORAH: Do you really think huddling around in the lobby is discreet! Don't answer that—I'll let you know when I want you to answer something! Do you think that a group of y'all who didn't know each other before should be standing around in the LOBBY? Why are you looking like that? What's wrong with you Shelby?

SHELBY*: I…I feel faint.

DEBORAH: Ugh, sit down Shelby. I don't need you *dying* on me.

Shelby took a seat.

DEBORAH: This is such a disappointment!

She approached the chalkboard and picked up a piece of chalk. She wrote "not discreet," "stupid," "replaceable," and "don't know your role."

DEBORAH: You all are *stupid*! You're not discreet, you are replaceable, and you don't know your role! You will not get into my chapter by being indiscreet!

She stepped down the line, getting into each of our faces, asking why we wanted to be TETs.

DEBORAH: Whitney, why do you want to be a TET?

ME*: So I can be an influential member of the community and join a network of women that will support me and my ambitions.

DEBORAH: Do you think it's weird that I'm yelling at you right now and in a few days we're going to be at a freshman leader meeting together?

ME*: No.

DEBORAH: Good! Teresa, why do you—you know what, I don't want to look at you! Go get in the corner!

Teresa walked to the corner.

DEBORAH: See! That's what I'm talking about! Why would you WALK to the corner? It's called SENSE OF URGENCY! Why did you just WALK?

TERESA*: I just—

DEBORAH: FACE THE CORNER! I DON'T WANT TO LOOK AT YOU! SPEAK UP! WHAT DID YOU SAY?

TERESA*: I don't know.

DEBORAH: Let's try this again. Go back to where you were and go back to corner with a sense of urgency…GO!

Teresa ran back to the line and ran to the corner.

DEBORAH: Didn't you used to run *track*? That wasn't running! Do it again!

Teresa ran back to the line again and ran to the corner.

DEBORAH: DO IT AGAIN! (pelting Teresa with Starbursts) YOU'RE NOT RUNNING FAST ENOUGH! PICK UP MY STARBURSTS!

Teresa began picking up the Starbursts and each time she picked up one, Deborah pelted her with others.

DEBORAH: Just stay back there until I feel like looking at you again. Amber, why do you want to be a TET?

AMBER: I want to be a TET because I want to be a part of a sisterhood and be able to use that sisterhood to create awareness in the community about important social issues.

DEBORAH: Eva, why do you—wait! Weren't you supposed to call and wake me up this morning?

EVA*: I—

DEBORAH: You made me miss my appointment and I slept through it! Do you know how important that was to me? Do you know that I now have to reschedule it because of you? Do you think I have you make wake up calls for *fun*? I really do have problems waking up and I trusted you to help me!

EVA*: I—

DEBORAH: Go to the other corner! I don't want to look at you either!

Eva ran to the corner.

DEBORAH: Jamie...how do you feel about *auxiliary* organizations? Don't you have friends in *auxiliary* organizations?

JAMIE*: I think they're fine if someone wants to join one, but they're not for me.

Deborah approached the board and began writing.

DEBORAH: What do you think it's going to take to get into Epsilon? What are some qualities that you all should have, but clearly *don't*? Are you okay now Shelby?

SHELBY*: I...need to eat something.

DEBORAH: Somebody give her some food or something! Don't look me in the eyes!

Britney Lynn entered the room. She looked at us in confusion and looked at Deborah.

DEBORAH: I came here to study for my O-Chem test, just to drop by and have small talk with the girls. But when I got here, half of them we're standing around in the lobby!

Britney Lynn shook her head.

DEBORAH: Brooke, do you tell your parents anything about TET?

BROOKE:* No.

DEBORAH: Oh really. So, if you're selected for pledging, you're not going to vent to anyone?

BROOKE*: I'll just pray.

DEBORAH: (suppressed a smile and got into Amber's face) Amber! Do you tell your Nu Pi boyfriend any of the stuff that goes on?

AMBER*: No, I don't.

DEBORAH: Sure you don't.

Britney Lynn began taking our bags from us one by one and placing them in desk chairs.

DEBORAH: Back to the qualities that you all are clearly *lacking*. What are some things that you should be doing? Vanessa?

VANESSA*: Being passionate.

DEBORAH: None of you all are passionate! (writing "passion" on the board) Do you realize how many other girls want to be TETs here? Do you realize that you can be replaced within a second with someone who really wants to be here? Eva! Turn around! What's another quality that you don't have? Better yet, what should you all be doing?

EVA*: Hustling…

DEBORAH: Ha! Hustle? (writing on the board) You all clearly don't have that one! Get back in the line—I mean that isn't a line! Get back in the *group*!

Eva ran back to her spot. Deborah continued to ask each of us to list qualities that she wrote on the board. She asked us to describe what each of them meant and how each of us was going to try and live out those words to get into her chapter.

DEBORAH: We have more to lose than you have to gain! Do you all realize that? Candace, what did I just say?

CANDACE*: You have more to lose that we—

DEBORAH: Pay attention! You all need to *listen*! (writing on the board) WE have way MORE to lose than YOU have to gain. I'm not tryna go to jail because a group of idiots want to stand around in lobby and talk about TET. Do you understand?

Britney Lynn removed Candace's bag last and Deborah continued to ask questions.

DEBORAH: (looking at her phone) Whoa. How long do you think you've been standing?

I thought forty five minutes.

DEBORAH: About three hours…Well, you all can sit back down. Make your circle again. Not you Teresa!

We arranged the circle and took seats. Deborah walked to the door.

DEBORAH: Teresa, come step outside with me. Someone wants to talk to you.

Teresa walked towards the door.

US*: Run!

AMBER*: Why aren't you running?

Teresa ran out to the hallway. She spoke to Sasha on the phone, and Deborah and Britney Lynn talked with her for a few minutes. When they were done, Teresa took her place in the circle.

DEBORAH: So, I've spent three hours of my life teaching you things that I shouldn't have to teach again. Don't let those hours have been a waste of my time. I'm going to go finish studying for O-Chem now.

She left, and Britney Lynn gave us a bit of advice before following suit.

Subject:	You are...
From:	"[Shelby]" <█████@gmail.com>
Date:	Sat, February 23, 2008 5:14 pm
To:	████████.edu (more)
Priority:	Normal
Options:	View Full Header | View Printable Version

```
YOU ARE:

Replaceable

Know your place and role, Listen

    -  Do your part!
    -  Liability
    -  Humble,   respectful,   sense   of   urgency,
       efficiency, punctual (early)
    -  Communicate with each other
** We have more to lose than you have to gain.**

          DISCRETE!!!!---
INDISCRETION!!!!!

Not intelligent

Lazy, don't listen

Don't know your role!

Learn/Expanding Horizons/ Not knowledgeable
```

The next afternoon we were sitting in Shelby's room, going over Deborah's lecture points, and making gifts in an attempt to apologize for Friday's mistake. Jamie, Mya, and I had purchased violet and green picture frames, wood markers, ribbons, and paper.

Mya took my sheet of paper.

MYA: Whit, your ivies look like marijuana leaves and they're making me...uncomfortable.

VANESSA: Yea, I don't know if any of us should attempt to draw the ivies. They'll play our lives. Let's just keep it simple with writing the sisterly words around the frame.

CANDACE: Okay, cool. Whose handwriting are we using?

MYA: I like Amber's handwriting.

AMBER: I like Mya's.

VANESSA: We can use both and anybody else who wants to write can write too, but we'll need to see a sample first. The rest of us can start tying the ribbons and cutting out the line numbers and stuff.

SHELBY: How much do we each need to pay for this Whitney?

I pulled out my planner.

MYA: (laughing) I don't know if I agree with us making Whitney the secretary. She owes every bank in Pittsburgh and that makes me...uncomfortable.

ME: Shut up Mya. I owe them each like a dollar.

MYA: Yea, plus an over withdrawal fee!

ME: Yea, plus that. It should be five or six dollars from everyone. I still need Jamie's receipts though so it might be a little less than that. We'll have to wait until she gets back for the set amount.

BROOKE: Guys, I can't do this anymore.

TERESA: Again?

BROOKE: I'm serious! I can't eat, I can't sleep, my hair's falling out, and I'm just stressed all the time. This is *too much* for pre-pledging.

VANESSA: Pass me the ribbon please.

AMBER: I need the other marker.

CANDACE: Well Brooke, I would really like for you to stay. Everyone else would too. Just think about everything before you decide to walk away. Spring Break will be here soon.

BROOKE: Okay, Candace.

We split up the task of delivering the picture frames. We wrapped them in green wrapping paper and tied a bright violet ribbon around each one. I delivered Cari's since she stayed on my floor and texted the SHs when my task was done. By the end of the night, each of us had delivered our gifts.

If I was a rich girl—na-na-na-na-na-na-na-na-na-nah. Tiffany.

"Hello?"

"Hi Whitney. I need you and one of your study friends to come clean my apartment this afternoon. You need to be here by four."

I asked Brooke to accompany me so I could ask her why she was acting distant from the group. She and I argued the entire bus ride. When we made it to the North side, we walked in silence until we reached Tiffany's apartment.

Tiffany told Brooke to clean the living room and the kitchen. I was told to clean her bathroom and bedroom.

"All of my TET stuff goes in the corner by that chest," she said. "And I need you to clean the tub too. Ivyana acts like she's incapable of cleaning up after herself. She thinks this is the Holiday Inn or something. I'm going back to campus. Make sure you lock my apartment when you leave if I'm not back when you get done. Bye."

I started cleaning her bathroom—the sink, the tub, the toilet. I hung all the shirts she asked me to hang, and placed her TET items by her chest. Curious, I opened the chest and looked through it. There were photos of her and her LSs, TET books, programs, and a dead rose. I spotted a book under her TV stand and yelled, "Brooke! Brooke! Brooke! Come here!"

JAMIE: Got Ivyana's email password, looking up stuff for her.

"What Whit?" she stepped into the room.

"This is their service book. Every TET gets one of these from nationals when she crosses."

"Let me see. Is this the book that Amber was talking about? The one they get when they go on line, the mind?"

"No, I don't think so. She said the mind looks like a planner."

I placed a pamphlet in the chest and then it hit me. I dug through the chest and found a small black book with spiral bound. I flipped through it and saw Epsilon lineage, poems, and history written in Tiffany's handwriting. As I flipped to the back of the book, I noticed that the pages were written like diary entries.

"Brooke…This is it…This is her *mind.*"

"Damn, Whit. What should we do with it?"

"Does she have a copier?"

"Nope. I didn't see one in the living room."

"There's not one in here either. Okay look, if you copy information from the service book, I'll copy information from the mind."

"Okay."

We locked her room door and prayed that we wouldn't get caught. My heart was racing. My fingers trembled with every word I copied.

If I was a rich girl—na-na-na-na-na-na-na-na-na-nah. Ivyana.

"Hello?"

"Where are you? Are you *lost*?"

"No, I just got to the library."

"Well, I'm on the third floor, hurry up."

I took the elevator to the third floor and walked into the study room where Ivyana was sitting. There was a freshman interest in the room. I handed Ivyana the food and took a seat. I didn't want to give away the fact that I was pre-pledging so I said, "I already ate my food but they gave me extra so I figured I'd come offer the extras to you."

"Why thank you Whitney," she smiled.

IVYANA: Sorry, you're stuck here dude. I need a ride to the North side when the lib closes. Figure that out.

ME: Hey Teresa, I hate to text you this, but Ivyana needs a ride to the North side at 2. Can you do it?

I was getting sicker every day. I always felt hot, even though it was freezing outside. I was drained and nauseous, but I always found the energy to complete any errand that I was asked to do. I headed to another study session, bowl of soup in hand, hoping that the TETs wouldn't show up.

At a study session:

ME: If Ivyana sends me one more smiley face I'm gonna scream! She sends at least five a day!

CANDACE: I really thought she was joking.

VANESSA: I'm glad I don't get those. When I brought her the fruit cup earlier, she looked like she was so happy about her little system.

BROOKE: That's ridiculous. Fruit cups are like three dollars each. Are you okay Whit? You look pale.

SHELBY: You don't need medicine or anything do you?

ME: Na, I'm good. I think it's just a cold. Are you alright from the other day, Teresa?

TERESA: Yea.

JAMIE: Why didn't you tell us that you had a panic attack?

TERESA: I didn't think it was that serious. Me and Felicia were just studying and all of a sudden I got weak and dizzy and I felt like...I can't explain it. She walked me to the hospital though. I guess I didn't immediately text y'all because I didn't know what was going on.

CANDACE: Well could you let us know if it happens again?

TERESA: Yea.

AMBER: Okay, good. I feel like they're going to show up this weekend so we should just go over everything tonight—the founders, charters, Greek alphabet, and the "info on them" document. Then when people post new info we can go over that in a few days.

EVA: (singing) *I wish I could believe you...*

JAMIE: Brooke and Whit don't forget to put up that info y'all got from Tiffany's place. Give it to me or put it up before Spring Break.

BROOKE: Okay, I will.

EVA: (singing) *Then I'll be alright...*

ME: Eva...

VANESSA: Let's get this info studying session over with. I need to study for my test.

EVA: (singing) *But now everything you told me, really don't apply, to the way I feel in—*

ME: SHUT UP EVA!

EVA: Huh?

ME: You were singing. We're supposed to be going over info.

EVA: Ohhh, my bad. We can start now.

We went over the information for two hours. Britney Lynn called and allowed us to leave at two. While we were deciding whose turn it was to leave first, Teresa's phone sounded.

TERESA: Hello? Hi Ivyana...Okay. Okay, I will. I'll call you and let you know (she closed her phone) Ivyana said I have to vacuum and straighten her apartment and check to see if the heater is working.

AMBER: What?

TERESA: (sighing) Yea. Can a few of y'all come with me?

Candace, Vanessa, and I accompanied Teresa to Ivyana's apartment. We each straightened a different room and when we finished we sifted through her TET memorabilia.

TERESA: Are we going to copy her mind too?

CANDACE: We could. Her mind is in her underwear drawer. I saw it there last week when I cleaned up.

ME: (opening her underwear drawer) I guess we'll just compare notes. I want to find those pictures that Amber was telling us about.

CANDACE: Their set pictures?

VANESSA: The pictures that show them pledging?

ME: Yea, where do you think she would put them?

TERESA: Not in her underwear drawer.

VANESSA: And not anywhere where we could find them.

We looked under her bed, under her couch, in her closet, through her photo albums, but we found nothing.

TERESA: Maybe she got rid of them.

ME: Doubt it. What's that basket on top of her armoire?

Teresa took it down and took out photo albums and books.

TERESA: Guys, I think this is it...

There were a handful of photos near the back of the album. In one of them, the girls from fall 05 were standing in a line dressed in white T-shirts, covered in what appeared to be vomit. In another they were dancing with looks of fear on their faces. They were holding ivy plants in orange pots in a few photos and in others they were doing exercises, appearing exhausted and miserable.

BRITNEY LYNN: Hey what's up?

ME: I'm just typing. How are you?
BRITNEY LYNN: I'm fine. Could you bring me a
Brisk tea?

At a study session:
SHELBY: Its 8:58. Where is Brooke?
EVA: Why is everybody looking at me? I don't know.
AMBER: Okay, its 8:59 now. Who's calling Britney Lynn?
CANDACE: I will.
            Brooke rushed into the room, angry.
CANDACE: Brooke, what's wrong?
BROOKE: I can't talk right now. Let me get my thoughts together.
AMBER: Are you okay?
BROOKE: Wait, I can't talk about it. I'm too pissed. Give me a
second.
CANDACE: Okay. (calling Britney Lynn) Hello? May I speak to
Britney Lynn? Are you available to speak? Hi, this is Candace. I
was calling to let you know that we're all here...Okay, goodbye.
She says she's going to stop by later. Are you ready to tell us what
it is Brooke?
BROOKE: Yea. Tiffany got mad because I wouldn't let her see my
paper from this class I took last semester. I'm not trying to have
her copy my stuff. Then, she tells me that I'm not going to get any
sleep tonight because she's gonna make me stay up until she
finishes it. Like, that's the one thing that I don't play about! That's
the one thing that you don't mess with! I need *my sleep*!
            We laughed.
BROOKE: I'm serious!

TERESA: Buying Ivyana Dippin Dots Ice Cream.
ME: She's lactose intolerant!
TERESA: I know lol.

If I was a rich girl—na-na-na-na-na-na-na-na-na-nah. Sasha.
    "Hello?"
    "Why do you sound like that?"
    "I'm sick."
    "Oh. I want Burger King— the usual, no onions and get me
an orange soda this time. I think I'm kind of addicted to that now."

She hung up and I lay in bed for a few minutes more, hoping that it wasn't snowing outside. I rolled over and drew the blinds: snow. It took me five minutes to get dressed. I put on two pair of stockings, a pair of sweats, three shirts, a hoodie, and a large gray coat. I tied a wool scarf around my neck, tucked my meal plan card into my pocket, and headed for Burger King.

As soon as the first gust of wind hit my face I started wheezing. I couldn't breathe. I couldn't move. Mucus was stuck in my throat.

I bent over and coughed out as much as I could. I continued walking to Burger King, stopping to cough when necessary. I was halfway up the hill when she called again.

"Are you at Burger King yet?" she asked.

"No, I'm still on my way."

"Isn't your dorm like five minutes away from Burger King?"

"Yea."

"Then you need to hurry up. You should have been at Burger King by now instead of taking your precious time."

She hung up. I kept walking and made it to the Pete, but I went to the restroom instead of Burger King. I bent over the toilet and tried to force more mucus out of my throat.

She called again. "Are you at Burger King now?"

"No, but I'm at the Pete."

"That's not what I asked you. Are you at *Burger King*?"

"No. I had to go to the restroom, but I'm on my way. I apologize that I'm running late but I'll be there soon."

"If you want to be on line, this little lax attitude you have isn't going to cut it! Hurry up!"

She hung up and something snapped. I thought, "Why the fuck am I *apologizing* for buying someone else *her* food? Did she not hear me say that I was sick earlier? She's lucky she's getting this within an hour!"

Once I finished coughing, I went upstairs to order her food. When her food was ready, I took the brown bag over to the far napkin station. I took out the burger and un-wrapped it. I took the patty from between the two buns and wiped it across the counter. I coughed on the top bun and scraped the inside of the bottom bun. I scratched my unwashed scalp and flicked the dirt onto the patty. I put the burger back together as neatly as possible.

I coughed on the carton of fries. I took a few of them out and dropped them in the cup of orange soda. I swirled the cup around a few times. When I was certain that the fries were mixed up well enough, I reached into the cup and pulled them out.

I threw the soggy fries away, placed the cap back onto the cup, and proceeded to walk up the hill towards Sasha's house.

I called when I approached her porch. Instead of answering her phone, she swung the door open and exclaimed, "Finally!"

She said thank you and closed the door in my face. I felt a tinge of guilt for playing with her food, but that feeling faded away as soon as I started to cough up more mucus.

I went straight to the student hospital. A doctor asked me to breathe deeply while she placed a stethoscope on my back. She looked down my throat with a light, shook her head, and wrote down notes on a clipboard.

"It appears that you have a bad case of pneumonia. Did you say that you've had this before?"

"Yes."

"And you didn't take any medicine for it?"

"No, I usually let it go away on its own."

"I don't think this will be going away anytime soon. I'm going to prescribe an inhaler with medicine for you, Sudafed, and nasal drops. If you don't know how to use an inhaler have the pharmacist technician show you before you leave today. Do you have any other concerns?"

"No, not really."

"I know that you have to attend class, but I need you to limit the time that you spend outside in this weather. You also need to drink plenty of water. Lay off the juice and drinks for the next few weeks."

She wrote down the prescriptions on a pad, insisted that I email her if I didn't notice a change in a week, and that was it. I picked up my medicine at the pharmacy counter and walked back to my room. I had a paper to write.

At a study session:
Candace and Amber walked into the room. Candace handed
Deborah a carton of McDonald's fries.

DEBORAH: What took y'all so *long?*

CANDACE: It was really icy outside.

DEBORAH: Oh.

Deborah talked to us for an hour and then she left.

TERESA: I'm not tryna come at y'all or anything but why did it take y'all so long?

CANDACE: Well, we got to the apartment and took down everyone's order—

BROOKE: Who is *everyone?*

AMBER: Sasha, Janet, Marilyn, Julia, and Nicole.

MYA: Janet and Marilyn? They don't even go to this school.

CANDACE: Yea we know, but they're TETs. Anyway we got to McDonalds, got the food, and then (laughing) Amber slipped on the ice but she held up that McDonalds like it was her life!

We laughed.

AMBER: But when we got there, they complained that it took us too long and they said that one of the bags was missing an order of fries.

CANDACE: They wrote down their order and we had to go back to McDonald's and have them remake the entire meal again because they wanted it fresh.

AMBER: When we got back the second time Nicole whispered, "Are y'all fucking up?" and laughed. Then they claimed that we got the order wrong AGAIN! But I knew we got it right so I pulled out the note they wrote and said, "DIDN'T YOU SAY YOU WANTED" whatever that paper said and they didn't have anything to say.

CANDACE: They just said that we should have gotten it right the first time. And of course we had to go to McDonald's *again* to get Deborah the medium fries so they'd be hot. That's why it took so long. It's extra snowy and icy out there too. We weren't trying to fall.

BROOKE: I just don't see why we should have to do anything for people if they aren't in *this* chapter.

TERESA: I feel you on that Brooke. That doesn't make any sense.

JAMIE: As long as the other TETs don't start calling us I guess it's okay.

TERESA: They better not. I just remembered something. Amber *always* falls or does something crazy when she runs an errand! When she and I had to go two different places to get Sasha food, she was running up that hill and taking sips out of Sasha's drink like she was in race or something!

AMBER: (laughing) Okay, back to business. Info time. Spring 07.

US: *Kamille Jackson, Sasha Irons, Latoya Riley, Julia Benson, Cari Jones, Britney Lynn, Nicole Ballard, Regina Addison, Tiffany Stringer.*

AMBER: Fall '05.

US: *Riana Lewis, Arizona Hilton, Felicia Cross, Deborah Parsons, Mila Thomas, Ivyana Tate, Amara Van.*

AMBER: Fall '04.

US: *Tanya Gaines, Tamera Clarke, Selena Lewis, Raven Black, Cassandra Turner, Hannah York.*

AMBER: Founders and charters…

Study sessions were increased from four days to five. Every Monday, Tuesday, Thursday, Friday, and Saturday night the ten of us were in the engineering hall or in the nursing hall. On the nights that we didn't have study session, small groups of us would meet to study information or talk about how excited we were about becoming TETs. We started to bond, and it didn't feel forced or insincere.

XV. Hold

"I'm so tired. Last night I was walking and I ran into a pole. My LS had to hold my hand and help me walk home. I'm sick of this! I can't wait for this to be over! I miss my life!"

I copied a couple of poems from Ivyana's mind and placed it back in her underwear drawer. I hung her pants and made sure that I locked all three of her doors.

CANDACE: Going to Sasha's house with Eva to clean.

I walked back to campus and went to the third floor of the union for a counseling appointment.

VANESSA: Is anyone near the Pete?

I put my phone on vibrate. Half an hour later, I found myself sitting in Sylvia's office.

"I'm glad that you came back, Whitney. I haven't heard from you in a while though. Is everything okay?" she asked.

"Yea, everything's great."

"How's the memoir about your dad coming?"

"It's going pretty well. I've realized a lot about myself by writing it."

"That's good. When you get done I'd love to read it."

"I'll be sure to email it to you. I meant to tell you, I got picked!"

AMBER: Going to get food for Tiffany.

"For TET? That's great! Are you pledging now?"

"Um, something like that...It's me and nine other girls. We're pre-pledging."

"Pre-pledging?"

"Yea."

"What does that mean?"

"We run errands all day and go to study sessions at night."

"Are you happy?"

"I'm happy that I was chosen, but I'm tired of all the errands. It's ridiculous. I just wish they would put us on line so we could get it all over with."

"Well, I'm glad you're happy Whitney. You've come a long way since last semester. I'm glad you're getting what you wanted."

"Thanks. Can I tell you something?"

"Sure."

"You're not going to tell anyone?"

"No, I won't."

"You promise?"

"I promise, Whitney."

"Okay," I sighed. "There's a part of me that just wants to throw my phone out of the window and never think about TET again. I'm not *learning* anything from what I'm doing. Granted, I love hanging with the girls in the study group, but everything else is just crazy. I know what I'm doing is stupid, but I'm too far in to just back away and say, fuck this. I just keep doing it because I want TET really bad. And, I've kind of started to realize that the TETs aren't who I thought they were. They're so into image and the process and all the stuff that doesn't even matter. I'm too logical for this sometimes."

"Why would you want to throw your phone away?"

"Because it rings all day. It's nonstop. If I'm not getting a call from a TET, I'm getting a text from a TET. If I'm not getting a text from a TET, then I'm getting a text from a girl in the study group telling me or asking me about something she's about to do for a TET. I need to pause everything and finish this memoir. I need time though, and I definitely don't have enough of that right now."

TERESA: Should I get B. Lynn pink lemonade or tea?

"Do you think you'll be able to finish it?"

"No."

"Why not?"

"I'll probably get enough pages done to satisfy the class requirements, but as far as finishing it for myself? No. I never finish anything."

"What do you mean?"

"If it's not for a class or for a writing seminar, I don't finish. I've got a closet full of notebooks with screenplays that I've started. I'll always get halfway done and then I'll think of something else and I won't finish. It's a cycle."

"Do you think that's part of the reason you want to finish the TET process? So you can say you finished something?"

"No. I don't think it's that deep. I *know* I'm going to finish this process. It's only the personal writing projects that I never finish."

"Well, I feel like if it's really important to you Whitney, you'll put in enough time and you'll finish it. Do you open up more to your friends about your feelings and your past now?"

"No."

"Why not?"

"Because I'll probably cry and people will think I'm weak. If I'm vulnerable, people will use that against me. I just can't be like that yet. I can't show emotion. I'm not ready for that. I'd rather just not talk about that kind of stuff at all you know? I just want to act like some of things that happened to me never happened."

SHELBY: Hey ladies, I'm going to be unavailable for the rest of today. I sprained my knee trying to run up Chesterfield St. with Ivyana's effin Veracruz burrito. Getting a brace put on. See you at SS.

"Hmmm." she paused. "How are your emotions towards your dad now? Have you found out or written down the things that affected you the most?"

"Yes. I think I finally figured out when it started."

"Have you already written that part? Can I read that?"

1997. Eight years old.

The three of them snatch tree branches from the ground and circle around him, beating him. They yell: "Where da fuck is my money?" "You're gonna pay for this shit!" "Bitch ass!"

They punch him, hard. He falls to the ground, and one of the three men picks him up and pushes him across the yard.

He tries to run away, but he's not fast enough—they grab him and move him towards the car. The short one slaps him across the head as the skinny one opens the back door of the car.

They stuff him inside. I hear his head smack against the rear. The third one slams the door shut. He looks up at me as I stare down from my window.

153

His skin is wrinkled, but not because of aging. He looks me straight in my eyes—as if he's ashamed, as if he's trying to say the "goodbye" that the beaten man cannot utter.

I watch as he slips into the car, as the other men close their doors and light cigarettes. I hear the engine start up, hear the men talking through closed windows. I watch the bruised man turn away from me, I watch him bury his head in his hands.

The car pulls away.

There goes my father.

XVI. True Bearing

Renee stopped talking to me. I would text and call, asking how she was doing and she would give me short responses or say that she was busy. When I asked why she didn't call me like she used to, she said, "I figured you wouldn't be free."

I knew she was hurt about not being chosen for TET and I knew there was nothing I could say to make her feel better. I wished I could have called her to vent about everything, but I knew that would only hurt her more. I continued to pre-pledge, hung out with my other friends when I got the chance, and eventually forced myself to realize that the friendship that existed between Renee and I had changed.

When the TETs asked about Renee, if she and I were still close friends, it pained me to say "no," but it hurt even more to hear them say, "That's just how it is sometimes. TET is more important anyway."

If I was a rich girl—na-na-na-na-na-na-na-na-na-nah. Sasha.
    I didn't pick up.
If I was a rich girl—na-na-na-na-na-na-na-na-na-nah. Sasha.
    I put my phone under my pillow.
If I was a rich girl—na-na-na-na-na-na-na-na-na-nah. Sasha.
`EVA: Where the fuck is WHITNEY! Sasha said that she has two minutes to call her back. Call her ASAP if you get this Whit!`
    I picked up my phone and deleted Eva's text. I called Sasha. "Hello can I speak to Sasha?"
    "Why didn't you answer your phone?"
    "I'm at the counseling center."
    "Oh, well why didn't you just text me that? I was just calling to check up on you and talk. Talk to you later."
    I put my phone on vibrate and slid back under the covers.
`AMBER: Getting Einstein's for Sasha and Tiffany.`

The more time I spent around the TETs, the more I realized that in any other circumstance, I would never want to be friends with them. Tiffany told me how she didn't even consider one of her close friends for chapter membership because "she wouldn't fit in." Although Julia and Deborah were my favorites, they always talked about the Epsilon process and how they had given up so much of their lives to become a part of it.

I couldn't picture myself giving up too much of anything to become part of a sorority. Nevertheless, I knew that I was willing to do anything to become a TET, so I ignored my morals and headed to another study session.

At a study session:

SHELBY: And remember that the other key goes to the third door of Ivyana's apartment. Just letting you know for future reference because I had a hard time with that today. I think she forgot I'm wearing a knee brace.

TERESA: Yea, she probably did. Just so you know, Sasha says that she's getting tired of orange soda and she might be switching back to Pepsi or Root Beer.

CANDACE: And she's into Sudoku puzzles now.

AMBER: And don't forget that one of Britney Lynn's eyes is lighter than the other. She's told us this like three times!

TERESA: Yea, I'm not even adding that fact to the account. Why didn't they just put us on line? Is there any time to put us on now?

EVA: (singing) *Amazing Grace...*

AMBER: I don't know. I hope so.

ME: Eva...

EVA: (singing) *How sweet the sound...*

JAMIE: If we don't go on line this semester, do you think they'll keep pre-pledging us?

BROOKE: No, they'll probably tell us it's over by Spring Break.

VANESSA: That'd be a loonngg time if they did that.

EVA: (singing) *Was lost but now I'm—*

ME: SHUT UP EVA!

EVA: Huh? What?

ME: You were singing.

CANDACE: Again.

EVA: Ohhh, my bad, what were y'all talking about?

ME: We were wondering why they didn't just put us on line.

TERESA: I think it's because they're selfish. They probably didn't want us to go to the centennial boule with them. They're so petty.

JAMIE: That's not it. They said that we're not ready.

Subject:	stuff we learned Saturday
From:	"[Teresa]" <████████.edu>
Date:	Mon, March 3, 2008 12:50 pm
To:	████████.edu (more)
Priority:	Normal
Options:	View Full Header	View Printable Version

Things that we need to do:
--Communicate with each other (if one person knows, all should know)
--Sense of urgency
--Don't talk back or use the word "actually"
--We all need to bring something to the table on your own ([TET] is not going to make you)
--Don't congregate/be discrete
--Do what you say you will do
--Woman of Substance (research it)
--Learn about "poems"
--Learn from everything they say
--Balance your schoolwork
--Don't leave voicemails? (Just [Julia] now or what?)
--Whatever you do or say, you will be wrong (again, be smart)
--Keep researching
--Marian Anderson and other famous women of sorority (learn about)
--Get to know each other
--Speak with confidence
--Follow directions and be smart about it

--Extra bit of information:

--Date of 1st study session: Feb. 3rd, 2008
--5's dad passed away on 9-██-05 (Do not use an as interesting fact)
--Everyone's email again [...]

Subject:	Your New Favorite Poems!
From:	████████.edu

```
Hey guys,

I found this website that has a lot of interesting
poems... and  one  of  them  has  a  "woman  of
substance".

Check it Out:
http://studo.████.edu/████████ files/poems.htm

[Amber Jackson].
```

---------- **Forwarded message** ----------
From :< [Candace]>
Date: Mar 6, 2008 2:10 AM
Subject: IMPORTANT Info from 1- what we need to do
To: <studybuddies040507@gmail.com>

So I had dinner (at 10pm) with 1, and she told me a lot of stuff
that really made me see what we need to be doing, and that we
are really behind. It's not just to make us feel bad, we really do
need to be working harder...A LOT HARDER.

-STUDY SESSIONS: We should be using our time more wisely.
When THEY are not present, we should be talking to each other
about what went on during the day, not joking around. She
showed me a packet of info they made the 2nd day of their study
sessions...it looked a lot like the document we made about each
other about our basic info. I told her we did make one and she
asked why we didn't know stuff about each other at the study
session over the weekend and all I could say is that we just aren't
reviewing it enough. She said it should come second nature to
talk about each other (that is the easy part), learning the official
info is the stuff we really need to worry about. She said they were

a "paper trail" group- they made sheet after sheet of so much info on the chapter, founders, each of the [TETs]...and went over them all the time. They would drill each other "Do you know this" "Tell me about that". They said [Tanya] would come to almost every one of theirs and they would usually have to meet afterwards to organize what needed to be done till around 3-4am. They are giving us plenty of time this year to talk when they don't come (they wanted to make that change FOR us), so we neeeeeedddd to use it.

-COMMUNICATION: She said that she isn't the only one that is worried about our lack of communication. They are wondering if we really don't care enough about this. She wants to know why we don't talk almost everyday, it can't be all texting. **She said they would sit down and make spreadsheets of who is calling the [TETs] at specific times so that someone isn't getting their phone blown up by 5 people at once. We definitely haven't done that. She thinks this e-mail account is a good idea, as long as we discuss the info still. It can't be like "oh, well I put it on the account, she should've read it". We need to still go over to make sure everyone understands things all the time. She re-emphasized the "if one person knows, we all should know" thing.

-DISCRETION: I know they say this all the time, but we really do need to stop hanging out and leaving our old friends with questions about where we are. She knows she wasn't the most social person, but she stated that we really need to be going to eat w/ older friends since we clearly can't see them at night most of the time. We have other friends, so even if we were friends before, we need to be with those other people as much as possible.

-BOOS: Anyone with a boo needs to make sure they are not caught, or else it will be a BIG problem later on. She dated the whole time she was on line and people still didn't find out till 3 weeks after they crossed, so she said it's possible. She says there is no problem having a boo, just DON'T let anyone see any sign of your relationship. She asked if the "boo in Duquesne" thing

([Vanessa] and [Mya]) was really a coincidence...I still don't think they believe it was. =/

-FREE TIME: There really shouldn't be down time. The time that we would have been hanging out before/chillin, should always be used for studying or refreshing up on info. If we're just sitting around, it's a problem.

-"TYPICAL INTEREST": It shouldn't always be "I have to call so-and-so, then ask to go to lunch" The "basic interest" thing is over. We shouldn't be getting bored with this, but instead use it to our advantage to do something social. Ask to go somewhere fun, where we like to go.

Side info more specific to me, since everything matters: She asked me how I felt about them saying I don't shine/don't have a personality. I told her I feel like I get caught up in trying to be respectful too much sometimes and that I'm ACTUALLY (lol) really sarcastic. She said well they should be able to see that, it isn't fair to me and it isn't fair to them if I'm hiding myself. I said I'm not hiding myself, she asked if I'm scared. I said no, maybe sometimes intimidated but definitely not scared. She said I sometimes come across as "I don't want to be here" and emotionless. I need to balance being respectful with being sarcastic and how I am with other people, as long as I'm not being a smartass.

Info on [KAMILLE}: She doesn't really like wheat bread or any bread with nuts in it, she likes potato bread. She was drinking pepsi or coke. She recently just decided to take a step back from NSBE b/c it was just too much butting heads w/ people. She didn't initially want to be in the role she was in, and then to get criticized about it made no sense. She is/currently in a "non-argument" w/ [her bf]...she is sick of going to his place and him never coming to hers and then she doesn't get back until it is really late. They are both verryyy stubborn. She is going to Bowie, MD (PG County) for spring break, most likely taking the Pitt Bus, staying with her Dad. Might go to Africa this summer, but doesn't want to get her hopes up[...] She never feels like going to classes or doing work. She is ready to "finish this shit and have some babies" [...] She all of a sudden would really like to try producing songs, since working w/ [Felicia] It seems interesting to her. [...] Mentioned "bitchassness" several times.

THEY REALLY ARE CONCERNED ABOUT US. THEY DON'T THINK WE WANT IT ENOUGH, SO WE NEED TO SHOW IT. WE NEED TO BE MORE ORGANIZED, COMMUNICATE, AND STEP IT UP FORREAL

nite loves.
sorry for writing a book, but it was that important.

---------- Forwarded message ----------
From: < [Brooke]>
Date: Thu, Mar 6, 2008 at 3:12 PM
Subject: Info from book
To: <studybuddies040507@gmail.com>

hey guys!
This is the info we copied from the pearls of service book. Hope its useful!
[Brooke]

Info.doc
35K   View as HTML   Open as a Google document   Download

I couldn't eat. It was the night before I was to leave Pittsburgh for Spring Break and the pneumonia had gotten worse. I meant to email the doctor, but I never found the time. I had to use my inhaler every time I went outdoors. I could only drink fluids and vomit, and my loss of appetite gave me a headache.

I called Candace. "Yo, I really need some Advil. I've got a headache. I also need some juice since I haven't eaten anything. Do you have any?"

"I don't have juice, but I have Advil."

"Okay, I'll come to towers in a couple of hours and get it from you."

I lay down in my bed and pulled the covers over my body. Minutes later, my phone rang. Candace.

"Hey...What's up?" I answered.

"Julia just asked me to bring her some tampons," she said. "She told me to bring them to her boyfriend's house, but I don't know where that is. Could you come with me since you have to get the Advil anyway?"

"Sure."

I dragged myself to towers and walked with Candace to Julia's boyfriend's house. When we were halfway down the street, Julia and Regina approached us. Candace handed Julia the tampons and Regina tilted her head to the side. "Call me when you guys get back since it's so late."

"Okay," said Candace, and we both walked away.

When we returned to her room, I crashed into a lounge chair. "I can't wait to go home. I feel like death."

"I gave her the slim fit tampons," Candace sighed.

"What?"

"I gave her the slim fit tampons. She's gonna be upset, I meant to give her the normal sized ones."

"Candace, please get real. Why do you care? She didn't specify so you're good. Beggars can't be choosers."

"Yea, okay you're right. What time is your flight?"

"I think it's at two. I'm going to be at the airport early as hell so I can get out of Pittsburgh. I'm sick of this shit."

"Yea, I think Ivyana's fruit cup runs are the worst."

"All of this bull is the worst. You want to hear something funny?"

"No, Whitney. It's probably not funny. It's probably something mean, especially if *you* think it's funny."

"Not even. I was going to say that the funny thing is, we're not even on line yet! We're not even on line! We're *professional interests!*"

I fell out of her chair laughing. I pulled her trash can closer and vomited. She looked down at me, shook her head, and continued arranging her closet.

"So...You want some water?" she asked.

"You think?"

I left Candace's room around six in the morning. I packed my suitcase and waited at the bus stop. An hour and a half later I was meandering through airport security. Since my flight wasn't until mid-afternoon, I found my gate and napped in a chair.

JAMIE: Guys, can somebody take Sasha's computer to technology help? You'll have to sit there for two hours while they fix it though. I can't.

AMBER: Is anybody near the union?

I woke up and started walking around the food court. Time wasn't going by fast enough.

CANDACE: Going to get Ivyana a week's worth of food. I might need to use somebody else's meal plan too. Is anybody available?

JAMIE: Candace is going to take Sasha's computer later.

VANESSA: Going to help Jamie and Candace.

I stopped looking at my phone. I felt it continue to vibrate but I ignored it. I was ready to leave, ready for a break.

I slept through the weekend preceding Spring Break, only waking up to take medicine or use the bathroom. When I woke up long enough to look at my phone, I had missed fifteen phone calls from the SHs, and collected thirty seven unread text messages.

I called each of the TETs in a row and sighed relief when they hit ignore or didn't answer.

CANDACE: I meant to tell you all that I missed Nicole's wake-up call the other day but she didn't get mad. She's definitely my favorite!

TERESA: Does anyone know what pro 11:22 means? I need to have an answer for Latoya asap!

From: [Teresa]
Date: Wed, Mar 12, 2008 at 6:34 PM
Subject: Just So Everyone Knows
To: <studybuddies040507@gmail.com>

Just so everyone knows:

What does Proverbs 11:22 mean?   Proverbs

What I said to [Latoya]: <u>New American Standard Bible</u> (©1995)
"As a ring of gold in a swine's snout So is a beautiful woman who lacks discretion."

The Israelites despised swine as filthy creatures, so putting a gold ring in the pig's snout was a waste of gold. A beautiful woman without morals is a waste as well, to be avoided as one avoids a pig (with or without a gold nose ring).

Also Discretion: the quality of being discreet, esp. with reference to one's own actions or speech; prudence or decorum

---

I spent the first few days of Spring Break extensively napping. My mom asked about TET twice and each time I told her that they would probably be having a formal rush in the fall.

AMBER: Whit, I need you to look at these photos I'm sending to Latoya asap. Look on the doc please!

ME: Okay, I'm going to look at them now.

    I fell asleep.

AMBER: Whitney! Did you look at them yet? It's been two hours and you didn't text me back what you thought.

ME: Oh yea. My bad, I'm headed downstairs now.

    I fell asleep.

ME: Hey Amber, my bad again. I dozed off again. I'm looking on the account now.

AMBER: Lol it's okay, I had Candace look at them and she approved them for me.

By Thursday of Spring Break, I was feeling better. I made calls to each of the TETs and texted each of the SHs.

CANDACE: Hey SHs, I spoke with Hannah today and got the whole story of what happened with fall 04. It's on the doc under the documents section cuz it's too long to put in a text! I'm also meeting up with her for lunch this weekend and I'll get more info.

[Hannah's] Story
Google Document
Thurs, Mar 13, 2008
<studybuddies040507@gmail.com>

So Fall 04 went through a 3-day process with 16 girls. (FYI: I remember seeing somewhere that they were called "The Bittersweet 16". Not sure if thats 100% right). They held programs and worked as a chapter for awhile, and she developed friendships with the girls but still wasn't satisfied. Her godsister and someone else she was close to were "made" and she would call them a lot... her godsister would tell [Hannah] the reason she wasn't satisfied was because she didn't go through a real process. She said "I mean, people were calling me soror and I was doing everything like a member but it didn't feel right." (She was planning programs and doing normal [TET] activities but went an entire year without a process as an [TET]). It had never occurred to her that she wouldn't get to pledge when she originally was interested in joining. The 16 got together and decided that they wanted to pledge even though some people were apprehensive. There were 2 attempts for people to pledge- 1) She said the first attempt "there were too many hands in the basket", she said it was all 16 so it never got started. Then 3 people graduated. 2) 2nd attempt was that summer after they were initiated. [Hannah] got offered an internship in Colorado with the federal government for the same summer, it was a tough decision but she chose the internship. She decided she would do the process alone when she came back. The summer process that some of the girls went through "wasn't legit", "was some whackass process" and was ELEVEN WEEKS! When she came back that fall they knew it wasn't right. She found the woman that would become her dean, talked to her, wanted to respect [Epsilon's] history, the woman said she would pledge them.[...] I believe this fall line was going to be [Tanya], [Selena], and [Hannah] but then some girls from the summer knew the process was whack and joined them

([Cassandra, Raven, Tamera]). 2 other girls from the summer process were heated and held animosity because they felt like [Cassandra], [Raven], and [Tamera] "abandoned" them, but [Hannah] said things just didn't work out. She doesn't talk to those girls, it was a mutual decision to not really be friends anymore. She said that other people are more forgiving, but she isn't one of those type of people. She'll usually forgive but not forget, so she still doesn't talk to them because they were so hostile over the girls going through a real process after summer. Anyway, she said from that point on the 6 of them (Fall 04) have wanted to have a clean-cut process, no split lines because she knows "split lines mean split friendships and turmoil". She's friends with a few of the original 16, but she's much closer to the 6 she was on line with. She also knows that people who don't pledge get hated on and "people will smile in your face then talk about you behind your back[...]" Another reason she wanted to pledge was b/c she knew that girls were coming behind her that wanted to join the sorority, and she didn't want them to have to deal with the same problems. The only reason Fall 05 was split because "some people from the summer were still here" <-- that was the part that confused me [...] But she said she was so glad Spring 07 wasn't split and wants "every line after that" to not have to deal with the drama she had. Aw...that kind of hints to us if we make it to that point, that they did that so we would not have to deal with the same problems. Shed a tiny tear...[...]

Bye loves, [Candace]

---------- **Forwarded message** ----------
From :< [Candace]>
Date: Mar 15, 2008 3:17 AM
Subject: New Info from [Hannah]
To: <studybuddies040507@gmail.com>

She doesn't come back to [Pittsburgh] that often; the step show will be the 2nd time, so I asked who else is coming. She said [Tanya] and [Raven], but I'm sure more people will. I asked casually if they'll come to study session, and she kind of smiled and was like "yeah...we might drop by...so ummm be prepared for that". She was basically letting me know she might not be the same nice person at study session. I asked if everyone should call and she was like "oh so they just want to call before I come to study session...I see the plan now" (she was laughing about it) and I was trying to play it off saying no, they want to get to know you too, and she was just like suuuureee. But she said it would definitely not be a good idea for study session to be the first time she talks to you "so they have 2 weeks to try to talk to me". [...]

**She mentioned how you need to keep everything tight and on point so no one suspects anything. At first I thought she was talking about US as far as not let anyone suspect we're pre-pledging/pledging but then she went on talking about if people see you putting on a bunch of programs and doing a bunch of community service, they don't think you have time to haze (SHE SAID HAZE NOT PLEDGE! ahhh) so then there are no investigations. She said as long as you project the image that you're too busy to do anything else, no one is in your business, "LUCKILY [EPSILON] IS GREAT WITH TIME MANAGEMENT...WE MULTI-TASK"...so read btw the lines, yeah she's saying they're great at putting up a front of "non-hazing org"[...]

**I asked how much the grad advisor knows lol...[Hannah] laughed! She said "Well...she came through [Epsilon] so she definitely pledged. She's kind of glad we do what we do, but I wouldn't say she knows each and everything we do. She knows we have this process but probably not what goes on each and every day." She mentioned how it's good to have a grad advisor "that has your back" so she can defend you, because undergrads aren't at the grad chapter meetings so she can keep people from getting too nosy. The grad advisor has authority over others for investigating the chapter so she can keep people from getting into your business too much.
**She discussed how the [Mus] just don't carry themselves well around campus, getting in too many fights. She said they have

too many issues and they hate on [TETs] cuz theyre the best. She said her org doesn't have to tell them, it shows through the way you carry yourself, your programming (she talked about how they held programs like spades tournaments, "that's not a program, that's a gathering labeled as a program"), and the respect you get on campus...it goes unsaid who's the best ([TET]). She was commenting on the issues that have happened with [Mus] this year (most likely the situation w/ [Tiffany], [Ivyana], [Sasha], etc) its a bad reflection on the org. "Now if you wanna go in the back alley or off out of the limelight I'll take my letters off and my shoes and then kick your ass...but just not in public" lol She was hating on the [Betas], I told her about how Im friends with a few of the girls [who are becoming] [Betas], she said "Whyyyy would you let your friends do that? Why would you let them go that way?" She says they carry themselves like men, and at their step show performance last year was boring. It was precise, but "who just wants to see you stomp your feet and clap your hands, babies can do that"...they didn't really have a theme. She said that the [last black fraternity and sorority] saved [Betas] and [Phi Beta Omicrons] from being the "who are you orgs"... I never thought of it that way! She said if those 2 orgs didn't come around they would be the people always forgotten. She said half the [Phi Beta Omicrons] aren't even in school so how can they have a line...[...]

**She mentioned how Fall 04 isn't as close with Spr 07 as Fall 05. She said "Fall 05 are my babies, we were with them every night, all the time" so she talks to them a lot more, but even though she was on campus she was too worried about grad school and other things to become as attached to Spr 07. She said she still loves them and there's no hostility, but she just doesn't talk to any of them that much except for [Sasha], occasionally, [Tiffany]. She said [Britney Lynn] is her spec, but she hardly ever talks to her. [Sasha] reminds her of herself, "a little rough around the edges" but still really friendly, spunky, good person. I agreed and mentioned how [Sasha] does spend a lot of time with us but still keeps us in check, and [Hannah] agreed like that's what she expects her to do.

**She asked how my grades are coming along. I said pretty well, study sessions are helping. She said good b/c she didn't think Spr 07 studied, and I said how we probably were studying too much-now we're balancing some of the time getting to know information. She said that's good, but of course this semester is the semester our grades should be on point. She said she heard all of our GPAs are pretty high anyway =)

That's all I can think of for now, I'll tell you if I think of anything else. Again, sorry it's so freakin long.

VANESSA: Hey ladies, I got my hair dyed! I am officially a chestnut blond!
JAMIE: I miss you guys! <3

XVII. Overreach

I lingered at the Pittsburgh airport. I stopped in a magazine shop and perused through shelves of books. I bought three magazines that I would never get a chance to read and a large bag of chips that would be devoured by one of the SHs later in the week. I was stalling. I didn't want to go back.

I forced myself to wait outside at the platform for the 28X. Once I was aboard the bus, a freshman interest sat down next to me. I remembered her from the Pink Rose Tea, remembered her telling me that she was a Bill Gates Scholar, that she was interested in the medical field.

She and I laughed about college for most of the ride, but as the bus drove into the familiar streets of Oakland, reality set back in.

```
IVYANA:  :-( Four fruit cups, two yogurts,
hummus, chipotle BBQ chips, three bottles of
metromint water. I will call for them later
when I get back.
ME: I need somebody's help in the next thirty
minutes.
AMBER: I just got to back to campus. I'm
going to Sasha's.
```

If I was a rich girl—na-na-na-na-na-na-na-na-na-nah. Tiffany.

"Hello?"

"Where are you?"

"Sutherland."

"Did you already buy the two trays of pasta?"

"Yea."

"Well, me and Ivyana are heading to the North side now. I'll call you when we get to my place and then you can come and drop off the food."

"Okay."

I sat in the lobby of Sutherland and sent out a mass text saying that I wouldn't be available for the next hour.

Tiffany called me again. "Whitney, I don't think I want the pasta right away. I want Panera. Go there and get me a bacon BLT. Then come to the North side."

I called Candace. "Hey Candace, I know you're probably busy but I'm leaving Pasta Plus with food for Ivyana and Tiffany but Tiffany just said that she wanted Panera and I don't have my wallet on me. Can you meet me there and buy it? Okay, I'll see you in a minute."

When I got to Panera, Candace was sitting down at a table. I placed the two pasta trays beside her and took her card to order the food. As soon as the cook handed me the bag, I brought it over to Candace and started taking it apart.

"Whitney! Tiffany's not even that mean!"

"Why do you have to have a *conscience* right now? She's not that mean, but she's still making me do shit and I'm tired of it. We just got back from break a few days ago. They need to chill."

"You don't have to mess with her sandwich though."

"Don't you do the same thing with Ivyana's tea? Aren't you the one who fishes your hand in the bottom of her cup to get the sugar packet?"

"I don't do that intentionally though. I only do that if the packet falls in the cup when I'm racing to mix it."

"I'll ask them to remake it then."

"Okay," she smiled.

I received a new sandwich and Candace placed the sandwich bag on top of the pasta trays as she waited with me at the bus stop.

"Are you not tired of this?" I asked.

"Yea. I'm really tired of it, but I just keep thinking about what I'm going to get in return after we get done with all of this."

"Alright, I'll keep that in mind."

I fell asleep on the ride to the North side. Instead of being able to drop off the food and leave, I was told to clean Tiffany's kitchen. I started putting the dishes in the dishwasher and felt Ivyana staring at me.

IVYANA: Explain something to me Whitney. Why is it when I ask you and your little study friends to get me a fruit cup or yogurt it takes forever or you all claim that the stores don't have it?

ME: Umm, sometimes Quick Zone runs out of stuff really quick and the student union doesn't really have that much yogurt or that many fruit cups so—

IVYANA: That doesn't make any sense. You know that I'm going to ask you for a fruit cup. You know that I like hummus and you know I like yellow tailed sushi. Don't you think it would *behoove* you to stock up?

ME: Yea…

IVYANA: Good, maybe you all should start doing that.

TIFFANY: Why didn't you get forks with the pastas, Whitney?

ME: I forgot.

TIFFANY: Perfect.

ME: Is there anything else you need me to do?

TIFFANY: No.

ME: Okay.

I put on my jacket and headed towards the door.

IVYANA: You're not going to ask us if we need anything else to be done?

TIFFANY: She did. She asked me.

IVYANA: Oh. You're not going to ask *me*?

ME: Is there anything else I can do for you, Ivyana?

IVYANA: What time is it Tiffany?

TIFFANY: 9:32.

IVYANA: And what time does the next bus come?

ME: 9:34.

TIFFANY: She timed it!

IVYANA: Bye Whitney!

At a study session:

TIFFANY: Vanessa, why did you do that to your hair? Are you going through an identity crisis? First you're confused about what color your eyes are and now you think you're a *blonde*?

SASHA: I wish my dean could see your hair right now. She would never let you get away with that. You're a pretty girl, Vanessa. You don't need to do that extra stuff okay?

VANESSA: Okay.

SASHA: I wish some of your friends would dress up like you or even try to look nice instead of…You know what, forget it. None of y'all are listening to me.

TIFFANY: Let's go Sasha, I'm running late for step show practice. Latoya's gonna get mad if I'm not on time.

SASHA: Okay, see y'all later.

They left the room. Jamie pulled out her computer.

JAMIE: Okay, so here's the email I was telling you guys about. It's from January but it pretty much says that Ivyana is going to be the dean of our line.

BROOKE: Dean?

VANESSA: What does that mean again?

AMBER: It means that she'll be like a mother to us when we pledge.

ME: Are they on *crack*? She's the worst choice for a dean! The dean is supposed to be the one that knows us a little bit better than the rest of them. She's too selfish.

CANDACE: I like Ivyana!

ME: As a dean though? She's the one who makes us do the most stuff *now*. Can you imagine what pledging under her will be like?

CANDACE: That's true. Maybe she won't be that bad though.

TERESA: If she's the dean, then who's going to be the ADP? And why are they talking about this stuff in their *email accounts*?

SHELBY: We do the same thing. Wait, what's the ADP?

AMBER: It's the assistant dean. That person is supposed to be a lot more mean and strict though.

JAMIE: It's supposedly Sasha.

US: WHAT!

JAMIE: Yea, it's Sasha.

AMBER: We're going to die. Let me see that email.

---------- **Forwarded message** ----------

From: [Ivyana] <█████████1908@gmail.com>

Date: Sun, Jan 28, 2008 at 3:01 PM

Subject: ...

To: [Tiffany] <█████████@aol.com>

Spec,

I just wanted to say thank you for stepping back so that I could be the dean of Fall 2008. For real, because you were the original choice. Love you.

It was official. We were going on line in the fall. I headed to another study session, hoping that the TETs wouldn't show up so we could talk.

At a study session.

ME: I can't believe we're not going on line this semester.

CANDACE: I thought you resolved that by now.

ME: I guess I was just hoping that we would.

BROOKE: Yea, Whit I thought they were gonna tell us something before we left for Spring Break.

AMBER: Me too. I was thinking the same thing. Oh well, maybe they won't make us run that many errands now since they're practicing for the step show.

TERESA: No, that means *more* errands because they're going to need *more* food and water.

JAMIE: I'm so ready for us to go on line guys! We're gonna be so much better than Spring 07! We're gonna be so *thorough*!

EVA: We definitely are!

ME: Aww, Jamie you're going to be the first person in your class to cross! (laughing)You're gonna have haters!

CANDACE: We'll take care of them for you though!

EVA: All of us are going to be what TETs should be. All of us have good grades!

MYA: Yea, we actually *want* to graduate summa cum laude!

BROOKE: We know what sisterhood is!

AMBER: We're all actually enrolled in school! Sasha isn't even a student!

SHELBY: None of us sleep around!

TERESA: None of us hit up Happy Hour underage and put up the pictures on Face book!

AMBER: We all get along most of the time! Spring 07 is broken up, they don't trust each other. It doesn't even seem like they like each other. Regina and Cari are hardly ever around the rest of them.

TERESA: We all have lives! We're involved in other stuff already so TET won't consume our lives!

EVA: You know what I was thinking the other day? Y'all watch *Making the Band* right? You know that scene where Danity Kane is singing, "I Love You Forever?"

BROOKE: What?

EVA: You know (singing) *I love you foreverrr...*

BROOKE: Oh, yea I know what you're talking about.

EVA: How about (singing) *Fall 08 is betterrr...Fall 08 is betterrr...I love you foreverrr!!!*

US: (singing*) Fall 08 is betterrr...I love you foreverrr!!!*

AMBER: Taking snacks to step show practice.
TERESA: Taking candy to Deborah.
MYA: Taking food to Britney Lynn and Julia.
VANESSA: Getting food for Cari???
JAMIE: Getting things for Kamille.
EVA: Hey, can I use someone's dining dollars?
I have to get something for Latoya.
CANDACE: Sasha and I are going to court,
literally...She tried to use my meal plan card
at MC today and the cashier reported
us...details at SS.
ME: Have to make a wakeup call for Tiffany.
Could someone make sure I'm up at like 6:55?

If I was a rich girl—na-na-na-na-na-na-na-na-na-nah. Ivyana.

"Hello?"

"Get me a quesadilla with two soft tacos, mild sauce from Taco Bell, and a sweet tea from Quick Zone. I also need you to get a double burger from McDonald's for Sasha with no onions and no cheese. I'm at step show practice and I need it in eighteen minutes," she hung up.

AMBER: I have to give Tiffany twenty dollars
for pictures frames. I'll explain later.

When I was halfway to Taco Bell I realized that Brooke still had my meal plan card. I called Candace, " Could you to go to McDonald's and get a double burger for Sasha with no onions and no cheese, and meet me at Taco Bell when you have it," and then I called Vanessa, "Vanessa, could you meet me at Taco Bell? I need to use your dining dollars for Ivyana's food."

I ordered Ivyana's food with Vanessa and went to Quick Zone to get the sweet tea. When I had finished paying for the tea, Candace passed me the McDonald's bag.

I made it to the engineering building with three minutes left and called Ivyana. "Hello, may I speak to Ivyana?"

"Are you outside?" she whispered.

"Yea."

"Are you outside the engineering hall?"

"Yea."

"Okay, come up the steps right now. I'm right there."

I went up the two flights of steps and when I reached the top, I saw Ivyana leaning outside of the door. I handed her the food, and as if she wasn't less than two feet away from me she spoke into her phone's receiver. "Did you get the mild sauce?"

"Yes," I spoke into my receiver.

"Okay," she took the bag from me and continued to speak into her receiver, "Drop off right here...Good...Bye."

JAMIE: Don't forget that Sasha said that we better have gifts for Spring 07's anniversary. Come with ideas to SS tonight and we can make them tomorrow night!

It was March 18, 2008, Spring 07's anniversary. I was having a horrible day. All I could think about was my father—about how in a mere forty eight hours, he'd be dead for a year.

The gifts that the SHs brought to study session were hand painted violet and green heart shaped trinket boxes. Each box featured calligraphic white words, twenty pearls glued along the frame, a candle glued inside the box, and a small ivy leaf and a mirror. Tiffany, Sasha, Nicole, and Latoya came by to look at them.

At a study session:

SASHA: Aww these are so cute! Y'all are creative!

LATOYA: They're alright.

TIFFANY (holding up a box) Next time, could y'all paint the bottom of the box too? Thanks, though. It's cute for an *attempt*. We're going to leave our gifts here. Y'all need to deliver them to me and rest of my line before tomorrow night.

They talked to us for an hour and then we were allowed to leave.

TIFFANY: Whitney, could you stay behind for a moment? You can leave with Vanessa.

ME*: Okay.

Mya and Candace left the room last.

TIFFANY: So, for the past few weeks we've been telling you about your attitude and we don't see any changes. I don't know who you think you are, but this is not a "take you as you are" deal. I'm president, which means that I have to sign off on everyone's paperwork and when Whitney *Gracia, Garcia,* however you pronounce it, comes across my desk I don't have to sign it. And if I don't sign it, you definitely won't get into my chapter.

SASHA: Is there a reason why you haven't worked on your attitude? You'll never be able to grow through the Epsilon process if you're not willing to change.

ME*: I am willing to change...I'm just having a really bad week and I'm not in the right mood to talk about this now. A year ago this same week my dad died. I'm sorry, but I don't think now is a good time to talk about this.

SASHA: Well, I think we need to talk about this *now*. We just want to know why you continue to have an attitude. Is there a reason?

ME*: Okay...I really apologize about my attitude, but it's not directed towards anything or anybody. I think it's being misinterpreted for me not showing emotion. That's just how I've always been. When I was little, my family was on welfare and...My dad and I had a rocky relationship and I think a lot of other things have just affected how I react or don't react to certain situations. Like, my dad—

SASHA: Whitney you are not the only one that has ever struggled! My boyfriend died when I was seventeen! I had to watch them pull him out of the car because the accident was so bad! I loved him! I told him everything! I still cry about him! Do you know what that's like? I grew up in the hood too! I went to twelve funerals when I was seventeen! When I was on line my mother had cancer and I still had to go to set! People are not going to care about your struggles when they're busy *making* you. Stop making excuses and stop using your past as a crutch!

TIFFANY: Wait Sasha hold up—

SASHA: You're not humble, and you're not passionate about this! You don't hustle—

ME*: I brought you Burger King *every* Monday, Wednesday, and Friday, even when I had pneumonia—

SASHA: I had bronchitis *and* pneumonia when I was on line and I didn't let that stop me because I had to get stuff done! Stop making excuses!

It took every muscle to control my body, to force myself to sit still, to not jump up and stab her in the eye with my umbrella. I told myself that I would never cry in front of the TETs, but I could feel the tears starting to well.

SASHA: Didn't you go to the counseling center before? Why don't you continue to go there regularly if you're having so many personal issues?

ME*: I do go to couns—

SASHA: It's clearly not working because you're still using your past as a crutch! You have to learn to let stuff go, Whitney. You're not the only one who has been through something.

I tried to keep the tears from falling.

SASHA: You can leave now. And don't forget those gifts!

I picked up the white bag and headed towards the door.

SASHA: Wait on Vanessa!

VANESSA*: Have a good night ladies!

I didn't say goodbye. I left.

I immediately called Brooke and told her what happened. I cried, "I can't believe she said that to me! The audacity!"

"She was wrong for that Whit, but you know what? It's going to be okay. Don't waste too many tears over her. TET is all she has and she thinks that gives her permission to say whatever she wants."

"I can't think straight right now."

"Are you going to be okay? You can come over to talk about it some more if you want."

"Yea, I'm gonna be alright…I'll call you back."

I couldn't sleep. I stayed up all night, rocking back and forth in my desk chair, trying to focus on my homework. I couldn't. All I could think about was what Sasha had said hours ago and how I wished that I wasn't an interest in that moment.

The next day I called Julia crying, attempting to explain what happened. She suggested that I speak to Sasha about it. I thanked her for listening to me, but when I snapped my phone shut I knew that I was going to hold off speaking to Sasha for as long as possible.

Sasha called me five minutes later.

I didn't pick up. I swallowed my pride and called her ten minutes later. "Hello, may I speak to Sasha?"

"This is she."

"Did you need me to do anything for you?"

"No. I don't want you to do anything else for me *ever again*. That was Tiffany calling you from my phone."

Click.

I called Tiffany. "Hello, may I speak to Tiffany?"

"Hi Whitney, I was calling to ask you to print off something for me, but that's okay I already did it myself. Did you want to talk about something with me? I know that whatever happened last night is bothering you and I wanted to—"

Her phone cut off.

I turned my phone on silent and went to Candace's dorm. She signed me in and I slouched in a chair. I waited for her to lock the door and yelled, "I hate Sasha!"

"Don't say that, you don't *hate* her."

"You're right. I *despise* her."

MYA: Printing off papers for Tiffany.

"Are you going to drop?"

"No."

"Are you going to do something crazy?"

"Why do you always ask me that? I'm *not* crazy."

"I just have to ask."

"I'm not going to do anything right now. I'll just wait 'til after our probate...I'm gonna beat her ass up."

"No you're not Whitney! Don't say that!"

"I'm not joking. I'm dead serious."

"After you pledge and after she becomes your prophyte, you're going to beat her up? At the probate?"

"You're gonna jump in right?" I sat up.

"Whitney!"

"What?"

"She probably didn't realize what she was saying."

"I don't care. She still said it."

"Maybe you should talk to her."

"Na, I'm good. You're not going to jump in though?"

"Yea, to pull you away and prevent you from killing her," she laughed.

"Yea, whatever. She's got a lot of nerve! I have to respect her but it's getting really hard. And I'm sick of them talking about my attitude. If it was that bad, then why did I get picked? I just don't show emotion, how is that an attitude?"

"Yea, but we all get attacked for something. I get attacked for being boring."

"And for wanting to be a...BETA!" I laughed. "Ugh, Teresa's calling me. Hello? What? Alright we're coming."

"Where are we going?"

"You're going to Market to Go and I'm going to Quick Zone. Teresa's gonna text us what to get for Ivyana."

If I was a rich girl—na-na-na-na-na-na-na-na-na-nah. Latoya.

"Hello?"

"Where are you?"

"I'm in towers."

"Okay, good. I need you to come and get my car keys from me. I'm in the dance studio at the Pete, hurry up."

I left my things in Tiara's room and headed to the Pete. I was becoming immune to the steepness of the hill. I didn't have to stop like I used to and I wasn't out of breath when I made it to the top. I swiped my card at the workout room and walked past the exercise equipment, through the door of the locker hall, and into the dance studio. Latoya was stretching on the floor when I approached her.

AMBER: WHO HAS IVYANA'S KEYS?!

"Use the key on top. I need you to get the canes out of the trunk. I parked across in the lot behind the Frick school. Do you know where I'm talking about?"

"Yea," I took the keys from her hands.

"Whitney, before you leave, I need you to get me some Quizno's," Tiffany walked towards me with a credit card in her hand. "Bring back the receipt."

"What type of sandwich do you want me to get?"

"Teresa should know. She got it last time so you'll need to ask her. And Quizno's closes at nine so you might want to hurry up."

"And I need those canes in like fifteen minutes. We're not gonna have this room reserved all night so bye."

It was 8:47.

I left the dance studio and immediately called Teresa. "Yo, Teresa, I need you to go to Quizno's and order whatever sandwich you got for Tiffany last time right now."

"I don't have my wallet on me."

"I have her card, I'm gonna meet you there. I just need you to order it."

CANDACE: Check the doc for new info!

"Alright, bye."

I raced down the hill to Quizno's. When I reached the shop, Teresa was standing outside.

"Did you order it?"

"Yea, but I didn't want you to come in. There's a Nu Pi inside and I didn't want him to see you giving me a card and walking back out."

"Oh, okay—here's her card. I've gotta run to the parking lot and get their canes. Wanna meet me at the Pete with the sandwich?"

"No, I'll get the sandwich now and we can both go get the canes."

Jamie told us that she would be spending Easter Sunday with her family in Monroeville and would be unavailable for any errands. At midnight, she dropped Ivyana's church clothes off at my dorm.

Ivyana called me around nine thirty. "Could you bring me my clothes please?"

I walked up the hill to her boyfriend's house on Chesterfield. I called her when I was in front of the house.

"Just slide them through the bottom screen," she said as she stood behind the door.

I unzipped the bag Jamie had given me and passed Ivyana a pair of shoes, a tie, and a shirt.

"These are the wrong pair of shoes. Ugh! Can y'all do anything right? And I told y'all to bring me the *mint green* shirt, not this one. This is not mint green. You need to go to my apartment and get the right shirt."

"Now?"

"Yes, *now*! I have to be at church in about thirty minutes so hurry up. Here are the keys."

I walked down the hill and remembered that it was a holiday. The buses wouldn't be running on a normal schedule. I called Teresa, "Yo, could you look up the bus schedule for me? I need to know when the next 71A comes."

"Okay hold on....The next 71A comes to towers in about five minutes."

"Okay thanks."

I hung up and walked to towers. I boarded the bus and got off at Melwood. I called Shelby. "Shelby, I'm at Ivyana's place. Which key goes to which door?"

"The small silver key goes to the front door, the larger silver key goes to the middle door, and the gold key goes to her front door."

"Okay thanks, stay on the phone with me—could you three way Teresa and have her look up when the next bus comes this way?"

"Yea, hold on."

I got inside of the apartment and Ivyana called my other line, "Whitney where are you?"

"I'm inside your apartment."

"You're just now getting there? Ugh, go to my room and get the shirt out of the closet."

"Okay."

"Do you see it?"

"Ummm there's a mint green polo shirt, is that what you need?"

"No! I don't want the MINT GREEN POLO! Does that even *sound* like something I would want to wear to church?"

"No I'm—"

"It's not that difficult Whitney. Do you know what mint green looks like?"

"Yes."

"Okay. Now that you know what color mint green is, pick out the shirt in my closet that is *mint green*."

"I don't see a mint green shirt, Ivyana. I really don't. There's a bright yellow button down, a mustard yellow button down—"

"Ugh! Just bring me the mustard yellow shirt."

I grabbed the shirt and clicked back over to Shelby and Teresa, "Teresa when does the next bus come?"

"In fifteen minutes."

"Fifteen minutes?"

"Yea."

"I need to get back quicker than that."

"Well, you're gonna have to run because that's the only way you're gonna make it. It's only like a mile and a half. You can make that in less than fifteen minutes if you start running."

I started running with Teresa and Shelby in my ear giving me directions on how to get back. I ran street after street. Block after block. Ivyana called me when I was halfway there. "Where are you? You just made me miss my ride!"

"I'm running....I'm...on O'Hara."

"When do you think you're going to get here?"

"In like five minutes."

"Ugh."

I clicked back over and thanked Shelby and Teresa. I closed my phone, sped up my running, and made it to Chesterfield. I approached Chesterfield and Ivyana called my phone again. "WHERE ARE YOU?"

"I'm about to be right outside your door."

"Oh," she opened the door and took the shirt from me. "Did you just *run* all the way from Melwood?"

"Yea."

"Wow. Well thanks," she looked off to the side and I backed away. I walked to the top of the hill and realized that I still had her keys in my hand. I didn't want her calling me later to ask for them, so I called her back.

She didn't pick up.

I called again. "Hello, may I speak to Ivyana?"

"What, *Whitney*!"

"I still have your keys. Can I bring them to you right quick?"

"Na nigga I'm goin' to church!"

I closed my phone. I walked back to my dorm and as soon as I unlocked my door, my phone sounded. Teresa.

"Hey Whitney, could you come to Market Central and eat with me, Kamille, and Felicia? You and me could type up the facts on the doc after we get done eating."

"Okay, I'm coming."

From :< [Teresa]>
Date: Sun, March, 23, 2008 at 1:28 PM
Subject: [Teresa] & Whitney's Brunch with [Felicia] and [Kamille]
To: <studybuddies040507@gmail.com>

[Felicia]:

-First job was at Old Navy in college

-Used to do ballet, gymnastics, cheerleading, figure skating

-Likes to try different things on her waffles at Market Central all the time (likes to switch it up)

-She attended a J. Holiday concert type thing and he came up to her and sang "imma put you to bed" (like dancing around her and stuff)

-Loves Trey Songz CD

-trying to go to law school when she graduates and if she doesn't get in, she's gonna take a year off and just pursue music

-In high school they had the academy awards and in high school she won most likely to be a hip hop star (or something like that/she couldn't remember)

-Won [best] athlete in high school

-Worked at Victoria Secret and got free bras and stuff (favorite bra was Very Sexy and doesn't like Body by Victoria)

-She thinks Lil' Wayne is attractive and that Chris Brown is "ALRIGHT" (lmao)

-In high school her and her boyfriend got nominated for "Best Couple"

-Loves Laser Tag

-Watches Making the Band 4

[Kamille]:
   -Her mom sent her an Easter dress
   -Used to be scared of Chuck E. Cheese
   -Doesn't really like Trey Songz
   -lost her favorite bra recently (but she thinks its at [Julia's] house)
   -used to go to Bible Center in Homewood but stopped going while she was online and now she feels bad cuz it was a small church and they know she wasnt there for a while
   -used to listen to Usher's Confessions album everyday the summer it came out
   -over spring break [Kamille] went to a birthday party at chuck e. cheese

If I was a rich girl—na-na-na-na-na-na-na-na-na-nah. Julia.
   "Hello?"
   "Hi Whitney. I need you and one of the girls from the group, *not* Shelby, to go to East Liberty and see if you can get Obama tickets for me and my sorors."

If I was a rich girl—na-na-na-na-na-na-na-na-na-nah. Latoya.
   "Hey, we're supposed to hang out today. Are you on campus?"
   "Yea, I'm in the library."
   "Are you studying for a test?"
   "No, just typing."
   "Umm, ok. Could you meet me at American Apparel?"
   I walked to American Apparel and found Latoya holding up a gray schoolboy-like sweater.
   "This is what we're going to be wearing in the step show. We're going for an old-school theme in certain parts. We just have to stitch on our letters and decorate them. I think I might have to go to the other store because they don't have any more of these in the right size."

As she was debating on whether she should get light gray or dark gray sweaters, Deborah walked in. I followed them around the store.

"Come with us to CVS," Latoya motioned for me to follow them.

"Okay."

"What's my favorite ice cream?" she asked.

"The ice cream pies from Burger King?"

"No," she sighed. "I told Candace what it was two days ago. Y'all don't communicate."

"I don't know how they would ever get into our chapter Latoya," Deborah laughed. "They *really* don't communicate. They really don't."

At CVS, Latoya purchased a stack of white poster boards and handed them to me. She told me to have every SH bring color pencils and markers to study session. She would call one of us later that night and give instructions.

I walked to towers with her and Deborah and paid for each of them to get into Market Central. I started walking towards the library and felt my phone vibrate. Amber.

AMBER: Do you still have my meal plan card?
ME: Yea, whats up?
AMBER: Where are you? I need it.
ME: Leaving towers.
AMBER: Don't leave. Meet me at Quick Zone.

I sat in front of Quick Zone for ten minutes but there was no sign of Amber. Tiffany called me. "Whitney, where are you?"

"Sitting in front of Quick Zone."

"Ugh, Amber Jackson is a liar," she hung up.

Amber descended from the steps and headed towards me. "I'm sorry; I had to run from Magee Women's Hospital because Tiffany just gave me this huge order. I got on the bus, but I didn't have my ID so I had to get right back off. I lied and told Tiffany that I was already here. Sorry."

"Oh, it's not your fault. You want help taking it over there?"

"Yea, I'll get everything. Just hold the basket and carry whatever can't fit."

Later that night at study session we designed and colored the TETs' signs for the step show.

The morning that Obama came to Pittsburgh to speak at the Soldiers and Sailors building, Vanessa called me. "Sasha said she wants you to go to Seven Eleven and get her and Latoya hot chocolate."

"Why can't she call me and tell me herself?"

"I don't know. Are you gonna be able to do it?"

BROOKE: Guys, how do I get to CMU?

"Yea. Talk to you later, bye."

I walked to Seven Eleven and prepared two cups of hot chocolate. I paid for them at the register and walked towards Soldiers and Sailors.

Vanessa called me again. "Hey Whitney. Um, they already went inside the building so Sasha said she doesn't need the hot chocolates anymore."

On Sundays, I usually rode the bus to Latoya's house and studied with her. I added her to my list of favorites and tried to call the other TETs to form some type of bond.

Ivyana and I didn't really have too much in common, but one day while we were "bonding," I ran down my list of random questions and asked, "What's your favorite flower?"

"What's my favorite flower?" she sighed. "I'll have to get back to you on that. My favorite *plant* is the ivy though. And it's not just because I'm a TET. They ivy reminds me of myself. It's always climbing and reaching towards the sky, attempting to reach its full potential."

My mother was a fan of ivies too. Although they were a beautiful breed of plant, I was never too enamored with them. They were a selfish plant.

Ivies killed grass. They envied the thin green blades that grew straight up without the aid of an erected or dilapidated building. They couldn't grow alone. They were inevitably dependent on each other and they always would be. They could rise and take over walls, creep into the smallest of crevices, and abundantly multiply. But what the ivies failed to realize, what they failed to see was that—once they reached the top of whatever building they were climbing, once they spread out across the crown of a rooftop's structure, that would be the highest they'd ever be able to go.

XVIII. Careening

CANDACE: Julia said that it's good idea that me, Whit, Amber, and Teresa are going to be living together in the fall.
ME: Went to the library and made copies of all the Epsilon chapter photos from old school yearbooks. I'll bring copies for each of y'all tonight.
JAMIE: Guys, I have an email to show you at study session. See you there <3

---------- Forwarded message ----------
From: [Ivyana] <█████████1908@gmail.com>
Date: Wed, Mar 26, 2008 at 1:21 PM
Subject: A note
To: [Hannah] <███████████████@hotmail.com>

Hi [Hannah],
I just wanted to throw some ideas your way and see what you thought about them. I think that there should be an outline of what is and what is not acceptable because sometimes sorors slip up, including me. So, for the rest of the school year:

* Food runs or basic tasks are acceptable
*Cleaning demands need to wait until Fall '08
* Errands during study sessions are not acceptable
* Wake up calls are fine
* Assigned calls are fine
* Any food requests need to be from someone's meal plan
* If you're requesting food from another type of restaurant then pay the person before or after.
* Each soror needs to tell the the dean or adp (who must then tell the dean) if: 1) they are having someone run an errand OR 2)they are going to be present at a study session...except for the dean of academics, whose presence at study session is habitual
* study session guidelines:

>>remember that if you are a study session, you may inhibit actual studying

*That said, limit your time there to 20-30 minutes and limit distracting interaction

* do not teach any lessons that deal with the pledge process please

* It is up to you if you want to be mean or nice but you should not be overbearingly brutal.

The following are NOT ACCEPTABLE and DO NOT 1) Throw items at people 2.) Tell people that they can't look you in the eyes 3.) Shout at people

What do you think of this?
[Ivyana]

At a study session:

JAMIE: And that's the end of the email I wanted to show you. She sent it a few days ago. Hannah responded by saying that we shouldn't be running too many errands and that the wake up calls shouldn't be done until we're on line. What do you guys think?

TERESA: They broke every rule already! What's the point in coming up with guidelines *now*? There's only like a month of school left!

EVA: Maybe they're trying to make it seem like they haven't been doing anything. You know, like trying to hide things from their prophytes.

TERESA: Seriously, I can go down the list and point out every mistake they've made. Eva weren't you just at Sasha's house a week ago cleaning her bathroom? Almost all of us have cleaned one of their houses! I just took Whitney and Brooke to East Liberty to stand in line for Obama tickets. Don't do errands during study sessions? Please. Eatn' Park, Panera, and McDonald's are not part of our meal plan. And *throwing* things? Don't let me get started.

BROOKE: Well, maybe we should tell the prophytes.

ME: Yea, let's just call them and say "Hey, we were going through Ivyana's email and we saw that we're not supposed to be cleaning their rooms, buying them food, or getting yelled at, but they're still making us do it." NOT! Bad move!

MYA: I agree. That'll just make things worse.

VANESSA: I think they're extra hype to pledge another line.

AMBER: It's about to be April, we've been doin' this for eight weeks already. They should have just put us on line!

CANDACE: They said that won't be happening until the fall. Well, they never officially *said* that, but that's what they're clearly aiming for.

BROOKE: So, we're just going to keep pre-pledging?

CANDACE: Yea, I guess. I was with Sasha and Ivyana earlier this week and Ivyana said, "So since we're not doing intake this semester, why don't we just keep having you guys run errands? And have y'all get to know us by doing it!"

BROOKE: Ughhhhh. This is some—

ME: Bullshit.

TERESA: Julia's calling me, put up that email and stuff. Hello? Yes, we're all here…We're on the ninth floor. Okay.

The TETs entered the room and surrounded us.

JULIA: (snatching the yearbook packet from my book) WHAT'S THIS?

TIFFANY: What is it, LS?

JULIA: This girl has a packet of TET information and she has her *name* on it!

SASHA: Wow, y'all are so dumb! Who else has one?

JULIA: They should all have one! Take them out, give them to us!

DEBORAH: (taking Candace's packet) Let me see! Who made these?

ME*: I did.

DEBORAH: Why is there information about *Mu Beta Xi* in here? I think Whitney is confused about what she wants to be! Are you confused Whitney?

ME*: No.

JULIA: She's just dumb for putting her name on the packet!

TIFFANY: They all have their names on them! They really are tryna get us sent to jail! Why are y'all so stupid?

Silence.

SASHA: My tail is asking you a question! Answer it! Why are y'all so dumb?

Vanessa raised her hand.

VANESSA*: It seems like we're dumb because we're just really confused about a lot of things. But we're learning to correct our mistakes and work on them. It's just taking us a lot of time because we have to learn so much at once.

SASHA: Vanessa just *sharted* on all of you! She's the only one who knows how to speak to us!

JULIA: I want to know who put the idea of gifts in your heads. If you make a mistake, *fix* it. Don't go out and get me and my sorors picture frames!

FELICIA: What picture frames?

DEBORAH: The picture frames with the ribbons and our line numbers…You didn't get a picture frame? Why didn't my LS get a gift?

TIFFANY: Where is Felicia's gift? Who has it?

SASHA: Y'all made everyone else a gift but Felicia? That's deep!

JULIA: Hello? Why aren't any of y'all saying anything? Where is the gift?

TIFFANY: WHERE IS THE GIFT?

SASHA: So all of y'all are just going to sit quiet?

BRITNEY: That's disrespectful.

KAMILLE: Say something. Anything.

SASHA: Y'all are so lame. For real though, y'all didn't make her a gift?

TIFFANY: So y'all are as *dumb* as we thought y'all were! We're gonna find out who has the—

SHELBY*: I HAVE THE GIFT!

TIFFANY: Of course, Shelby Layton. You have the gift?

SHELBY*: Yes.

TIFFANY: Where is it?

SHELBY*: At my house.

TIFFANY: And where is that?

SHELBY*: On Coltart Street.

TIFFANY: Hmmm okay. Let's go get it. Come on, get up. Let me take off my paraphernalia. I'm not tryna' run into people while I'm around you.

Tiffany and Shelby left the room. The remaining TETS continued to talk to us. After ten minutes, Tiffany returned to the room.

SASHA: LS, please don't tell me that Shelby didn't have the gift!

TIFFANY: (pursed her lips) Nope.

SASHA: (laughing) Wow, y'all are unbelievable! Where is she at?

TIFFANY: She's coming. I told her to take her time since she's got that brace on her knee.

JULIA: They're so wack!

SASHA: Y'all disappoint me for real.

Shelby entered the room, holding her knee, freezing her face in agony. She paused before she sat down.

TIFFANY: She just wants us to feel sorry for her! That's why she twisted her face like that! (laughing) I told you that you could walk Shelby. Why are you in pain if I told you that you could walk?

SHELBY*: I was trying to...have a sense of...a sense of urgency.

TIFFANY: Whatever. I wonder what Shelby was thinking when she got inside her house and realized that she didn't have the gift. She was probably thinking about that walk of shame!

JULIA: She probably was, LS!

TIFFANY: Shelby, why did you say that you had the gift when you knew good and well that you didn't? Better yet, how did you feel when all of your so-called *friends* allowed you to get up and waste my gas on you when one of them knowingly has it?

SHELBY*: I was... *disappointed.*

TIFFANY: Why Shelby?

SHELBY*: Because the other girls *knew* that I didn't have the gift.

I sighed and resisted the urge to throw something at Shelby.

TIFFANY: Look at how Whitney is looking at Shelby!

JULIA: Why did y'all make Shelby get the gift when y'all knew she didn't have it?

TIFFANY: They thought they were just gonna go make another one tonight and give it to us tomorrow! They didn't think I would take them to go get it!

JULIA: Wow, that's wack!

SASHA: They're all wack! Except Vanessa! She's the only one who remembered that I was on a diet! She called me back after I asked her to bring me a Pepsi and suggested green tea! The rest of them didn't care!

TIFFANY: There are too many of them anyway. We need to get rid of at least one of them. Let's have an America's Next Top Model moment for a second. Let's see. Who are two people that wouldn't matter? Whitney versus Mya. So, (imitating Tyra Banks) who's it going to be? Is it gonna be the girl with not enough personality (she placed her hand over Mya's head, then moved it over mine) or the girl with *too much*? I have one photo in my hand, and it belongs to the girl who is still in the running to be a part of the Epsilon chapter. The other girl must immediately leave study session and never come back. And the photo belongs to...Oh, it's BLANK!

SASHA: No, wait. It's *Vanessa*!

DEBORAH: (laughing) My LS needs to have her photo frame by the end of the weekend. Whoever has it needs to get it to her ASAP.

JULIA: And y'all really need to learn what discretion means. Get rid of all those documents. Mya, aren't you the one who won the pink tea rose scholarship?

MYA*: Yes.

JULIA: Good. Tell me who the award was named for and why it's named after her.

MYA*: I don't know why.

SASHA: WHATTT? You're going to have to give us that scholarship money back! We are *scholarly* women! Why wouldn't you think to research the person that the award is named after!

TIFFANY: Wow, I'm shocked. That's *wack* Mya!

JULIA: You are WACKTASTIC!

TIFFANY: Brooke, where are my cups? I told you that you needed to replace them since they just magically ended up broken after you cleaned my house. Did you get them yet?

BROOKE*: No.

TIFFANY: Well, I need to have them in the next few days. And you need to get them from *IKEA,* not the dollar store. They need to be the exact ones that I had before. I can't believe that *these* are the girls we picked. Our legacy is not looking too promising. We've got *unsisterly* people like Amber Jackson—

SASHA: Amber Jackson thinks she's a STAR!

TIFFANY: We've got boring people like Candace. We've got Tweedle dee and Tweedle *dumb*, we've got Jamie—
DEBORAH: What did Jamie do?
SASHA: We saw Jamie walking around the other day in pajama pants and UGG boots!!
TIFFANY: Yea, we had to immediately tell her to go change clothes.
SASHA: Don't forget about Teresa! You know she's Oliver Twist!
I zoned out for the next twenty minutes. I had homework to do and we had a sleepover planned after study session. By the time I snapped back into reality the TETs had left the room and the SHs were making fun of Shelby.
SHELBY: I really thought one of you had the gift.
TERESA: How were we supposed to know that? That was the most confident you've spoken since I've known you! I thought you had it!
AMBER: I HAVE THE GIFT!
EVA: NO, *I* HAVE THE GIFT!

After study session, all the SHs with the exception of Shelby and Eva packed into Jamie's car and rode to her house in Monroeville. We claimed sleep spaces in the basement, and after eating food from Sheetz, we became quiet.
VANESSA: (tying a scarf around her hair) Are we still studying this info or not?
ME: No, Brooke is already half sleep.
BROOKE: I'm not half-sleep Whit.
ME: You're wrapped up in a blanket on the floor.
BROOKE: I'm still awake though!
ME: Yea...We're not studying info, everybody's too tired. We'll just do it on our own Sunday I guess.
VANESSA: Works for me.
TERESA: Me too.
AMBER: Yep.
CANDACE: Me too.
MYA: Wait, we're just going to study on Sunday? How are we going to make sure we all know it if we're studying alone?
CANDACE: We can study in pairs or whatever, but I don't think anything is going to get done tonight.

ME: Me either. Let's just sleep. Nobody answer your phone until after eleven. Got it?

TERESA: Good idea. It's Saturday so they shouldn't call us until afternoon anyway.

BROOKE: Well, I'm turning my phone off so I won't get their calls even if they do call me. I'm going to sleep. I'll see y'all when it's light outside.

I woke up at nine in the morning to Amber saying, "Latoya just called me."

TERESA: She called me too. And Tiffany called me ten minutes ago.

ME: (looking at my phone) She called me too. Did she call anyone else?

The other SHs checked their phones for missed calls while Teresa paced the room.

TERESA: Okay, I don't think any of us should call them back until after eleven still. Like, we could really just say we were sleep. What are they gonna do?

We mumbled variances of "yea," and "true," and went back to sleep. Fifteen minutes later Vanessa's phone sounded.

VANESSA: It's Tiffany. (flipped open her razor) Hello? Oh, I don't know where the other girls are…No, I'm not on campus…the parking meter? Oh okay…I'll call around and see if I can get someone to do that. (closed her phone) Someone needs to go put money in the parking meter down the street from the Pete in the next twenty minutes.

ME: (trying to keep my voice calm) I'm sorry, didn't we just agree to not pick up our phones? I could have sworn that was the deal.

VANESSA: It was Tiffany.

ME: Did you think she was calling to have a *conversation* with you on a Saturday morning?

VANESSA: No, but—

TERESA: But what? We agreed to not pick up our phone because *one*, we didn't want to run errands until later today and *two*, because we're in Monroeville! We're thirty minutes away from campus as is, how are we gonna get that done in *twenty*?

VANESSA: I'm gonna call and tell Shelby to do it.

TERESA: Yea, you do that.

Vanessa called Shelby and asked her to run the errand, but minutes later Tiffany demanded that someone else complete the task since Shelby's knee was still hurt. Jamie drove Candace, Mya, Amber, and Vanessa back to campus. When she returned, she sighed, "Guys, I'm not going back to campus right away. I can take y'all back in an hour but I have to get a little more sleep."

CANDACE: Paid the parking meter, now I'm going back to do something else.

BROOKE: That's cool, I'm not tryna go back anyway. Whit, what time do you wanna get up?

ME: Let's get up in like two hours. Turn your phone alarm on.

Her phone alarm went off at 12 p.m.

BROOKE: Are we getting up?

ME: Hell no.

BROOKE: What time then?

ME: Two!

We didn't wake up until four. Jamie dropped Teresa off on campus, and drove Brooke and I to IKEA to buy Tiffany's cups. While Brooke went to look at glasses, Jamie and I walked around the store.

"Why would she pick up her phone?" Jamie asked. "That type of stuff is not gonna work when we get on line."

"Maybe she just wants to shine subconsciously and doesn't realize what she's doing. Either way, it looks like she's gonna do what she wants regardless of what the group decides," I sighed.

"That stuff is so annoying! Especially when she answers rhetorical questions! She's done that at least six times! If they ask why you're stupid, don't answer because you're *not* stupid!"

"You know what she reminds me of?"

"No, what?"

"That Rocko song—the one where he's like *Ima do me! Ima do me!*"

"She does! Hold on, hold on. We gotta come up with some lyrics to this!"

"Ima do me! Ay! Ima do me!"

"You run an errand, but I run ERRANDSSSSSS!"

"You bought her Pepsi, but I bought her green tea!"

"You rock that black hair, but I'm a blonde bombshell!"

XIX. Headway

---------- Forwarded message ----------
From: [Shelby]
Date: Sat, Mar 29, 2008 at 3:05 PM
Subject: IMPORTANT INFORMATION FOR THE COMING OF THE PROPHYTES
To: <studybuddies040507@gmail.com>

[Cari] says the prophytes are going to tear us apart. She says it shows that there [is] dissension between us and we should be willing to stand up for each other. She said someone should have gone with me last night or even taken my keys, and that when no one moved except me it showed that we don't really all know or like each other (her words not mine..).. **We need to know stuff about the people are coming**; they want us to know everything about the prophytes..we should have a gift for example: [Mila from fall 2005] likes orange starburst so we should have for [Mila] **five orange starburst**..Find out favorite candy..Its already going to be bad... **prepare yourself to be attentive** when they get here **SENSE OF URGENCY HUGE FOR OLD SCHOOL SORORS!** we need to be listening to everything they say even when they're talking all at once...we need to understand that no one is going to make it alone ..We all need each other..Everyone is going to be broken down..to stand up for someone: you're always going to be wrong; it's OK that you stuck up for someone rather than not stick up for someone..don't let someone get in trouble by themselves..know stuff about each other really well and talk about each other as if we were old friends **like i told her how I cut my hair really short when I was younger but i just meant to trim my bangs and my dad flipped out** [Cari] *knows that story, so you can use it as a fact/you should know it*
KNOW [TET] FOUNDERS KNOW GREEK ALPHABET
NO OTHER COLORS OF ORGS...wear white grey brown tan black orange. DONT ALL WEAR BLACK we can wear jeans.

"We really need to have gifts for the prophytes," Amber said to me over dinner. "Shelby keeps stressing that."

"I know, but we're not going to be able to find out all their favorite candies and crap within a week. The step show's on the 4th. We're going to have to do something else."

"Well, a few of us were talking earlier and we were thinking about cookies. We could make sugar cookies, frost them in green, and decorate them with icing."

"Sounds like a good idea, we just need to get everybody's money together."

"Isn't that your job?"

"Oh, yea..."

ME: Cookies for the prophytes. Everybody chip in like two dollars so we can get the cookies and icing after Thursday night SS...sprinkles maybe.

"I can't wait 'til this is over," Amber shook her head. "Fall needs to hurry up and get here."

"I feel you. I'm excited though. We're going to be so *thorough*!"

"Yea, I'm so hype!" she smiled and then she changed her tone. "Do you think I'm unsisterly, Whitney?"

"No, why would I think that?"

"They keep telling me that. They say that all the time."

"I don't think they're in any kind of position to tell us *anything* about being sisterly."

"Yea, you're right."

The rest of the week went by just like the others—errands, study sessions, phone calls, and mass text messages. After each study session, we stayed additional hours to quiz each other over the founders, the chapter's charter members, the Greek alphabet, poems, interesting facts about each line, and facts about each other.

Thursday night, April 3, 2008, we met at Eva's apartment to plan what we wanted the cookies to look like. When Jamie finished baking the cookies, we agreed that we would frost them in green and use white icing to draw their respective line numbers on top of each one.

"These taste like crap," Amber sighed. "Jamie, why did you keep making burnt cookies? You made three batches exactly the same way! Did you think they would turn out differently? They're hard like *gingersnaps*, not cookies."

JAMIE: (laughing) Yea, they're pretty bad.

VANESSA: I told y'all I didn't know how to cook so it's not completely her fault.

AMBER: They're not going to like these. We need to have something else, and we're going to have to make some more batches.

JAMIE: Ugh.

MYA: This is going to be a long night.

ME: I can make a cake. I think we have everything we need—cake mix, oil, eggs—wait do we have eggs?

CANDACE: No...

ME: I don't think I can make a cake without eggs. Where's Eva at?

AMBER: She's not answering her phone.

CANDACE: She didn't answer my last text either.

ME: Okay, maybe she's doing something else. We can go to CVS. You coming, Candace?

When we arrived at CVS, we went straight to the dairy section. I shook my head. "Whoa. These eggs are four dollars. I'm not feelin' that."

"Me either, we only need three," she pulled the door open and shut it.

"You wanna steal them?"

"No, not really but—"

"Do you wanna pay for them?"

"No, but—"

"Great."

"How are we going to steal three eggs though? Put them in our coat pockets?"

"We can use your umbrella, I'll be right back."

I took a carton of eggs out of the glass refrigerator and walked to the front of the store.

"Excuse me?" I said to the store clerk.

"Yes?"

"Um, I was wondering if you all sold medium brown eggs or just these white ones?"

"I'm sorry. I think that's all we have. Giant Eagle in Shady side is twenty four hours though. They should have some."

"Oh okay. Thanks."

He walked past me, and when he settled behind the register I went down the cookie aisle. I placed the eggs on the shelf and pretended to be interested in a box of caramel popcorn. I placed three eggs within the folds of Candace's umbrella and passed it to her as I put the eggs back in the refrigerator.

When we returned to Eva's apartment, Jamie had left, and Mya was organizing cookies onto a tray. We stayed up baking and frosting the cake until four. The end result was a slime green colored concoction that resembled a sponge.

The morning of the step show I waited at the bus stop to catch a ride to the Southside. I needed a new outfit for the night and a chance to be away from campus. Within half an hour I found myself inside of Forever 21 buying jeans and tops.

Mya came into the store and walked towards me. "What are you doing here?"

"Buying a new outfit, you?"

"You didn't get my text? Deborah told me to come here and get her tights in a medium size. I saw some in H&M but I wanted to see if they were cheaper here."

"She waited until the day of the step show to get those? Interesting. I ran into Hannah from fall 04 a few minutes ago."

"Did you speak?"

CANDACE: Going to pay Mila's parking meter.

"Yea, and I shook her hand," I laughed.

"You're so weird. I've got to catch the bus back soon, are you leaving now?"

"Yea, I think I'm done."

"Alright, let me think about which store I'm gonna get the tights from and we can ride back together."

"Okay."

AMBER: Going to get shoe polish and a case of bottled water for Ivyana.

When I returned to my room, I set my alarm clock for five. I got into bed and my phone rang. Amber.

"What's up?"

"I'm so pissed right now!"

"What's wrong?"

"Ivyana called me and told me to get her a case of bottled water and black shoe polish. She told me to bring it to her at Soldiers and Sailors, so I went to Rite Aid and bought everything. I walked to Soldiers and Sailors with the stuff, called her, and she told me that she didn't need the stuff anymore!"

"What are you going to do with it?"

"I don't know. I just needed to vent. I'm going to call you back later, I have to carry this stuff back."

"Alright, bye."

I turned my phone off. Fifteen minutes later, there was a knock on my door. Cari.

"Hey Whitney, are you busy?"

If I was, would it matter?

"No, I'm not busy."

"Okay, want to come with me? I'm going to get something to eat."

"Sure."

ME: Going to get food with Cari.

Cari and I walked to Wendy's, and afterwards I sat in her room and talked to her for an hour. By the time I finished talking to her, I had one hour to get to the step show.

I hadn't done my hair. I hadn't showered. I curled my hair as fast as I could and showered for three minutes. I pulled a new top over my head and ripped a hole in it by doing so. I panicked. I knew the SHs had already agreed that only three people could wear black shirts, but I didn't have a choice. I put on a black blouse and a black and silver blazer. I strapped on a pair of heels and bolted towards Soldiers and Sailors.

The show started late. Mu Beta Xi stepped first. The theme of their show was commercial advertisements that had been altered with Greek themes. They wore white dress shirts, burgundy ties with sparkling letters, and black pants. They made fun of the TETs, paid tribute to each of the black fraternities, and garnered enthusiasm from the crowd.

Beta Phi Chi stepped next. The girls that stepped were from another chapter and their theme was secondary school. Their steps were average, and they received moderate applause.

Theta Eta Theta stepped last. Dressed in the old school gray sweaters with their letters stitched on the front, they took the stage. Ivyana was positioned on a table, and the others were planted on the stage. They began to step, and within the blink of an eye Ivyana pulled Kamille from under the table. They continued to step and then they paused.

A video was supposed to appear. Sound was supposed to come from the speakers. Nothing happened. The TETs remained in their stances, frozen.

CANDACE: Damn.

SHELBY: I don't want to show up tonight.

EVA: OMG!

They started to step again without the music. For a few minutes the music played, but then they were left to complete the show without visual effects on the screen. At the end, they party walked off to Shawty Lo's "Dey Know."

I couldn't focus on the fraternities that stepped, I was too nervous about what would happen at study session later that night. I saw Sasha storm out of the auditorium and shook my head at Candace.

EVA: I have to leave the show for a few minutes. Sasha said I have to buy alcohol for her prophytes. Does anybody have money?

I thought the Mus were going to win. I thought their show was more entertaining, and I knew we would have to listen to the TETs complain about how they were cheated. As the host stood at center stage, she begged the audience to quiet down. She smiled, "Okay so for the sororities…second runner up, the lovely ladies of Beta Phi Chi!"

The crowd clapped.

"The first runner up is….Mu Beta Xi!"

My jaw dropped. I couldn't believe it. I didn't even have a chance to gather my thoughts before she announced Theta Eta Theta as the winner.

ME: What the…

JAMIE: It's good for us that they won though!

CANDACE: Maybe the prophytes won't be mean to us now.

AMBER: Who's going to get the cake and cookies for SS tonight?

After the step show I went to Taco Bell with my friends. Tiara and Michelle offered to pay for my food, Alexis and Raya bought me cookies from Quick Zone, and they all seemed disappointed that I wasn't going to the after party.

"Son, don't you think this is getting ridiculous? You're not even on line. Why can't you go out?" Alexis sighed.

"I mean…Yea, it's ridiculous, but it'll be over in a few more weeks, and then I can chill for the summer and I'll only have to get through eight weeks in the fall."

"I hope so son. I feel like we're losing you—not like as a friend or anything, but this pre-pledging stuff isn't you and I really want you to know that."

"Okay, I'll keep that in mind."

Michelle handed me a bag of Taco Bell and I immediately turned away to go to the engineering building.

At study session we set up a table and covered it in a decorative table cloth. We placed pink lemonade, cups, and plates at the end of the table and put the cookies in the middle. Candace and I attempted to pull the plastic wrap away from the cake, but the frosting came away with it so we left the cake wrapped.

We organized our desks into a circle and called Britney Lynn and Sasha. Fifteen minutes later Ivyana opened the door to the classroom and rolled her eyes. "What the hell is this? Ugh, you guys aren't going to believe this!"

Spring 07, Fall 05, and Fall 04 entered the room.

RAVEN: Awww look! This is so cute!

RIANA: They made us cookies!

The TET prophytes snacked on the cake and cookies and asked us questions. Despite Spring 07's many warnings about "how mean" their prophytes were going to be, they were actually nice.

Spring 07 sat with frowns on their faces as their prophytes laughed and joked with us. The only mean comment that was said to me came from Spring 07's dean, who tapped me on my shoulder and said, "You have an attitude. I don't like you."

Ivyana and Tamera from Fall 04 came to the next night's study session. Tamera asked each of us to introduce ourselves and give our majors. She told us information about herself, which a few us wrote down. After about twenty minutes, she and Ivyana left. We pulled up the account and went over what we learned about the prophytes that weekend. While we were in the middle of listing Tamera's comments, Jamie's phone rang.

"Hello? No, I don't have my car...Teresa doesn't have hers this weekend either...Okay," she closed her phone. "They just wanted to know if one of us had a car to take Riana to the airport."

EVA: Wow, they're so extra. Didn't some of them drive to get here? Why can't they do it?

JAMIE: I don't know. They'll probably have to do it now though since me and Teresa don't have our cars.

AMBER: I'm still mad at Ivyana for making me get all that stuff and saying that she didn't even need it! She definitely told me that she needed shoe polish and a case of bottled water!

EVA: Yea, that was a mess. Do you think Sasha will pay me and Candace back for the alcohol I bought yesterday?

ME: Um no.

AMBER: Please.

MYA: No.

VANESSA: Doubt it.

CANDACE: You're joking right?

TERESA: You know what? You want to know why—

JAMIE: Wait a minute guys, they're calling me again. Hello? Okay....Okay...We'll figure it out. (snapped her phone shut) We need to figure out a way to get Riana a ride to the airport at 5. Does anyone have friends with cars?

TERESA: Yea, I do. I'll just call them and say I need to use their car at 4 in the morning, and when they ask what it's for, I'll tell them that I can't let them know because I have to be discreet. Are they being for real?

JAMIE: Well, I can't go to Monroeville to get my car this late.

It's already twelve. Some of us might have to ride on the 28X with her or put in money for a cab.

AMBER: The bus is free.

EVA: I have friends with cars but I don't know if they'll let me use them this late.

After proposing ideas, the plan was made clear: Jamie's friend Bray would help us out. Jamie would use Bray's car and Teresa would ride along with Jamie to the airport.

We finished putting things on the document, and Britney Lynn called and allowed us to leave at two. I was elated, ready to get sleep. I walked back to towers with Candace, and as soon as we walked through the first door, my phone rang. Mya.

"Whitney, do you want to help take Riana to the airport?" she asked.

"Are you seriously asking me if I *want* to? Hell no, I don't *want* to. What happened with Teresa? I thought her and Jamie were doing it."

"Teresa's sick and I'm going to stay with her for a few hours to make sure she's okay. Jamie is still going to drive, but she said she doesn't want to drive alone. I called you first."

"Okay, I'll do it," I sighed.

"Thanks, Whit."

I closed my phone and went to a friend's dorm. I sat in the lounge with my head in my hands. Pre-pledging was wearing on me again and I wished that I could somehow fast forward to the end. I had expressed my feelings to a few of my friends who already crossed in other organizations, and although they agreed that the TETs were "taking it too far," they encouraged me to stick with it.

At 3:45, Jamie called me and told me to meet her outside of towers. I got into the car and tried to keep my eyes open. When we reached the address the TETs had given us, we got out of the car and knocked on the door. We carried Riana's suitcases to the trunk, and opened the front door of the car for her.

"I knew you ladies would come through for me. I knew I didn't need to worry. What's your name again?" she turned towards the backseat and looked at me.

"Whitney."

"I thought so," she pulled the seatbelt across her shoulder. "And you're Jamie right?"

"Yes," Jamie flipped her hair and began driving towards the airport.

"I'm very impressed in what I saw of you ladies," Riana went on. "It was very smart of you to look nice for us and have the room set up nicely. My dean said that she's not sure if you guys are ready for the process, but I think you guys will definitely be ready by the fall. Do you have any questions?"

"Did you ever have any doubts about the process?" I asked, not intending for those words to actually come out of my mouth.

"Oh, sure! There were times I thought the process was absolutely stupid, but I kept going, because I knew that my prophytes cared about me and were trying to make me a better person. I went in with limits. Sometimes they would have frats come see us and I told my LSs that I wasn't going to do anything sexual, but my prophytes never allowed anything like that to happen. You just have to go in with a strong mind. Know who you are before you start, and at the end you'll be fine. When I pledged, my prophytes yelled at me, but my mind would be elsewhere. I'd be thinking about what I was going to wear the next day, or going over homework assignments in my head."

"Did you ever want to give up?" Jamie asked.

"I don't know anyone who didn't want to give up at one point. That's part of the process though. It's going to push you to your limit, to where you think you can't take anymore, and then your passion and your spirit will carry you through. I think that's one of the most important things that I learned—that they can break me down mentally, and they can hurt me physically, but they can't touch my spirit."

Hearing a TET talk about how the process had shown her so much about life pushed my logic and skepticism to the side once again. We continued to ride to the airport, asking Riana questions. Eventually, she started asking about our summer plans and the other SHs.

When we arrived to the airport, we pulled her suitcases out of the car and gave her a hug. We wished her a safe flight, and waited in the car until she disappeared behind the sliding glass doors.

"I'm so tired," Jamie said. "Thanks for riding with me. I probably would be sleeping on the way back if you weren't with me."

"No problem. I'm so ready for this to be over. I was okay with the small stuff here or there, but I feel like they're just using us most of the time. Why couldn't they take their own prophyte to the airport?"

"Exactly! Tiffany has a car! She could have easily driven her instead of making us go through all that trouble. At least we got it done though."

"Yea. Do you think you'll haze people after we make it?"

"Well, since I'm the youngest, that would be really weird. I have a lot of friends who are going to be interests so I don't know. I probably will though since I had to do all this stuff. Do you think you will?"

"Probably not. I have an attitude apparently so if I act normal interests will be intimidated."

"Yea," she laughed. "You wouldn't make people run errands for you?"

"I can't see myself doing that. That's just not me. Plus, as much as I've played around in their food, I would never want to take that chance you know? I'd rather just do the stuff myself."

"I feel you on that. Someone's gonna have to do it though."

"You and Teresa," I reclined the seat.

"Do you think Ivyana will be a good dean?"

"Hell no."

"Why not? You don't think she cares about us?"

"Ivyana only cares about herself. If it isn't about Ivyana, it isn't relevant to her life. I could see her taking it really serious in the beginning, but I think she'll just fall off and she'll be the one hazing us the most, not protecting us."

"I don't think so. I think she'll be really caring. It's Sasha that I'm worried about."

"Yea, Sasha's probably going to try her best to kill me."

"No, she—Yea, she probably will, Whit."

"And that's fine, because I'm still going to beat her up after our probate."

"I think all of us will be so happy to be done that we won't even care about what happened this semester or whatever happens in the fall."

"For her sake I hope so," I laughed.

"Do you want to put up everything that Riana said on the doc' or do you want me to do it?"

"Let's just do it together at the next study session. She's not gonna pop up and quiz us about it anytime soon so there's no rush."

"True."

We rode the rest of the way with soft music playing, interjecting every five minutes or so with thoughts about the step show or things that needed to be put up on the document.

A few days after the step show, Deborah told me to bring her a couple of tacos and a Dove chocolate bar to her house. She had me wash a few of her dishes, and when I informed her that I was done, she asked me to talk with her for a few minutes.

"Do you think we deserved to win the step show?" she asked.

Um, no.

"Yea, I think you did."

"Really?"

No, not really.

"Yea, I really think so."

"People are getting so upset about it. We weren't the judges so don't blame us. I hate the fact that we had technical difficulties, but that's not our fault. Our show was still better. Don't get mad because you had to dedicate your entire show to dissing TET and you still couldn't win."

"Yea, I thought that they could've come up with a better theme," I froze my eyeballs in their sockets.

"We just have so many haters here. I hope you know that if you ever get into my chapter, people are going to hate on you just because you're a TET. And that's fine. I've accepted the fact that our process is what it is and people wish they went as hard. Don't talk about our process when you came off the sands looking the exact same way you did before you started and I lost ten pounds. Anyway, let's not talk about people that don't matter. Tell me one interesting thing about each girl in the study group."

---------- Forwarded message ----------
From: <[Amber]>
Date: Thu, Apr 10, 2008 at 3:55 AM
Subject: Wednesday Lunch with [Deborah] at Red Oak Cafe
To: <studybuddies040507@gmail.com>

[DEBORAH] SAID...
- All the girls got calls for the first night of set to go to [Tanya's] apartment (she lives on the FOURTEENTH floor!)
- Not everyone chose to come to set
- She was with [Felicia] when she got her call but she still hid it from [Felicia] and acted like she was leaving to go get something to eat
-[The CMU grad advisor] was trying to bust [Epsilon] then too, even though she came through [Epsilon]!
- She had braids when she was online because she didn't want to walk around campus looking like "who shot John"
- She was never big on caffeine but tried no-doze once and considers it to be dangerous
-[Riana] is currently getting her master's degree in Public Health and plans on going to Pharmacy school afterward; everyone loves her, she is always smiling
- While Fall 05 was online, they each had different techniques for staying awake:
  2. [Arizona]- coffee
  3. [Felicia]- energy drinks, but more so Gatorade
  5. [Mila]- coke
  7. [Amara]- vault
- She strongly believes in the tradition of the [Epsilon] process, but naturally, every line will have a slightly different process (IE. Fall 05 post-pledged, Spring 07 pre-pledged in the Fall and

transitioned into pledging in the Spring, & we pre-pledged in the Spring and will possibly pledge in the Fall or Spring)
- She always thought that I was the shortest (IE. potential ace) until she had [Brooke] stand next to me and compare that one night at study session
- When I told her about the [Nu Alpha Pi] grad advisor knowing my first and last name, she said that she thinks [Ivyana] runs her mouth TOO MUCH
- feels it is good that the organization wants to raise the GPA requirement, but believes it should be raised to a 2.75 and not a 3.0
- Said that you never really fall completely asleep when you're online because you're always ON EDGE, expecting a phone call
- [Mila] lost 20-25 lbs when she was done pledging
- [TET] shield is always on the left side on paraphernalia (over your heart)

That's it!
[Amber]

I was hungry and I only had twenty three dining dollars left on my meal plan. All of my friends were in class and I didn't want to ask any of the SHs to buy me anything. I walked to an Einstein's bagel stand. I stood in line and when no one was watching I took a fruit cup and placed it in my purse. I walked to the cathedral and went to Chick Fil A. I picked up a student newspaper and folded it. I slipped a chicken sandwich within the folds and tossed a bottle of water into my backpack. I relied on this system for the rest of the semester.

XX. Leeway

I was helping Candace clear out a room in the engineering hall. We were gathering all the things that the TETs used in the step show.

"Thanks for helping me," Candace said. "I think Ivyana will be calling me soon."

"Ugh, she's so extra."

"Right on time," she opened her phone. "Okay, I'm coming."

We carried the trash bags outside and Ivyana told Candace to get inside the car. I closed her door and started walking back to my dorm.

If I was a rich girl—na-na-na-na-na-na-na-na-na-nah. Ivyana.

"Hello?"

"WHITNEY! Your feet are ASHY! Go put on some lotion NOW! That is not cute! That is not *sexy!*"

TERESA: I have to take Latoya to the bus station next week. She offered to give me gas money!
CANDACE: With Mya and Vanessa at Deborah's house making a cake.

At a study session:
Sasha asked each of us what our GPAs were going to be at the end of the semester.
SASHA: Well, sounds like you all are going to be okay. Brooke, can I have a sip of your juice?
Brooke passed her the juice.
SASHA: Why are all of y'all double majoring, getting minors, buttons, stickers, and stamps?
We laughed.
SASHA: Well, it was nice talking to y'all I guess. See y'all later.
She got up and left the room.
AMBER: What was she saying about her favorite thing to eat? Did anyone catch that?
JAMIE: I did. I'm putting it on the document right now.
CANDACE: Okay, good. Just to let y'all know, I was with Tiffany today and she said that—

BROOKE: She drank my juice.

JAMIE: What did you say Candace?

CANDACE: I was saying that Tiffany—

BROOKE: She drank my juice! Sasha drank my juice and she didn't give it back! That was *my* juice!

We laughed.

CANDACE: (laughing) I'll just put it on the document later.

VANESSA: Hey guys, I'm thinking about living with Kamille for the summer. The rent is affordable.

TERESA: Why would you do that?

AMBER: That's suicide! If they know where you live, especially if you live with one of them, they'll make you do stuff all the time.

VANESSA: Okay, good point. Does anybody know why they call Nicole the "charm" of the line?

ME: Maybe it's because she's number seven. Lucky number? Lucky *charm*?

CANDACE: Maybe. Or maybe it's because she didn't get beat a lot when she was on line.

VANESSA: Oh, well if that's the case, I'm tryna be like that.

CANDACE: Are you saying that you're not going to take wood?

VANESSA: I want to be the charm.

Silence.

Candace left the room.

VANESSA: I was joking.

AMBER: It didn't *sound* like you were joking.

BROOKE: Sure didn't.

VANESSA: Well, whatever. I was.

ME: Anyway, what are the plans for the summer? How are we going to keep studying the info?

JAMIE: I'll make a syllabus. Since all their lineage is already up on our account, I'll just divide it up and break it down so it's easy to study.

EVA: They're gonna hate us because we're already going to know everything!

AMBER: Oh well. We've been doing this long enough. We know everything else so we might as well learn that too.

SHELBY: They're going to call us skaters!

AMBER: SKATERS!

EVA: (singing) Big ups…to all MY SKATTTERRSSS!

If I was a rich girl—na-na-na-na-na-na-na-na-na-nah. Tiffany.
"Hello?"
"Where are you?"
"I'm in Candace's room."
"She lives in towers, right?"
"Yea."
"Okay, come down to the lobby. I'm going to need your ID to get into Market Central and then you need to help Ivyana get stuff from her house. Go meet her at my car after you give your card to me."
"Okay."
ME: Candace, Ivyana said that she needs your laundry detergent, could you bring it outside? I'm in Tiffany's car.

At a study session:
AMBER: I'm starting to run out of dining dollars.
ME: I have twelve.
BROOKE: I haven't had any in forever.
EVA: Me either.
VANESSA: I'm almost out too.
TERESA: Why don't we just lie and say that nobody has any more dining dollars? What are they gonna do? They can't hit us, we're not on line.
CANDACE: Well, Deborah might throw Starburst at us.
JAMIE: (laughing) Yea, she might. I have dining dollars so if any of you need me to get you anything right before study session I can get it.
MYA: Aww, we love you Jamie!
EVA: I love all of you! (singing) *Fall 08 is betterrr—*
ME: Come on Eva. Really?
TERESA: I just wish us telling them that we didn't have dining dollars would stop Ivyana from calling me in the morning and getting her Starbucks. That's *real* money and she acts like I don't have a job to go to.
ME: Well, why don't you just tell her that you have a job?

TERESA: You really think it's that easy? You don't think I tried telling her that?

JAMIE: Did you?

TERESA: Let's take this morning for an example. She calls me at 8:30 and she asks me if I have to go to work. I say yes. She says, when? I say, 9:30. She says, Good you have an hour.

AMBER: Julia's calling me. They're here. Hello? Yes, we're on the seventh floor...Okay.

Julia, Sasha, and Latoya came into the room.

JULIA: How is everybody today?

US: Fine.

JULIA: Good. Do you all *still* not understand that we have something that y'all want? I don't understand why you all rush me off the phone or act like you don't want to talk to me. That's fine though, because you know what? (she pointed to her TET broach and tapped Brooke on the shoulder) You'll *never* have one. (she tapped Amber on the head) Hey Amber, you'll *never* have one. Candace—I mean, BETA! You'll *never* have one.

SASHA: Y'all are so wack. And I'm not saying that just to be saying that. I mean that from the bottom of my heart. I just don't get y'all sometimes.

LATOYA: You all are just *lax*. Y'all are going to have a rude awakening *if* you make it to the pledge process.

JULIA: Who can make a McDonalds run real quick?

Candace raised her hand.

JULIA: Okay, go to my apartment and get Nicole's card.

LATOYA: And bring me back an ice cream please.

Candace left the room. One by one, Julia called us over to the other side of the room to discuss what we needed to work on during the summer.

SHELBY: Whitney, could you come get the black thread from me and give it to Kamille when she asks for it?

The errands began to fall off. For the last two weeks whenever they called me I would say that I didn't have dining dollars. If they asked if someone else had any I would say no.

CANDACE: Going to get an omelet for Ivyana.

ME: What? I thought we agreed to just tell
them that we didn't have dining dollars.
CANDACE: I did tell her that. She said that I
still have swipes. She told me to go to
Market Central and get her pancake mix in a
cup and an omelet. I'm going to sneak the
omelet out in my purse.

The TETs showed up to our study sessions less often. We spent
our time singing, joking around, and imitating their behavior at
past study sessions.

Subject:	Lunch with 1 and 7
From:	wgw█████edu
Date:	Mon, April 14, 2008 1:30 am
To:	studybuddies040507@gmail.com
Priority:	Normal
Options:	View Full Header	View Printable Version

So on Friday I had lunch with 1 and 7, and in the middle of our lunch [Chris] showed up and starting talking about "his sorority"--it's called "FM"...lol but anyway..

--[Kamille] was in the "sci-fi" club (Im assuming in high school)
--she likes to sew things and the black thread was for [her boyfriend's]backpack which "has a huge hole in it"
--said she doesn't own any polo shirts, and when she said this [Nicole]said she would buy some for her
--said [Selena from fall 04]spec'd "like almost everybody on the line except me.. and two or three others"
--thinks trey songz sounds like "a little girl"
--doesn't like thunder--when we walked back to lothrop she asked if she could come up to my room, but the thunder stopped so she said she'd try and make it to her house quick

[Nicole]
[...]
--addicted (according to [Kamille]) to energy drinks
--out of nowhere said, "Omg, Whitney, your ears are SMALL!!!"
--lied to [Chris] about being in a sorority
--claimed that pledging affected her life as a member of BDW
--said she has all the requirements for pre-dent but is going to just be a sociology major "the things I sacrifice for [TET]..."
--likes trey songs but thinks he's too skinny (went to his concert in ATL over Spring Break)
--was dying to get her nails done after lunch (she goes to "Hot Tips")
--when she was younger she asked her Dad for a tennis bracelet, he gave it to her, and then she lost it.....
[Chris] came over and the conversation got cut short lol

For Fall 05's anniversary we bought blank violet Chinese takeout boxes and glued pearls in the shape of an ivy leaf on each one. We wrote their line names and ship names in green, and filled each one with their favorite candy.

The day that we were supposed to present them, I found myself slumped on a bench outside the library. It was a beautiful day.

"SANDBAGZ!" I heard my friend Andrew call out.

"That's not my name, Andrew."

"Yes it is, *Sandbagz*. It's been your name since freshman year."

"Whatever," I laughed. "How's your life?"

"Life's good. It's good. How's *your* life?"

"I don't even want to talk about it."

He and I discussed the Literature and Race final, and as he started talking about poems he had written, I flashed back to his probate.

He was a member of Nu Alpha Pi and he had crossed in the fall. His fraternity had held the probate at a nightclub. I remembered how perfect the recitation of information had been, how the cane twirls and shimmies were in sync, how happy he was after he crossed. I remembered his line brother Trey smiling for the entire night, smiling as if it was the happiest day of his life.

"Are you and Trey closer after crossing together?" I asked. "Like, I know y'all both knew each other from Jersey, but do you think Nu Alpha Pi made you closer?"

"Um, I don't know how to answer that. Me and him were always tight so I guess—"

"Hold up, is that Ivyana?"

"Yea."

"Ugh."

She and Teresa walked over to us. Ivyana smiled, "Hey Andrew, how are you today?"

"I'm alright, how are you?" he asked.

"I'm great. Whitney, what is up with your hair?"

"I didn't have time to do it. I'm going home soon though. I'll get it done then," I sighed.

"That's not the issue. Your hair isn't done at this moment."

"You want some sunflower seeds?" Andrew interjected.

"No thank you," she went on. "I just don't understand Whitney. Like, why is your hair not done?"

I cracked. "It's a beautiful day outside Ivyana. Why don't you focus on *that* instead of my hair?"

She rolled her eyes and smiled. She and Teresa walked away.

"I'm not gonna make it Andrew. I can't put up with this crap for too much longer."

He laughed. "You'll make it Sandbagz."

Later that night at study session we presented the gifts to Fall 05. They laughed and joked with us, and reminded us that we needed to send our grades to Britney Lynn within the first few days of May. After Ivyana told a story about Jamie and Candace, she put on a serious face. "Whoa wait a minute. I've got to stop the fun festivities for a second. Let me tell y'all what Miss Whitney said to me today. I was asking her about her hair and she tells me that she's going to get it done *soon*. You know that's not a good excuse, so naturally I inquired further and she said to me, in front of her little Nu Pi homie, it's a nice day outside Ivyana, why don't you focus on *that* instead of my hair!"

"Whoa," Deborah looked at me.

"I don't know if you think you have something right now because you got picked or whatever, but you don't. You do not need to disrespect me. It's called *deference* and I'll be sure to help you out with the definition in the future. I'm going to remember what you said to me. It may not be today, it may not be *tomorrow*, but I'm coming for that ass. I have the tendency to black out and when I come back to my senses someone will end up being hurt. I won't know what I actually did or how it happened…Wait til the fall, Whitney. Anyway," she changed her tone. "Thanks for the gummies girls! Next time get the Black Forest brand."

The last study session was April 19, 2008. We all thought the TETs would show up, so we didn't bring Candace's surprise birthday cake to study session. After we had been sitting in the room for two hours, Kamille walked in and handed Teresa a box of cake mix.

"Felicia said that y'all need to make her a cake for tomorrow," she said before leaving.

CANDACE: I'm going to the bathroom real quick. I'll be back.

Candace left the room.

ME: We all owe you like two dollars for the birthday cake and stuff right, Teresa?

TERESA: Yea and I *need* the money.

ME: I told you I lost my debit card today. My mom's overnighting me money so can I get it to you tomorrow?

TERESA: Who can cover Whitney?

MYA: I will.

JAMIE: I'll cover you when we go to Sheetz later, Whit.

TERESA: Are those your last two dollars Mya?

MYA: Yes.

TERESA: Fork them over.

AMBER: Wow, son.

Candace walked back into the room.

SHELBY: (handing Candace a card) We wanted to give you something, Candace—

AMBER: Yea, but we were gonna wait until midnight when it was her actual birthday Shelby!

SHELBY: Oh, sorry.

CANDACE: (laughing) Okay, I'll wait to open it.

At midnight we sang Candace "Happy Birthday" and she opened her birthday card.

EVA: Your favorite artist is Alicia Keys right, Candace?

CANDACE: Of course!

EVA: (singing) *Some people live for the fortune...*

TERESA: Let's take photos!

We posed for Teresa's camera and hugged Candace.

SHELBY: Take some on my camera too!

EVA: (singing) *Some people live just for the fame....*

ME: EVA! Take pictures with the rest of us!

After we finished taking pictures, we continued to study, and wondered if the TETs were going to show up.

AMBER: It's about to be four! Do you think they're just keeping us here because it's the last session?

EVA: I don't know. We're not going to have much time for the sleepover if they don't hurry up and call us though.
JAMIE: Guys, I'm ready to leave!
BROOKE: Me too!
TERESA: Okay, let's just call Britney Lynn and tell her that a janitor kicked us out.
JAMIE: Yea! Good plan! Do it!
TERESA: Okay (opened her phone) It's ringing....She didn't pick up.
CANDACE: What? Could you try one more time?
TERESA: Okay. It's ringing again...Hello may I speak to Britney Lynn? Hi Britney, I was calling to let you know that a janitor just walked by and he said that he has to clean the room...Oh. Oh, okay. Good night.
AMBER: What did she say?
TERESA: She was half sleep! She said we could leave though.
ME: Cool, let's bounce.

We left the room and got our overnight bags. We crammed into Jamie and Teresa's cars and rode to Jamie's house.

We partied until the wee hours of the morning—party walking, singing, and drinking—living in perfect harmony. Little did we know, we would be living one of the last notes.

The next afternoon, Candace and I went to Eva's apartment to bake Felicia's cake. Candace monitored her Face book wall and I attempted to stay awake as the cake cooked in the oven.

"I can't believe I'm making someone else a cake on *my* birthday. I can't believe study sessions are over either."

"Me either," I sighed. "I'm happy as hell though—I'm getting out of here."

"You're not going to take your finals?"

"Yea, I'm just more focused on going home."

"I can see that," she laughed. "I'm glad we're done too. I can't wait til we get back in the fall. We're finally going to be TETs!"

"Yea finally, but we still gotta go through a lot more bullshit."

"I won't care then. It'll only be *eight weeks*. Eight weeks after waiting for almost a year isn't bad."

The timer went off. I took the cake out of the oven and started searching for a tray.

"Candace, Eva doesn't have a tray in any of her cabinets. She has small ones but not one that's big enough."

"Well, what do we do?"

"We could cut the cake in half and put it on two separate trays."

"No, that won't work," she shook her head. "I'll go get one. Be back."

When she returned, she slammed the tray onto the counter.

"Candace, that's a McDonald's tray."

"I know. I stole it from *McDonald's*."

"Okay, it's whatever. Just wash it off and then we can put the cake on there."

"I'm not even going to attempt to make the cake look decent. I'm slapping the frosting on there," she said as she washed the tray.

"That's fine with me. Refresh my memory," I took out a knife. "What exactly did we learn from everything we did this semester?"

"I think that aside from all the reckless stuff, we learned how to communicate better and work together to get stuff done."

"Oh, that's what we were learning? I thought we learned how to lie, cheat, and steal."

Although we did not have to go to study sessions anymore, we still ran errands during finals week.

I almost slept through my first final. Candace came over and helped me stay awake to study. If it hadn't been for Amber's text about getting an envelope for Ivyana, I would have slept through my second final.

Beyond this place of wrath and tears
Looms but the Horror of the shade,
And yet the menace of the years
Finds, and shall find, me unafraid.

XXI. Making Way

I arrived in Memphis for the summer in late April. I was exhausted, but I felt free. I turned my phone off for two days and slept. I thought that my summer would be free of doing anything TET related with the exception of calling them every now and then, sending them my final grades, and emailing them my class schedule for the fall. A couple of days went by without an errand until Vanessa called me.

"Hey Whitney. I'm calling to let you know about our first assignment," she said.

"Wait a minute. Did you just say *assignment*? And did you say *first* assignment? As in there will be *others*?"

"I'm just the messenger Whitney. I'm just doin' what they told me to do. I've got to call everyone individually because we all have different themes."

"Go ahead," I sighed.

"Okay. You have to create a program, a budget for your program, and a way to execute whatever you create by outlining where the event will be, how many people you'll need, et cetera. The platform you have to address is 'finances of the black family.' It's due May 11th. I'll call you back later to make sure you've got everything down."

"Alright, thanks."

I immediately called Brooke to ask what program she had been assigned to construct.

"I got—you know what?" she said. "I'm not even thinking about what program I got because I'm not doing it until May 10th!"

"Are you serious?"

"Yea. I got stuff to do Whit. I don't have time to be doing this in the summer."

"I feel you. I was looking forward to not having to deal with them so much. I see why they would give out an assignment since we'll have to do it when we get in the chapter, but it's the *summer*. Oh, and I was talking to Julia the other day and she said that none of them have heard from you. She said that you need to step your game up, or it might be a problem when we get back in the fall."

"What? Julia needs to fall back! It hasn't even been two weeks! I can't take a break for *two weeks*? Please! I'ma get my two weeks!"

"I mean—"

"Whit, its summer break. I'm going to take a *break*. Last semester was way too crazy. I need time to be away from all of that. I'll call them eventually."

"I can understand that. I'm not looking forward to going back anytime soon."

"Me either! That's why I'm gonna make the most of my summer because I know that when we get back they're gonna go way too far. I'm tired of them right now. They just want to see my name on their caller ID. They don't really want to talk to me so, whatever."

```
JAMIE: I have to go to the Southside with
Sasha in a couple of weeks and I've been
running a few errands a week ever since
school let out. Miss u guys! <3
```

---------- Forwarded message ----------
From: < [Candace.]>
Date: Wed, May 7, 2008 at 8:26 PM
Subject: [Candace's] lunch and mall extravaganza w/4
To: Victoria Benedum <studybuddies040507@gmail.com>

Ok, this is extremely long, but we were together for 5+ hours and I probably asked hundreds of questions, no lie. Later on I'll separate this more into "facts" vs. "information" if that makes sense, so some of it can go on the regular document about them. So set aside some time to read this when you can...you might want to take breaks, or grab a snack =)

*she named stuff we should know: founders, charters, dates of other frats/sororities founding, greek alphabet, great lakes regional director (the only one I told her I didn't know), she asked who [the executive director] was (I checkmated the shit outta her, she wasn't expecting me to know lol), I said we're trying to know more [Epsilon] info and single letter chapters...she looked at me with this weird smirk and asked why single letter chapters- I said b/c they said it at her probate-she just nodded her head and smiled

*she said she's not into the whole drama between orgs, she thinks all the facebook stuff is dumb and feels that all orgs are really the same except for colors/founders/maybe a few platforms[...]

*Prophytes are sooo different from them, they wouldn't accept the excuses we make, they would just say don't come back to study sessions or "oh ok, see you in the cut"

*she didn't understand why we would ignore phone calls from them or not call back for hours and hours/sometimes the next day ([Amber] she brought up you in particular), she said we should just text them and say we're busy doing whatever instead of just letting it slide by

*she says her prophytes were different b/c of all that they had to go through- her dean ([Cassandra]) was on line 3 times to get to where she is now and it's amazing to her how hard they worked to become a member of [TET] and to get the [Epsilon] process, it's an honor that they did that-so future lines would not have to hear shit about being paper or would not have split lines, that's why she feels that they were so hard b/c of all the respect they've built up for [TET] and the process so it has made her respect them for everything

*she still doesn't understand why certain ones of us hardly ever call her, even if you're on vacation you should be able to slip out for a few minutes

*she feels that some people rush her off the phone like "well, okay just wanted to say hi" and at first she was so surprised but

now she doesn't even care b/c if we don't want to get to know her then its whatever, she feels like we think it's a chore to call them and we should want to get to know them, she wanted to slap Whitney for asking how much we should call over the summer-that's like asking how much should I want to get to know you...she really wants us to ask her questions b/c she feels as though she's an honest person and pretty open about everything, "don't you all want to know things?! i don't get it!"

*she said like 10 times that she thinks we treat this like a "checklist"...like "well I called her and her and her so I'm done, I ran errands so now what". She doesn't like getting 1 call then seeing her LS get a call 2 seconds later, it seems impersonal (I don't get why that's a problem but whatever)

*she asked me what I was worried about-I just said that I was worried that some of my connections with ppl don't reflect the amount of time I've been calling them, she said yeah she had called [Cari] to see if she wanted to come with us to eat and [Cari] said she didn't have a way to get there and [Julia] offered to call me to see if I could pick her up and apparently [Cari] said she doesn't know me that well and that made [Julia] upset. I also said I sometimes worry if we still communicate as well as we should (I was tryna dig for stuff) and she asked me to explain. I just said sometimes text messaging doesn't get responses from everyone and she wanted me to say names but I wouldn't say any, she just said there's no excuse to not be able to text so we should work on that. I really don't think it's a problem I just had to say something!

*she talked about how some of her line sisters were too non-chalant and didn't understand the "team" aspect while they were on line-they sometimes were still more focused on themselves, but you can't help that b/c that's how some people's personalities are. You really just have to work through it together or else everyone suffers. She feels like she should have asked for help more

*I asked how she thinks it makes a difference how a lot of us knew each other before study sessions: she knew [Britney Lynn] a little bit but they were in different circles of friends, she knew [Nicole] of course, and then she mentioned how [LATOYA] WASN'T IN STUDY SESSIONS...so it just meant they had to talk to each other a lot to get to know one another, she said they got close really quick but I don't believe it [...]

*she said we're not hungry and all that crap, she said they did anything and everything they could [...]

*she said they can tell who the nonchalant people are/the people who think "things will get done whenever they get done"...those are the people she doesn't want in her chapter or then if you do make it, it will just be hell

*she doesn't wear a lot of skirts-she said "b/c I have a lot of scars on my legs now"   umm ok. damn. [...]

*still feels uncomfortable around [her prophyte Raven] b/c she still feels like she doesn't know her, it's awkward

*has a Tommy Hilfiger perfume, loves Coach and Dooney+Burke, used to love Wet Seal and Forever 21, now she likes Express, H&M, Pink, still Forever 21, thinks Urban Outfitters is hit or miss [...]

*felt that she was attacked while on line for her health, she talked to [Tanya] sometimes about it when she felt that things had gone too far, talked to her line sisters

*her parents knew a lot of what was going on while she was on line, she would call her mom crying sometimes and her mom would threaten to come down to the basement (mainly joking), no parent wants to know that their child is going through

something like that but her Dad was proud of her for pledging (he's still active so he has an idea of what was going on), her Dad said he would have been able to tell she pledged b/c of the probate even if she didn't tell him [...]

*she says the whole process isn't normal, you always feel overwhelmed b/c that's just how it is, every day is extreme and you're asking "is this really happening?" [...]

*when she has a birthday she wants to get a gift in a cool Hallmark box...we were getting a gift for [Raven from fall 04] and she was obsessed w/ all the cute boxes. She ended up getting [Raven] a pink compact mirror with a little flower on the front...I'm not sure if it was Juicy or not but it was over by all the designer stuff and the total came out to like $40 (stalking, I know)

*she likes to scrapbook, wants to do an [TET] book but hasn't gotten around to it

That's all I can think of for now, I'll keep coming back b/c I'm sure more random shit will pop up

---------- Forwarded message ----------
From: <[Whitney W.]>
Date: Fri, May 9, 2008 at 5:01 PM
Subject: SUMMER PROGRAM ASSIGNMENTS
To: Victoria Benedum <studybuddies040507@gmail.com>

So, from a reliable "leak" in the greek life community, and one of their misplaced flashdrives, I was given this:::::
These assignments are more than likely tentative, but it's good to have an idea of what is expected----hope your programs are going well!!! :-)

Summer Assignments

The purpose of these assignments is to prepare the candidates for chapter responsibilities. There will be three different projects for May, June, and July. In August there will be a reading assignment.

Terms:

The candidates will have two weeks to complete each task. If the project is not turned in on time then they remove themselves for a spot on the Fall 2008 line. The candidate will be told that they are no longer being considered and that they should take deadlines seriously. Therefore, you should try again next time. However, they may redeem themselves:

Sorors will not answer phone calls for at least 1 week (7 days) after the candidate fails to turn in an assignment. If the candidate still continues to call after the week of no response from sorors, they can be reconsidered for Fall 2008. They must have contacted at least 2 sorors on that Friday to be considered. However if they miss something else again they will no longer be considered.

Assignment 1:

Please notify candidate on May 4, 2008 about assignment.

Assignment is due no later than May 17, 2008 at 11:59pm

Event Planning and Execution

Candidate will be assigned a platform or community service effort to plan. Candidate must include the following:

350 word explanation of program that describes the purpose of the event/program.

Location and time

Target audience: who, how many?

What materials will be needed---where can you get these materials (place, address, and phone number, etc.)

Guest speakers? Provide name and contact information.

Make the event come to life

Create a program for the event

Make a PowerPoint presentation or supplemental visuals or materials for the event (handouts, etc.)

The goal is to create a product that could be done "tomorrow" if needed be.

Please assign each candidate the provided platform/task:

[Amber]: Sisterly Relations amongst African American Women Event
[Teresa]: Platform #2 Economic Keys to Success
Whitney: Platform #3 Economic Growth of the Black Family
[Eva]: Platform #4 Undergraduate Signature Program: Economic Educational Advancement Through Technology
[Vanessa]: Platform #5 Health Resource Management and Economics
[Brooke]: Breast Cancer Awareness Event
[Jamie]: Voter's Awareness Event
[Mya]: Founder's Day Program
[Candace]: Scholarship Tea
[Shelby]: Platform #1 Non Traditional Entrepreneur

Assignment 2
Please notify candidate on June 8, 2008 about assignment.
Assignment is due no later than June 20, 2008 at 11:59pm
From the event that was created in assignment 1, create a budget that includes every expense needed to put the event on. Then create a fundraiser that will fund the event. The fundraiser needs to be planned out the same way as the event.

Assignment 3
TBA

Reading Assignment: Candidates must read The Divine Nine and report on something on the book...more information to be defined.

Subject:	Hi!
From:	wgw██████.edu
Date:	Sun, May 11, 2008 11:11 pm
To:	████████@yahoo.com
Priority:	Normal
Options:	View Full Header	View Printable Version

```
Hi [Julia]
     hope everything is going well--- Here is the
information I've been meaning to send to you.
Looking forward to speaking with you soon,
Whitney Gracia W.
```

Attachments:

flyer.doc	**222 k**	[application/msword]	Download
Program-platform 3.doc	**58 k**	[application/msword]	Download
Powerpoint for Relevance Section.ppt	**469 k**	[application/vnd.ms-powerpoint]	Download

---------- **Forwarded message** ----------
From: <[Whitney W.]>
Date: Wed, May 14, 2008 at 8:34 PM
Subject: What [Julia] said
To: Victoria Benedum <studybuddies040507@gmail.com>

Okay, so as you all know, I called [Julia] yesterday to ask what she thought about the programs and she said: (there are going to be some typos...im tryna remember everything real fast lol)

--that she was disappointed, that some ppl's look like they put time and effort into them and others looked like "crap"

-- [Vanessa], she said that your program was okay, but your flyer looked like you had done it in five minutes, "like there was nothing on it..."

--[Jamie], she ranted on and on for like 8 minutes about how you turned yours in at 11:59 and how she just couldn't believe that you did that

[Candace], she said that you had the scholarship program and that you should've made a scholarship application to go with the program

--She said that some ppl put an actual October date on the programs, and that if we were smart we would've all chosen the same week, and made a collective flyer together

---

--She said how dare we put "[Theta Eta Theta Sorority, Inc]" on some of thát stuff? especially the [EPSILON] chapter"?

--She said that we were "lax" and that this was supposed to show us how to work together in the chapter but she doesn't think we succeeded at that

--She made a comment like, "the other girls will be hearing from me," so I'm not sure if she meant that she'll be calling you all or that when you call her she'll be going off on you...I don't know lol

--She said that we should've turned the assignment in a day early...or like during the daytime if we were going to turn it in on the 11th

--She said that we were selfish for not checking everybody's ([Vanessa's]) program before we sent them off and for not telling ppl what they needed to change...and I quote, " if you all are so called LSs as [Brooke] likes to call yall, then why didn't you check each other's programs? When I talked to [Jamie] she said y'all we're proofing each other's work, but that's [clearly] not true because I got some *crap* from y'all"

Whitney (gotta keep this third person theme goin lol), she said you left out the program along with other ppl (she didn't name anybody else) who left certain stuff out

She said that we had a week to do this and that she didn't understand why she got them "so late" because "a lot of y'all don't have jobs or internships so it's not like you're doing anything anyway"

She said that we wouldn't make it on line with the attitudes we have now, and that she finds it hard to believe that we want to be on line

She said that when you're on line you only get a few hours, or sometimes a few minutes to do an assignment, and that handling it the way we did wouldn't cut it

ALLLSSSSOOOOOOOO (Whoa can't believe I forgot to say this yesterday)::::

She said that some ppl will be doing their programs over and that you won't have a week to do it, and that it better be on time or else....but I'm not sure how she's going to assign that out

She asked why nobody had heard from [Eva] or [Brooke] (said that [B.Lynn] told her that she has yet to receive a call from [Brooke] at all) (but, I already called you [Brooke] so, as you would say, "fall back, it's only been two weeks" lol)

She told me to stop asking questions about the programming part of her chapter because I might not get in

She said that [Brooke's] and [Mya's] fliers were very good

She said "yall must've thought that [I] wasn't going to read all of your programs? No, I read *every single word*!" (umm....calm down...lol)

She said she's not really enjoying her internship so far and that she still needs a job...refuses to talk on the phone at work but talks to [her boyfriend] on her lunch break...her week has been "kinda slow"

She also threw in the classic, "if yall aren't tryna get to know me that's fine...that's fine.."

---End scene---

---------- Forwarded message ----------
From: <[Whitney W.]>
Date: Wed, May 21, 2008 at 5:36 PM
Subject: 2 and 4 called me last night
To: Victoria Benedum <studybuddies040507@gmail.com>

So last night, I spent 50 minutes of my life to speak to [Sasha] and [Julia] after they interrupted my phone conversation with [Mya]— (didn't realize I was on 3-way until [Sasha] said [Julia's] name and [Julia] started laughing :-/) I'm gonna write out the convo the best way I know how (in script form lol) and summarize their lecture points... Looking back, it's actually pretty funny, since they clearly had nothing else to do lol[...]

***THIS IS LONGGGGG—MAKE SURE YOU HAVE A SNACK OR SOMETHING WHEN YOU READ THIS LOL (or print it out, read it, then BURN it, especially [Jamie] and [Vanessa]!)
**sidenotes/laughter are in parentheses

11:03 pm
Me: Hello?
2: hello, what are you doing?
Me: (lying) Getting some stuff ready for work tomorrow
2: Why do you sound like that? Like you're annoyed?!
Me: I'm not annoyed
2: I told you, I told you—[Julia]!
4: (laughing)
2: I told you Whitney didn't like me, she sounds like, "why da hell is [Sasha] callin me right now!" She's annoyed!
Me: (lying) I'm not annoyed, I'm just tired
2: After all that stuff you said, oh no Whitney doesn't dislike you, oh no! Not Whitney!
4: She doesn't dislike you, she likes you
Me: (silence)
2 : (laughing) She doesn't like me...Anyway, where do you work?
Me: UPS
2: She works at UPS!
4: (laughing) Do you get to wear the brown?
Me: What?
2: She gets to wear the brown!
Me: Oh, no, I don't get a uniform
2: Why not?
Me: I just unload trucks (2 and 4 laugh)
4: Isn't that why you didn't want to work with Northwest? Why are you doing that for UPS?
Me: They pay more
2: How much are they paying you?
Me: ten dollars an hour
2: Oh Okay
4: Yea, that's okay
2: Do you like it?
Me: No, not really, but I'll stay (I'll probably quit after three days) until I find something better in a week or two
2: A week or two?

4: No, let me give you some life advice, you know [Sasha], I'm always giving them life advice—don't keep quitting jobs, you never know when they're gonna do a background check or ask you for that information. If they ask, 'well why did you quit?' and you just say, 'I didn't like it' they're probably gonna assume that you won't like your new job and they won't hire you
2: She probably doesn't put her old jobs down there
Me: yea, I don't put them down

Summary: She told me about Mya calling her "[Jules]"
4: You know, your friend [Mya] called me and was like, "What's up [Jules]?" I had to pause and look on my caller ID to check, and then I had to make sure I wasn't hallucinating. I had to ask, "Who is this?"
2: (laughing)
4: You all are NOT on my level, Did she tell you that?
Me: Yes
4: And what else did she say?
Me: She told us to never call you that and to stop being lax and that—
2: And yet, you all still don't listen...like, where did me and [Jamie] go last week?
Me: I thought y'all were supposed to go to the Southside, but yall ended up going somewhere else...I'm not sure though...
2:Yea, we definitely weren't anywhere near the Southside last week...
4: Do yall talk about us?
Me: (lying) No, not really
2: She's lying! She probably says, "I hate [Sasha]! I can't stand her!" (close...)
Me: We just repeat what you all tell us to do
4: No, you know what they do ? After they call me, they'll call everybody in their little circle and be like, "I just spoke to [Julia], and she sounds sick...call and check on her so you can get that call out of the way"
2: (laughing)

4: They don't communicate..they're [Brooke's] LSs (laughing)

2: Whitney, do you know the single letter chapters?

Me: Well, no, but I know the Greek alphabet, and we're all studying where each of the chapters is located...

4: I mean, why?

2: Yea, why are y'all trying to learn that stuff?

4: I don't know what made them think that they need to know that, [Sasha]

2: Well, could you [something incoherent] it right now?

Me: What?

4: Do you know the whole alphabet now?

Me: Um, yea

2: um yea?!!!!!

(2 and 4, laughing)

4: try saying "um yea" in the basement, I'm gonna "um yea" give you a few taps with the wood

Me: Oh, you meant could I say it right now?

2 and 4: YEA!

Me (the Greek alphabet extremely fast)

(silence)

4: It was okay, still not as fast as we used to do it...You think we could still spit it as fast as we used to?

2: Yea, we could

4: That's something I still have stuck in my head—I have it on call, so I'll know when...(didn't finish her sentence) [...]

Summary: Birthdays

2: my birthday is coming up—June 24th, remember that (even though I don't want to, I'm going to send her a big ass card with all our initials signed on it—is that cool with everyone?)

Me: Okay, I will

2: When is [Julia's] birthday?

Me: August 16th

2: you would know that....whose birthday is coming up?

Me: Out of us or out of yall?

4: we don't care about *yall's* birthdays

2: Duh, hint, it's June 1st

Me: I apologize, I don't know

2: isn't she the one who called and gave them the assignment? ([Cari]) So disrespectful...I'm definitely going to tell her about this

Summary: Asked me if I had been saving money. I said yes, and they were like "we hope yall all have been saving money...it's gonna be about $1,000, and that's just for [nationals]...for the [Epsilon] chapter, it's gonna be more than that...)

4: DO you want to know how much I spent when I was on line Whitney?

2: No, she's not privy to that information

4: Oh well, I was going to help you out. But, Let me put it this way, if you're on Jeopardy, you wouldn't want to go into the finals with this amount (I didn't get it... and I LOVE jeopardy)

2: You need to save at least $1200.00 but it's def gonna be way more than that...

4: Waaayyy more

2: There is NO "I'm gonna pay you back" or "come and use my card and get me..." when you're on line

4: (laughing) Yea, you just have to get it, and you BETTER get it

Side note: I think we're used to that already...

2: If you could pick the top 6 people to be on line with, who would you pick?

Me: I couldn't do that...

2: Yes you could, and you *will*, you don't have a choice

Me: I can't

4: We don't want to hear that, u HAVE to

2: Yea there aren't any options here

Me: Do I have to include myself?

4: You don't have to, but that would be really *dumb*, and would make us think that you don't want to be on line

4: hold on, wait, and let me go get a pen and paper to write down who she says

(10 seconds)

4: Okay, go

Me: I—

2: Go!

Me: [Amber Jackson]

4: You know, everybody always says [Amber Jackson] first, because they think she was on her grind for such a long time

2: Yea, like, there are paparazzi out there who just KNOW that [Amber Jackson] is an interest and if she doesn't make line, it's over!

4: Yea, whatever, who's next?

Me: [Brooke]...[Shelby]....[Eva]...Me... I can't do this...

2: You don't have a choice

4: Why didn't you pick [Candace] first? Y'all aren't friends anymore?

Me: [Candace]

4: That's six! I think we should call the other girls to see who's in their top six, [Sasha]—that should be interesting

2: Why didn't you pick [Shelby]?

4: She did, she picked [Shelby]

2: Oh, well why not [Mya]? Why not [Vanessa]? Why not [Teresa]?

4: Yea, why didn't you pick them?

Me: I picked all the seniors because if they weren't a part of the next line, I'm not sure if they would be able to do it in undergrad.

2 and 4: Oh...

Summary: They asked what I would do if they told me I wouldn't be chosen for the fall 2008 line.

Me: I would ask why

(SILENCE)

4: You expect us to answer that?

(2 and 4 laugh)

Me: I would probably ask why, and be really sad and hurt

2: I'm mad she said she would actually ask us "why"! She probably would ask us why though, knowing her... do u know [some character] from Flavor of Love?

Me: No, I don't watch that show

2: Oh, well there's this one girl that just says crazy stuff all the time and Flav just blinks at her ...that's what I would do to you if you asked "why?" I would just sit there and blink at you

4: You wouldn't tell on us if you didn't get picked?

Me: Probably not

4: Probably not?

2: Did she just say probably not? That scares me...The only reason you got picked is because we were scared that you might tell on us...Probably not? Ugh...Would you try again?

Me:(unconvincingly) Yea...

4: She's like these bitches better pick me! I sat up in a hot room a whole semester and did stuff for them, I better get picked! You know, they actually got upset over the small stuff we asked them to do for us last semester?

2: That's nothing, wait til the fall

Summary: They wanted to discuss programs

2: If you could give Whitney a grade on her program what would you give her?

4: I'd give her a B....plus...a B plus...

2: Why not an A? What held her back from the 4.0?

4: Well, she left out the program

2: What?

4; She left out the program that we hand out at every event that shows the order of ceremony and stuff. But, the program was very creative; she just left out a very important part

2: Hmmmm

4: I didn't really have a problem with too many of their programs, just the whole [Jamie] 11:59 thing and [Vanessa's]

2: Yea that was too much

4: And you know something, Whitney was asking too many questions about programming last week

2: (laughing) what was she saying?

4: She was asking all this stuff about the [black greek council on campus] and how they changed the rules about programming, and how we structure programming duties--I mean, I'm glad she's inquisitive, but you don't need to know that much 'bout MY chapter

2: Yea...deep [...]

Summary: [Sasha] started talking about how she didn't like me (big surprise) and how my ambiance should change over the summer

4: Yea, I told her that when I spoke to them all individually that day

Me: I'm really working on that

2: And sometimes, the clothes you wear...it just looks like, not bad, but just rough, do you really want that to be your legacy?

Me: No

4: I don't need people calling me after I graduate telling me "hey, Epsilon is looking rough wit these new girls y'all picked" (*once again, she's not saying "if"!*)

2: Yea, like uhh...

4: I would say something, but it would be mean

2: No, say it

4: No, I can't

2: sayyyyyy ittttttt!

4: Whitney, What's up with that black hoodie?

Me: I don't know

4: Wait, does it have sentimental value?

Me: (laughing) no, it's just COLD up there

2: (laughing) Whitney has cute clothes-like, I've seen them! I saw her dressed up one day [and] I almost passed out, but then other times, she'll have on a cute outfit, and then she'll put on a hoodie and mess everything up

4: Your assignment when we get back to Pittsburgh for the fall, as soon as you get off the plane, as soon as you get back, me and you are going to H&M and I'm going to pick out a few different hoodies for you to wear

Me: (laughing)

2: You can laugh at that, that's funny —but NO, wait, nothing beats [Jamie] in those damn pajama pants and the 300 dollar UGG boots

4: Yea, that was a mess. I mean, I grew up around white people but I would never rock their style, especially some UGG boots like she does

2: Yea, what is up with that? And Whitney, like you just gotta stop wearing that one hoodie, you know which one I'm talking about right?

Me:(laughing) Yea

2: I mean, don't feel bad, I tear down everybody and I'm probably going to do the same thing to everyone else, so don't feel like "Oh, they just decided to pick on me b/c they don't like me, and they're trying to make me feel bad" [...]

Summary: the usual we're lax and wack bullshyt and we'll never get into the chapter, but if we do they'll be disappointed. At one point 4 said that we're a "boring group of girls" blah, blah, blah, def not writing out a script for that shyt...

2: Your ambiance better be different tomorrow

Me: It will be

2: What time do you have to go to work tomorrow?

Me: [(lying)] 10

2: What time do you [Julia]?

4: I need to get up at 8

2: well....

4: It's like 11:45, who do we wanna call next? Let's call [Brooke]

2: No, I don't feel like talking to [Brooke], let's call [Shelby]

4: Okay

(silence)

2: Hang up the phone Whitney, so we can use the three way!!!

Me: Oh, okay

4: You could say, nice talking to you all, have a good night ladies and then say bye

Me: (nicely) have a good night, bye

I immediately called [Shelby] and told her to expect a call, and then I sent out that text about them calling me---
Also, at some point 4 said, "Can I have a top model moment? Let me say that," and said something but I was closing the garage door so I couldn't hear what came after that...oh well
LAMMMEESSSS!!!!!!

From: <[Amber]>
Date: Fri, May 30, 2008 at 7:19 PM
Subject:sorry this took so long
To: <studybuddies040507@gmail.com>

Hello my lovely SHs!

Here is what i learned about [Selena from fall '04] when we spoke last Saturday, may 24th, from 7 to 7:30 pm:

- Wants me to re-do my resume because it has the wrong lay-out; said she would re-do it for me and have it to me in about a month
- Thought it was **weird** that we were buying lunch and mailing things etc. for them last semester
- Worked with career services as an undergrad doing resume-building, so she considers herself to be very good at it
- Says that "[THETA ETA THETA] STANDS ALONE! Men do NOT define you. Do not be influenced by thetas!" I'm not really sure what this means... I'll leave it up to you to interpret lol
- Asked me to say something interesting/describe about all of you... and i said the same wonderful comments about each of you
- Graduated with a 3.8 GPA, worked as a pathfinder, and was a member of the band (played clarinet and saxophone). said, "[TETs] have no reason NOT to take me. but if they don't, i already know i got it goin on!"
- Says "When you talk to a [a TET], be mindful of who you are talking to. [...] figure out their personalities and speak to them accordingly."
- She will do her BEST to make sure you drop during rush because she doesn't want anyone in the chapter who is not on her level.

but she says she gives good advice, you just have to ask. people were scared to talk to her because she is very strict and always used to tell them "get on my level!" (guess that's where [Julia] got that shit from lol)

- Was President of [TET]
- Business major
- One of her many goals of the year is to be influential with Fall 08. She already said she was impressed with what she has seen thus far. So therefore, she expects us to be ON POINT!
- We need to have two main goals: 1. (always first on the list) educational aspirations as well as 2. [TET] aspirations. she said that she already saw on paper that we have the #1 goal in common, now we just have to prove to her that we have the #2 goal in common as well.
- Has 2 sisters
- Said everyone will eventually have to call her at 3 pm everyday...something she made Sp07 do as well
- Another metaphor she said was, "[TET] is a glass house. don't throw stones." and what she meant by this was "keep what's in your line/chapter to yourself!" don't go talking about your line sister to your best friend or your boyfriend.
- Her Mom is also an [TET]- 5 years away from becoming a golden soror but her Grandmom was a [Mu].
- Went to all the sororities' events. Encourages us to go to all events so that people won't know exactly what we're interested in. (not as easy as it seems lol)
- Says, "we don't program for interests. people should not be intimidated when they come to our events. They are for the general public, not just interests." (that *does not show* lol)[...]
ALSO...
i spoke to [Hannah from fall '04] briefly today and she said:
- she wants to get a humming bird tattoo on her ankle but hasn't got the courage yet to get any tattoos. her mom's nickname was bird when she was younger because of her skinny legs.
- went to Cancun, Mexico last week with one her best friends.

... and every time I call [Riana from fall '05] she doesn't pick up or she'll say that she will call me back but never does. that's really pissing me off lol. i wish she just wouldn't answer.
ok love you all,
[Amber].

From: <[Candace]>
Date: Sat, May 31, 2008 at 9:44 AM
Subject: Re: sorry this took so long

wow she seems pretty cool and strict at the same time. a few questions/comments...

When she [thought it was weird that] we were buying lunch/mailing things, is this [because] she never pre-pledged or pre-pledged people under her? [...]
Do you think she'll say anything to them about the errands [?] we should tell her more lol
Did you post the things you said about us somewhere, I don't remember, just so we know what to mention or if she asks about one of those facts
So during rush shes gonna try to make us drop if we aren't dedicated enough, or we don't have the GPA/activities? and that get on my level shit should only be used if you're actually on a different level like her. [Julia], I beg to differ.
Aww she wants to be influential to us! and she called us Fall 08!
How does everyone call at 3pm, I'm assuming we take turns?
Spr 07 broke that glass house a long time ago. Their names are in the streets 24/7
[Candace]

On 6/4/08,<[Amber]> wrote:

Hola!
well, [I don't know] why she thought the errands and such were weird. She didn't exactly say, "wow. that's weird." that's what I interpreted through the inflection in her voice after i told her

some of the things we had to do last semester. I never posted the things i said about you all[...]

And yea, I'm assuming she thinks we are all capable of becoming [TETs], but she still wants to make it harder during rush to see who can last. I was also elated when she said the words "FALL 08"! lol

I have been thinking a lot lately about [EPSILON] and the whole process. I'm not happy with what I have seen thus far, especially Sp07. I would be waaay more excited to join the sisterhood if there were people like Fa04 present. Instead, we have hoes ([Ivyana]), unscholarly ppl ([Sasha]), etc...Like I'm really not excited about the bull shit we are going to have to face. I don't wanna do undergrad with these LOSERS! I'm not even joking...I'm really not looking forward to becoming Sp07's sisters, only you guys [because] you all have real goals and aspirations and know that [TET] is not #1 in your life. Why am I doing this again?

[Amber]

From: <[Jamie]>
Date: Wed, Jun 4, 2008 at 2:59 PM
Subject: Re: sorry this took so long

awww [Amber] ur little message about you only wanting to be our sisters [because] we have real goals in our lives touched my heart and almost brought a tear lol... yeah but i agree. I dont even respect spr07 too much. [Sasha] told me that we should trust the people pledging us that they won't put us in true danger and that everything they are doing is for a reason and that she trusted Fa04 and Fa05 with basically "her life". But to be honest I do not trust spr07 and their intentions on pledging us at all. Like i feel they hold [TET] too high on their priority list and one (if not more) of us will really be hurt. Like, I can feel it happening. And it's like we shouldn't be getting seriously hurt to join. Like i understand taking wood and eating wild stuff and all the crazy exercises, but I

know they're going to cross the line because they already have and I really think it's only going to get worse. But anywho, I TRUST you lovely ladies and i KNOW we'll ALL make it to "the lovely land of [theta]". And I believe Fa08 "is better **sang to the Danity Kane I Love You Forever beat lmao! [...]**"--and that we can help to change things around and truly make the chapter better. Well I feel like I'm getting long winded now.... LOVE U ALL <3
-[Jamie]

XXII. Abandon Ship

Shelby called me one afternoon. "Hey Whitney, did you know that Vanessa was living with Kamille this summer?"

"WHAT! No, I didn't know that. Shelby, are you—"

"I'm sure. I just got Jamie's text about it, and you should get it soon too. I could have sworn that we all urged her not to live with Kamille when we were in study session."

"We did, and she said that she wouldn't. Wow. Maybe she had no other choice. I wish she would've just said something like 'I moved in with Kamille today' or *something* to give us a heads up."

"True. I don't know about her sometimes. I swear she thinks that she's doing this alone, or that she has to outshine everyone else. I've talked to a few other people about this and we agree. I've grown to respect her, but she keeps showing her selfish side."

"I'm going to give her the benefit of the doubt. I don't—"

"I'm not going to do that anymore. I think she's selfish and I don't think she cares about the rest of the group. I think all those 'golden child' comments went to her head and she hasn't realized that we're all going to be in the basement and *even she* is going to get hit. I really don't think she understands that part."

"Why don't you just tell her how you feel?"

"I don't see a point."

"You're just going to remain mad at her and let us get to the fall and show the TETs that you don't like her?"

"*You* can tell her how I feel. I don't want to talk to her. Do you want to know what she said to me the other day?"

"What?"

"She said, while y'all are in the kut getting beat in the fall, I'm going to be staring off into the Theta light."

"That's...I'm not even going to address that. Are you getting upset because she didn't tell us that she was living with Kamille?"

"No, this is about everything that she's done. She doesn't talk to us, she doesn't text us, yet so much information is around her because she's living in Pittsburgh and she's around the TETs a lot. Don't you think that we should have a lot of new information about Kamille on the document?"

"Yea, but she did text us about 2, 7, and 9 thinking about getting key tattoos."

"Okay, she's texted us *twice* about TET and she still has nothing to say about Kamille. I really think she's in this for herself. I'm not trying to be petty, but I'm getting this weird vibe about her and my vibes are usually right."

"Alright. I'll talk to her later this summer and try and get her to be more open with the rest of us."

"Alright Whit."

Candace was studying abroad in Costa Rica for the first part of the summer. Although she didn't have a cell phone, she still managed to call the TETs using a program on her computer. She stayed abreast of what was going on with the study group by reading the Gmail documents and sending emails to the SHs. Yet, there were no emails on the account that could have told her what was about to unfold in our group.

I eventually called Vanessa, and in the nicest way possible, tried to explain that people in the group felt that she was being distant and standoffish. I told her that I honestly had no idea that she was living with Kamille, to which she replied, "I told y'all that I was living with her when were in study session. I swear I did. Maybe y'all didn't hear me, maybe you weren't paying attention, but I definitely told y'all and I refuse to take the blame for that."

I tried to tell her that we were not angry, that we just wanted her to open up more. But before I could finish my explanation, she began to cry and hung up.

JAMIE: Hey guys. I made a mistake and Sasha told me that I have to write a twenty page paper on the founders. Can each of you guys help me out? Can 2 people do three founders since Candace is out of the country?

I woke up one day in June. It was a day after my sister said, "Maybe if you have a good experience in Theta Eta Theta, I might consider it. I still honestly think it's a cult, but if your college ever gets back to me with a decent scholarship offer, I might try it there too."

Hearing her speak those words made my heart hurt. I couldn't picture her doing the same things I had done in attempts to get into the Epsilon chapter. I couldn't picture myself allowing someone to treat her badly in the name of a sorority. I couldn't fathom standing in the basement while my potential prophytes or line sisters abused my own flesh and blood.

I pulled out my planner, my wallet, and took out all the receipts from the spring semester. I found the gift purchase calculations, ran down the list of all the errands I'd ran, and flipped through my black notebook to calculate how much money I'd spent on the TETs: $781.63. It was nearly $800 and I couldn't believe it. I re-calculated the amount over and over, slower and slower, trying to make sure the figure was right. It was. It wasn't a mistake.

I called and expressed my concerns with Shelby. She said, "Don't worry about that. We all know that they went too far with us last semester. We all know that they're not ideal women of TET, but think about how much better the chapter will be once we get in. Don't think about what Epsilon made you do or how much money you've spent. Think about how much better we're going to make it for the next group of girls. Think about it that way. All of Spring 07 are going to graduate in 2009, so even though I'll be gone too, the rest of you will be immune to their influence."

She was right. I would get through the pledge process regardless of how much money I had to spend, regardless of how much physical pain it caused, and when I got into the chapter I would do my best to make it better for the next group. I dropped my doubts.

One day while I was away in St. Louis on vacation, a day after I wished Deborah a Happy Birthday and posted interesting information about her to the document, Shelby and Amber called me on 3-way. They revealed that they had talked about what I said earlier in the summer, and they agreed with my thoughts. They told me they were thinking about whether they wanted to become a part of the chapter and felt that the process was "for the insecure." For three hours we went back and forth about how much we had done in the spring, how little we had learned, and how we weren't looking forward to pledging. After speaking with them, I forced myself to take a step back and think about what I might be getting myself into in the fall.

Amber called me a few days later, sounding extremely happy. "I'm calling to let you know that I'm done being an interest. I thought about everything a lot, and I don't think that the process is for me. I've called all of the SHs today and I'm going to call the TETs and tell them about my decision when I have time. Oh, and I finally told my mom everything."

"Whoa, I mean wow. What did she say?"

"Well, at first she was mad at me for not telling her how long this had been going on, but then she was disappointed with the people in the chapter for doing everything they did. She said she pledged and I shouldn't have to. It's against the rules."

"Do you think she'll say something to them at the centennial boule?"

"I asked her not to, but I don't know. She was pretty upset."

"Do you feel better now that you've told her?"

"Yea, I was so tired of hiding things from her. Plus, I don't think it's fair how I was treated. I've been doing this stuff for a long time and I'm no closer to being a TET right now than I was two years, or maybe even a year ago. And I don't see what I was supposed to have learned from pre-pledging, and I doubt any of us would learn anything significant during pledging because of the type of people that they are. How much more do I have to prove to them?"

"I feel you. Are you *completely* done though?"

"For right now I am. I feel so free—no more lies, no more assignments, no more wasted phone conversations, money, anything. Everything is so much clearer now."

"What did the other SHs say?"

"Well, I still have to send Candace an email. Teresa, Eva, and Shelby were sad about it but they felt where I was coming from. Mya, Jamie, and Vanessa just didn't understand. I told them that they were brainwashed."

"What?"

"Jamie told me that if I changed my mind she would pledge me on the next line."

"Was she joking?"

"No. She wasn't joking. I sent everybody a text about what she said because I want people to see how messed up that was."

"Oh, I haven't looked at my text messages in a long time. I'm on break. What did Brooke say?"

"You *know* she understood!" she laughed.

"Yea, true. Do you think you'll regret it in the fall?"

"There might be a few times when I regret things. If y'all probate and start having programs I might feel like 'that could have been me,' but I think I'll be okay with that. Are you done?"

"I'm on the fence. I know that everything we did last semester was pointless in the grand scheme of things, and I'm tired of putting up with them and stroking their egos. But I've put in too much work. I don't know if I'm going to be able to walk away without *something* you know?"

"I understand that. I'll support your decision either way."

Sasha instructed everyone to call her by midnight and explain why we were still interested in becoming members of her organization. All of us called, all of us except Amber and Shelby.

On Friday, June 20, 2008, our second assignment was due. The assignment was due by midnight. All of us turned in our assignments, all of us except Amber.

Over the next few days the TETs began to call each of us nonstop, but we didn't pick up our phones.

From: <[Shelby]>
Date: Fri, Jun 20, 2008 at 8:53 AM
Subject: From [Shelby]...
To: studybuddies040507@gmail.com

Hey ladies--

So as I'm sure you guys know, I have decided that I do not want to be a part of Fall 2008. I had been thinking about how good it was to be home, away from all the shit, but then when I came to Pittsburgh to visit [my boyfriend] and those of you there - I couldn't even relax! I cannot live my life like that anymore. I sincerely applaud the accomplishments the organization has achieved since its inception in 1908, however, at an undergraduate level, I would be first a member of the [Epsilon] chapter...I cannot sleep at night under that title. I would be wholeheartedly embarrassed by my chapter's lack of unity, volunteerism, and overall morals. While I know that with [the] addition of the Fall 2008 line, [Epsilon] will receive AMAZINGLY TALENTED, NOTABLE, FINE AFRICAN AMERICAN WOMEN, change will not come immediately and there is a reason why the process is still what it is. Those involved do not want it to change, or have lost the gumption and patience to do so. There is someone who will be a part of this chapter to change it...but it will not be me. I look at this last year of my undergraduate career as a gamble. I am trying to do so many things with very few resources (financial, physical, emotional), that a non essential, taxing 'extracurricular activity' would not be the smartest risk.

I have been thinking about this all summer, and have been going back and forth because I want this. I really really do. Learning more about the history of the organization, being apart of something so integral to the Black experience in American history would be phenomenal. But I need to live in the present to secure my future and realize I do not [have] the ability to take this particular risk. So much so, I want [TET] even more - I fully intend on being a part of a graduate chapter (mark my words). But right now? No thank you.

I am so proud of you who continue to pursue membership with the organization at this stage of your lives. I just ask that you really think about what you're willing to risk for this..you don't necessarily have to have this now. Please know that I am here for you always...if you need somewhere to hide out, someone to wash clothes, get you food (YOU...not them), I will do anything for you. You are my SHs, my sisters, no matter what anyone says. I hope that you guys will still feel comfortable speaking with me about whatever and do not feel as though I have abandoned you.

I just need to do this for me.

I will be emailing [Julia] this weekend (at my own leisure haha) about my decision. Please call me if you want to talk...I am super busy with work, but texts really work wonders lol...and then I'd be able to call you later.

Sincerely and lovingly,
[Shelby]

From: <[Whitney W.]>
Date: Sat, Jun 21, 2008 at 1:47 PM
Subject: A letter
To: studybuddies040507@gmail.com

"Life is but a dream to me, I don't wanna wake up, thirty odd years without havin' my cake up"--Jay Z, "Beach Chair"

Dear SHs,

I am writing this letter to express my feelings about my participation in the Fall 2008 intake process. First, let me say that I've wanted to be [a TET] since I was a little girl. All of my mother's memorabilia has made my heart smile over the years, and I've always dreamt of becoming her soror. I'm just not sure if I want to get it *this* way.

I know that this timing is terrible, but better now than later. Over the past few weeks I have learned that I am not complacent with the "process" that the [Epsilon] chapter has in place, or with the potential prophytes that are supposed to have **"[excellent] moral standards,"** or demonstrate *"a true [genuine] sisterhood."* I know that if I continued I would be unhappy with their negative insecurities surrounding me, and I would not have a real relationship with a single one of them. I do feel that the process they have in place doesn't teach you anything unless you secretly believe that the process is right. It's not. I'm to the point now where I am not intimidated the slightest bit by any of them, and I am annoyed to the point of no return.

I know that [TET] is in all of our hearts, but is it really worth being degraded, beat, and torn down for? Is it really worth tears, irreversible emotional damage, financial drama, and unnecessary stress? Is it really worth eight weeks of hell and obscurity so that people who don't even know you can call you *"thorough"?* I don't believe that, and I know that deep down most of you don't believe that either. It's one thing to have a "process," it's another to have a process that dehumanizes you and places you in a position to be harmed. (They say that they "break you down to build you up," but the truth is evident in the attitudes and actions of Spring 07: They break you down, and leave you to build yourself back up.)

Fall 08 is supposed to be the *"change"* and the rebirth of what a chapter of [Theta Eta Theta] Sorority should be, but I don't know if we would be able to pull that off. In all honesty, I don't think so. Two reasons: 1) we're human and I feel that some of us will revert to the demented ways of 04,05, and 07 and treat the new interests the way that they treated us 2) they've burned the chapter into the ground and it's going to take more than a year to change that, time that a lot of us won't have because we're involved in other organizations, and their influence and lack of lives outside of [TET] will cause them to resist change and continually interfere.

At this point, *logically,* I do not wish to be a part of this line. Although I would love to call each of you my "LS" and have that special bond, I have to wonder about what I've gone through thus far and what will take place next semester: I have learned nothing significant from any of them these past few months, I've lost time and money, and I've become something I thought I would never become: *brainwashed.* (Since when is it okay for me to think, "Yea, all I have to do is let them beat me up, let them harass me, and let them demoralize my character for eight weeks and then I'll be an [TET]!" It's not okay, and clearly my thought process has been warped.)

However, another part of me, a part that I cannot deny and/or explain, does wish to be involved with fall 2008. As of now I'm 50/50, and I will not contact any [TETs] for the next few weeks or so...I need more time to think so that I will make a decision that I can live with for the rest of my life.

Yet, if I do so choose to become a part of fall 2008 _**I will not endure slapping, hair pulling, punches, or any unnecessary degrading acts. I will not participate in ANY form of financial hazing: meal plan or money related. I refuse. No exceptions. There is no such thing as "you have to when you're on line," because you don't. I WON'T.**_

I've grown so close to you all and I value all of your friendships. I hope that you value mine just as much and respect my decision either way. I've spoken in detail about this situation with a lot of you, and I'm taking all the positives you offered into consideration.

I'm not really one for emotional stuff, but I've cried about this for the past two nights and I don't know why. I didn't know that I could cry in my sleep or that this affected me that much. I've wanted this for so long, but I'm not sure if I'm willing to sacrifice everything I stand for to become part of an organization.

> I love you all,
> Still 50/50
> _Whit'_

Candace called me first. "Whitney, are you seriously saying that you're done? I'm about to cry in a Costa Rican computer lab over this!"

"I'm not done. I'm just tired and I need to think about some things. I still want to get into the sorority."

"First Amber, then Shelby, now _you_? Really? You're just going to walk away without getting _anything_?"

"I'm not walking away. I _still_ want to get in. I just need some time away. I'm tired of thinking about them, worrying about how many times I need to call, and stressing about when the next assignment needs to be turned in."

"Okay, I understand that. Whatever you decide to do I'll be there for you regardless."

"Thank you."

Hours later, Mya called me crying. "How did all of this happen? You said you were still going to do it two days ago, Whit. You said that you were still going to go through with it."

"And I might Mya. I never said that I was *completely* done like Amber and Shelby. It's just like having a job and getting sick of it. I'm still interested in TET. I just need to think about some things because this doesn't feel right anymore. It's taken up too much of my time, and I still don't have anything to show for it."

"I just think that we need to get through this. Like, we started out together and we need to end together. I can't imagine doing it without you. The TETS are scared about Amber's mom and they don't know—"

"How do they know she told her mom?"

"I don't know. This stuff really hurts. It's not healthy for me to be crying like this. We *all* need to figure something out."

--------- Forwarded message ----------
From: <[Whitney W.]>
Date: Sat, Jun 21, 2008 at 8:11 PM
Subject: SH's PLEASE READ!!! UNITY BABY :-)
To: <studybuddies040507@gmail.com>

AS OF TOMORROW JUNE 22ND 2008, WE NEED TO UNIFY AND WORK ON OUR OWN INNER PERSONAL ISSUES AS WELL INTERPERSONAL ISSUES BECAUSE ALL TEN OF US NEED TO MAKE IT THROUGH THIS. SO, IN ORDER TO MAKE THAT HAPPEN:

DO NOT CALL ANY MEMBER OF [THETA ETA THETA SORORITY, INC.] UNTIL JUNE 29, 2008 (ONE WEEK ABSENT OF CALLS)

DO NOT PICK UP ANY CALLS FROM MEMBERS OF [THETA ETA THETA SORORITY], INC UNTIL JUNE 29,2008

RESPOND TO THIS POST WITH TWO OR MORE GRIEVANCES THAT YOU CURRENTLY HAVE/HAD WITH THE [EPSILON] CHAPTER (DO NOT REFER TO ANY THING THAT HAS NOT ALREADY OCCURRED I.E. BASEMENT THINGS)

AFTER A WEEK WE CAN **ALLOCATE** WHO WILL CALL MEMBERS OF [THETA ETA THETA SORORITY, INC.] TO READ OUT THE GRIEVANCES, AND AFTERWARDS REGULAR CALLING CAN BEGIN

IF YOU HAVE A PROBLEM WITH AN SH **CALL HER** AND LET HER KNOW THIS WEEK. SISTERS ARE SUPPOSED TO BE ABLE TO TELL EACHOTHER *THE TRUTH* REGARDLESS OF IF IT HURTS FEELINGS. SO, TO PREVENT FALL 08 FROM BEING LIKE SPRING 07 WE NEED TO GET ALL THESE BAD FEELINGS, RESENTMENTS, AND ANGER OFF OUR CHESTS.

DO COMMUNICATE WITH EVERY SINGLE SH THIS WEEK

DO TAKE TIME OUT AND REFLECT TO MAKE SURE THAT THIS IS WHAT WE REALLY WANT AND COME UP WITH WAYS WE CAN MAKE THINGS BETTER

*IS EVERYONE **DOWN** WITH THIS? PLEASE RESPOND*

On Sat, Jun 21, 2008 at 8:13 PM, <[Vanessa]>wrote:

I'm down for the cause :-)

[Vanessa]

On Sat, Jun 21, 2008 at 8:28 PM, <[Teresa]>wrote:

I'm down too...[Teresa]

On Sat, Jun 21, 2008 at 10:02 PM,<[Vanessa]> wrote:

Oh yeah so i'll be talkin to [Kamille] on a casual basis NOT ABOUT ANYTHING [TET] related until thursday when I leave.....i just feel like it would jus be awkward to jus like ignore her and stuff....but if she does ask anything about yall I" DONT KNOW ANYTHING".....but no phone calls and stuff

But my grievances are:

1) I hate when they call us and we are legitimately busy with stuff, like our jobs and school and act like we are just supposed to walk out of class and work to entertain their phone calls
2) they always say " u need to call me so u can get to kno me...but when we call just to say hey.."do u want to hang out"...they seem more interested in just getting some task done

** and another thing these last few days have made me realize that unfortunately we are not as close as we all think, and for a while i felt like it was more than just us against them and more like us and against us. I know personally, i care more about my relationship with you guys than with any one of them. with all of the issues that have come to light, not ever was i angry, but just saddened and even hurt by some of the other preexisting issues. I want us all to make it, and above all else i want us all to feel comfortable enough to express our feelings positive or negative with one another in the name of progress

[Vanessa]

On 6/21/08, <[Teresa]> wrote:

[Epsilon] Chapter grievances:
They are not great role models in scholarship, service, and sisterhood and have driven themselves as well as friends and others to the point that nobody wants anything to do with them. The [Epsilon] Chapter does not have a good reputation in public anymore because of what Spring 07 has done this past year. (fights, etc)

I do not appreciate being spoken to like I am not even human. Being degraded and belittled, etc. I had to go the emergency room last semester because of a panic attack. (That speaks for itself, why ELSE would i have a "panic" attack)...Furthermore, we were completely taken advantage of last semester regarding money from our OWN paychecks, our parents' money, as well as our meal plans. They say we need to get to know them, but they only want us around when we're doing something for them. They dont answer the phones when we call, yet, they'll call you when they need a ride to their MOTHER'S house so they can get money because THEY have no money, and when they're on one side of pittsburgh and need u to come get their keys to go to their house on the OTHER side of pittsburgh to get them a bra and take it back to them. (sry im venting...more than 2 grievances but there ya go...and theres ALOT more where that came from lol) ....

[Teresa]

On Sat, Jun 21, 2008 at 11:13 PM, <[Jamie]> wrote:

[Jamie] is down for the cause-----

On Sun, Jun 22, 2008 at 3:22 AM, <[Mya]> wrote:

Yea...I'm down. But Whit, I already told you my concerns: if we don't contact them for a week, I'm scared that if [Amber] does want to continue in light of this new unity concept they won't "accept" her back (this coming from that "leaked source" we found earlier this summer about what happens when one person doesn't submit an assignment). I know it's a game, but I feel like there's no need for them to play games amongst themselves when it comes to "business". So yea...

And don't be mad at me for asking this, but does this mean NO calls/texts on [Sasha's] birthday (Tuesday), just to say Happy Bday?? Cuz I feel like bdays are special, and usually an occasion to the rule?? Yes... no... maybe so?? But anyways.. I'm down for the cause. Whatever we decide goes.

*[Mya]

On 6/22/08, <[Mya]>wrote:

Grievance #1: I don't feel as if their programming is sincerely geared towards EVERYONE, like they should be, and like [Julia] claims they are. Example: Asking for a fact about [Theta Eta Theta] Sorority, Inc. during the first or second book club meeting of the month turns away people who may have been genuinely interested in reading/discussing, but not necessarily interested in pursuing membership. Not cool. Thus, Book Club quickly dwindled from like 20 ppl... to 3/4 during the last meeting of the semester.

Grievance #2: Community service?? Where is it?? Because I only see it in the week during October celebrating Breast Cancer week, that one time WE clean up a street [in] Oakland, and supposedly the "Computer Girls" program which I haven't heard anything about since January. It is now June.

I have more... but when it comes to talking to them about it, I guess I just focus on #1 and #2.

Grievance #3: How are we supposed to get to know them when some of them REFUSE to answer our phone calls? I call when I get a chance, so clearly I'm making an effort. But I don't have time to be calling people 3 and 4 times a day just so they can feel "loved". Negative.

Grievance #4: Some people don't practice what they preach. Service organization? Women of substance? Academic excellence? That's not what it seems when community service is a chore, when reputations are trash and nights of drunken valor are the regular ([Tiffany] clearly is NOT 21, but schedules Happy Hour into her daily activities), and when [Julia] tells us that if we're looking to graduate Summa Cum Laude we might as well get up and leave the room.
*[Mya]

On 6/22/08,<[Whitney W.]> wrote:

Grievances:
#1--**It is not my job to keep a member of the sorority (2) alive** because she can't afford to buy her own food. It is not fair (as [Teresa] mentioned) that my funds are used to help out other grown women who are capable of supporting themselves and buying their own meal plans and/or getting jobs to buy their own

groceries. Furthermore, it is a bit uncanny that they "demand" that we buy them food and seriously think that we're so scared of them that we wouldn't dare say "no." Please. Last time I checked, "Prospective [candidates should not partake in humiliating, undignified or ruthless acts. Should members of Theta Eta Theta Sorority ask you to carry out tasks or partake in actions other than those stated in the official membership process, they are breaching the Sorority's guidelines and procedures and do not symbolize the morals of our organization. This conduct will not be accepted."] Can't and won't [accept] it anymore.

#2--I thought we we're joining a sisterhood, but it seems as if it's just a group of women who do the minimum, wear [violet] and green, and think that just because there are three letters on their chest that they are above everyone else. I don't think a sisterhood can operate if the big sisters don't look out for the little sisters and are only concerned with what they can get out of them. We all have talents and **I have yet to see any of those put to use for the good**. Also, sisters are supposed to know eachother very well, but as [Mya] mentioned, our calling them doesn't bring us any closer to them. It has to be a two way street--they need to be trying to get to know us as well...phone calls feel like one sided interviews...I can ask one of them a million questions, but I still wouldn't know her any better. Just because I can give you a few interesting facts about someone does not mean that we are close.. (I can give you twenty interesting facts about Beyonce...does that mean me and her are sisters? lol)

#3--**It's summer time, bitches**. Do not call me just to harass me and tell me that I am "wack," "lax," and "incapable of being a member of your sorority." Instead, either call me and talk to me like a human being or take that time and come up with some things you could actually be doing to better the mess of a chapter that is [Epsilon]. I am too busy to be bothered: I chill from 9 to 5 and I relax from 6 to 10. I don't have time for nonsense.

Whit'
PS---[Mya] I think people should email [Sasha] a happy birthday if they want to and still not call b/c if any of us call her she won't be saying, "thanks for the B'day wish" she'll be wanting to yell and ask questions........

On Sun, Jun 22, 2008 at 5:37 PM, <[Whitney W.]> wrote:

Ohhhh also, Me and [Mya] were talking earlier today and decided that we shouldn't "call" each of them with the grievances (to prevent backtalk lolol) and should instead nicely edit all of our grievances on one document, make them look and sound very [professional], and then create a random email address to send the doc to [Britney Lynn]. Then one of the SH's could call her at 6:06 on Monday and tell her that we sent her an email for her and her sorors to read.

What do y'all think?
 WGW

And yoooo why am i walking around with half of my head in braids and the other half nappy as ever??? lololol

On Sun, Jun 22, 2008 at 10:24 PM, <[Amber]> wrote:

i agree with all of you lovely ladies...

in addition to your grievances, i also have a few of my own. all of you know my thoughts since i have personally spoken to you throughout the week on the phone, but here are 2 in writing:

1) why are we doing chapter work during the summer when we are not part of the chapter? they already know they want us. if they had doubts, then they wouldn't have put up with all of us during the spring semester. It would be a lot better if they GUIDED us through the tasks. But instead, they give us a task and demand that we figure it all out by ourselves. Then we get yelled

at and told it is "lack-luster" but we have no foundation! it's all a guessing game!

2) I'm sick and tired of paying for them to survive basically. Everyone has said it. We all agree on this one. The first lunch I had was with [Sasha] during finals week the spring semester of my freshman year. That was April of 2007. It is now JUNE 2008!!! This is a prime example of how greedy she is and shows her true character: master-hazer. Why should I have to buy you lunch for you to get to know me? Why do I have to drop off pizza, ranch dressing, and a pink lemonade ([BRITNEY LYNN]) off at tower c lobby? I'm not getting to know you that way. All of us have been slaves... it is slavery because there is no reciprocation. They don't take us out to lunch to get to know us. We don't even get a simple THANK YOU!

There are so many more grievances. I could go on and on, as you know. But here are two. I hope this gets to them.

U-N-I-T-Y! UNIFY FOR THE [TET] REVOLUTION!!!
[Amber]

On Sun, Jun 22, 2008 at 10:30 PM, <[Teresa]> wrote:

[Amber] I completely agree..I wanted to add onto your first one about chapter work. You brought up a great point. It seems to ME like they just dont want to do it so, once again, they're using us. Also, you would think that as "big sisters" or our so called "makers" (lol) they would GUIDE us through certain things. You would think that if we really do screw up, they would sit down and HELP us figure out what went wrong and what we could possibly do to make it better, or how we could have done something different to achieve a better result. Also, I wanted to add, WHY DO THEY KEEP CALLING US LIKE THIS?!?! All of a sudden they're interested? When we're not?...confuses the hell outta me...maybe if things were a bit different ...well aLOT different...we would have never gotten to this point. ([Teresa])

On 6/22/08, <[Teresa]> wrote:

[Sorry] I just thought of this too lol...I think they are extremely 'SELFISH, RUDE, OBNOXIOUS, and GREEDY" for going a WHOLE year and a half without having another line...clearly they wanted to USE and ABUSE people and hold onto their NEO-dom (lol) longer than clearly necessary...and THEN they blamed it on us saying that WE'RE not ready...we were alot more ready than they ever were.

From: <[Mya]>
Date: Mon, Jun 23, 2008 at 12:43 PM
Subject: Something to reconsider.
To: Victoria Benedum <studybuddies040507@gmail.com>

Ok... I'm on the phone with [Vanessa], and we all know she's not technologically savvy, so I decided to type this up.
I have a change of heart. I'm still down for the cause, but I think that some parts should be reconsidered.

[Epsilon] is really concerned. They ([Kamille], [Tiffany], [Sasha], and [Britney]) sat down with [Jamie] and [Vanessa] on some realness. They are concerned/hurt that if these questions and reservations arised about them and the process that we didn't ask. Granted, they are sometimes on some bullshit, but when we ask questions they generally do give us a straight answer.

The grades situation was brought up, and [Kamille] apparently said that they understand that our grades are important to us. And they've taken that into consideration. But the fact [was] that a lot of us were in study sessions and didn't take advantage of our time, and some of our grades suffer. They said that they KNOW that parts of their process hurt them, and those may not be included in ours.

By picking us for study sessions... they liked us, and clearly want us for their organization. And clearly... they trust us with the future and continuity of their chapter. But when we don't pick up and ignore them, to the point that they don't know what is going on with their organization... I can see why they would be upset.

They don't trust us anymore. And that might just bite us in the ass later.

And not talking to them is not going to fix the problems. And I know that we have our grievances... but we should talk to them about it. NOT talking to them and avoiding them is creating even more of a distance between us and them. If we thought that we weren't close to them before, we REALLY aren't now. A week is a long time.

By separating ourselves, it kinda seems to them as if we WISH to be paper. Some of our grievances are understandable, but some of them are not going to be well-[received], someone said that we are trying to CREATE our own process without having experienced one. To an extent, I think that's kind of true. I believe that they understand where we are coming from, because they were here last year. They even brought up [the girls that dropped when they were in study session]. So... I think they know the feelings we have right now. [Sasha] (I know how some of you feel about her, but please, read on) said that if we really and truly want to be a part of this chapter/organization it's okay to quit when it's TOO MUCH, but not when it's just hard.

Call me brainwashed, or say that I actually believe in a process... because maybe I do. But bottomline is... I think we should talk to them. Instead of trying to figure it out on our own, they might be the only people to offer advice, because they can tell us from experience. We can ASK questions about the process. We can ASK how they felt when [the girls from their study session] decided to drop, and how they coped with it between themselves etc... Some of them may not be as open... but we can try to talk to them on a human level. Because all of this affects them too.

This is not to say that we don't need to still work on our inner relationships with each other. I just think that picking up one of their phone calls may not be a bad idea. I think I told Whitney yesterday that... when [Britney Lynn] calls us... I don't think its to yell, and belittle us. She's usually the softspoken one who is usually willing to help/offer advice. And when someone spoke to [Hannah]... she was honest, open, and concerned.

Please don't jump down my neck for saying this, or wanting to "break the pact." Because that is not the case. A part of our promise was to speak to each other honestly... and this is me being honest.

**[Mya]

On Mon, Jun 23, 2008 at 1:35 PM, < [Shelby]> wrote:

I certainly [understand] what you're saying about how it could be considered that [we're] being selfish about how were handling things..but do you really think if we hadn't [brought] any of this up anything would have changed? I truly believe everything they say is in their best interests ...which are the interests of [Epsilon]. It sincerely alarms me that suddenly now they want to talk sensibly about the process...where is that logic when you're slapping an interest who isn't online..or grabbing the face of another at study session..or eating up the monies of people who you don't even know their middle names? i can't understand that. How superficial are you[?] The longevity of their chapter depends on you guys...are you willing to sacrifice integrity for someone else's wishes? This conversation would be different if this wasn't [Epsilon]...but they gain way more than you ever will by being apart of them..And you(this you is plural lol) know that..Hence why there is such discord with the entire situation in the first place. Please respond back with thoughts disagreements whatever...Im trying to understand the logic...or lack thereof.

sincerely,
[Shelby]

On 6/23/08, <[Mya]> wrote:

Ok... here's my thing. For those of us who wish to continue on with the process, we are going to have to talk to them at some point. I understand that everything they said is in their [own] interest, but I wouldn't expect anything different. In the same regard, what we say/think/write is in our own interests. And regardless of how it sounds, they still have something that we want.

I know that some of you are having serious doubts, and [Shelby], it sounds like you're completely done :-(However, I hope that everyone has taken a step back, and made sure that this is something that they still want (or not).
>> And to be honest, some of the shit is not logical. I can't explain that. But what I do know is that if WE still want to pursue this, we are going to have to pick up the phone. And I just feel as though sooner is better than later.

Oh... and I also wanted to point out: " they gain way more than you ever will by being a part of them" - damn. that was deep. lol... and I'm still trying to decipher the meaning behind that.
**[Mya]

On 6/23/08, <[Whitney W.] > wrote:

> Hey Mya, I appreciate your honesty, I just want to know **which parts** we are reconsidering….Like, I really just feel that they are **scared** and know that we've discovered that they only have as much power as we give to them. I wanted to touch on every point so I had to break it down this way. Long, but I needed to get everything out:

1.)   "*[Epsilon] is really concerned*". **They should be.** They deserve to be. But I'm not buying their "ask us questions" and if we have "reservations" they'll accommodate point because 1)they don't pick up the phone when we call 2) when I try and ask questions about the chapter work and/or process they get snappy and say, "you don't need to be asking that because you may not get in" or, my personal favorite, "you're not privy to that information" As far as "straight answers" go, I'm not buying that either. When [Mya] asked [Tiffany] why she wanted to become [a TET] she said "because it fit my personality," that is **not a straight answer.** When I asked [Deborah] how the process made her a better person she said "because it's better than any other process on this campus." That is **not a straight answer.**

2.) *"But the fact [was] that a lot of us were in study sessions and didn't take advantage of our time, and some of our grades suffer. They said that they KNOW that parts of their process hurt them, and those may not be included in ours."* I'm confused here...are they seriously trying to say that "**we**" didn't take advantage of "**our**" time and that's why our grades suffered? Really though? Some people can't study in that type of environment, and how can we get a lot of study time outside of study session if we're constantly being asked to run an errand every five minutes? We can't and we didn't.

3.) *"But when we don't pick up and ignore them, to the point that they don't know what is going on with their organization... I can see why they would be upset. They don't trust us anymore. And that might just bite us in the ass later......."* *First off, we don't trust them either, or if people do trust them, they shouldn't. **How can you trust someone** who constantly demands that you buy them things and gives you nothing (nada. Zilch.) in return? How can you trust someone who doesn't really know you, and when you try and get to know them they don't offer much? It might bite us in the ass later...literally ("get in the kut!!" lol) but so what. I value our friendships more than their so called "trust." Also, I'm not buying the "when we don't pick up and ignore them.." deal because when we call them they don't pick up and they hit ignore and we don't know what's going on with them. I mean, I personally don't care [about] what's goin' on with them, but they only care [about] what's going on with us now because they're **scared** that we might get them in trouble.

4.) *"And not talking to them is not going to fix the problems. And I know that we have our grievances... but we should talk to them about it. NOT talking to them, and avoiding them is creating even more of a distance between us and them. If we thought that we weren't close to them before, we REALLY aren't now. A week is a long time...."* Okay, I'm not saying that we shouldn't talk to them.

I'm just suggesting that we need to work on our own shyt since we all might be on line together. **We need to get our kitchen clean before we invite company.**[lol] It is about us NOT them. "More of a distance" between us and them?" We were never close, and quite frankly we're not ever going to be close because we all have morals and they don't. We have respect and they don't. We believe that using people is wrong and they don't. A week is not a long time if you consider the fact that when we all we're calling them, we would go two weeks without any of them picking up the phone...It's not that deep, and I refuse to believe that if we "talked" to them about our grievances that they would listen without interruption. They're just going to come up with a bunch of points (like they did last night) and make them sound believable. They're **scared.**

5.) *By separating ourselves, it kinda seems to them as if we WISH to be paper. Some of our grievances are understandable, but some of them are not going to be well-[received], someone said that we are trying to CREATE our own process without having experienced one. To an extent, I think that's kind of true. I believe that they understand where we are coming from, because they were here last year. They even brought up [the girls that dropped when they were in study session]. So... I think they know the feelings we have right now. [Sasha] (I know how some of you feel about her, but please, read on) said that if we really and truly want to be a part of this chapter/organization its okay to quit when its TOO MUCH, but not when its just hard.* No, by separating ourselves it seems as if they won't get the chance to BEAT us like they got their asses beat. However, we haven't been in the basement yet, so I can't speak on that. But I will say that we are not trying to CREATE our own process. We are simply setting boundaries, and we need to because they've crossed them several times and we should've spoken up a LONG time ago. True, they were there last year and they went through it...do you see how they turned out? I don't want us to turn out like them, and I don't care if some of our "grievances" are[n't] well received. That's why they're called

*GRIEVE*ances because one party is not going to like what the other party says. No one wants to be paper, but as I said in my other letter, "It's one thing to have a "process," it's another to have a process that dehumanizes you and places you in a position to be harmed."

6.) *Call me brainwashed, or say that I actually believe in a process... because maybe I do. But bottomline is... I think we should talk to them. Instead of trying to figure it out on our own, they might be the only people to offer advice, because they can tell us from experience. We can ASK questions about the process. We can ASK how they felt when [the girls from their study session] decided to drop, and how they coped with it between themselves etc... Some of them may not be as open... but we can try to talk to them on a human level. Because all of this affects them too.* Brainwashed? No. Convinced? Yes. I understand where you're coming from, I honestly do, but nothing can ever ***change*** if we always back down and ***accept*** what they say. They only want to talk to us now because they are ***scared ***that we are going to tell on them. They only want to talk to us now because they want to become prophytes and have the sickly pleasure of saying "we made y'all." We can ASK them as many questions as we want...***after*** we get our own stuff together. They can't tell us how to get along better or how to call another SH to talk to her about beef you have with her first instead of going to the other SHs. We've been trying to talk to them on a human level, but, as [Julia] so eloquently said, WE ARE NOT ON HER LEVEL so there's always going to be a bit of "I know this little girl is not telling me what to do" mindset in them. They're not going anywhere, and they can suffer for a bit. Please don't buy into their "emotional appeal" bullshit because they don't know us enough to truly and deeply care about us that much.

7.) *"This is not to say that we don't need to still work on our inner relationships with each other. I just think that picking up one of their phone calls may not be a bad idea. I think I told Whitney yesterday that...when [Britney Lynn] calls us... I don't think its to yell, and belittle us. She's usually the softspoken one who is usually willing to help/offer advice. And when someone spoke to [Hannah]... she was honest, open, and concerned."* One of their phone calls....last night was equivalent to four phone calls because it's four people, and they (according to what I'm reading) are only concerned with themselves (It's all **fear**...see through it). Once again, they only want to "talk" to us about what's going on now. We're not going to be building a relationship with them by calling them this week because they just want to ask questions, and we're not going to miss anything by skipping a week of calls. (Logically, if I don't call my friend/sister for a week...I'm STILL her friend/sister...)We are far more important than them right now because we are not all [on] one accord. How dare we try and talk to **them** about "us" when we're not sure if all of **"us"**agree? I'm sure [Britney Lynn] wasn't calling to yell, but at the end of the day, she's [a TET] and my allegiance is to my SHs and not to her. So, regardless of how nice she is, she's still one of them, and she abused her power last semester too. [Hannah from Fall 2004] told [Vanessa] that "this is the first line we've put through so they're going to make mistakes..." No, spring 07 was a **mistake**! She was open and honest, **only because** she heard about [Amber Jackson]! Any other day she doesn't even try to pick up our phone calls, let alone **call** one of us...

8.) *"Please don't jump down my neck for saying this, or wanting to "break the pact." Because that is not the case. A part of our promise was to speak to each other honestly... and this is me being honest."* I really appreciate your honesty, and I hope you return the same respect for my honesty ☺

9.) I know that they have something that we want...but they have to offer it to us at this point because we pre-pledged (we're already NOT paper). No, they're not **obligated** to take us, but if they don't, and think that we're going to sit quietly and never utter a word about what went on last semester then they are severely **disturbed**. I stared at the *"they gain way more than you ever will by being apart of them"* phrase for like fifteen minutes and it's very **deep**... I remember the other phrase, "They have more to lose than we have to gain"...We have way more power than they do, we determine how much we will take, and how much crap we will put up with.

 If a few of us pick up the phone and the others don't **that's not unity**. I'm not calling [Sasha] for her birthday (not my fault she was born this week), I will send her an email. I am not calling any of the [TETs] this week, and I'm still not answering their phone calls because I don't trust them, and I know they don't sincerely love me and care about me...

Fall 08 is supposed to be "better" but we won't be **"better"** if we accept the **same** things that they did. Change is not easy. It's hard work, and it has to start in the beginning, not the middle, not the end. We're not all going to agree on everything (sister's can't and they don't), but if we sincerely want change, we need to start NOW and we need to stick **TOGETHER** regardless of the consequences
Whit'

On Mon, Jun 23, 2008 at 3:48 PM, <[Teresa]> wrote:

I responded to this earlier, but I wanted to post it on here so that everyone could see my response to [Mya's] email. Basically it came down to this:

How are we supposed to have talked to them about this shit when they don't answer their phones, and we're either scared or too intimidated to voice our concerns [?] Of course, they're gonna say this now. They don't wanna get in trouble.

Furthermore, I just don't understand how they could possibly think that none of the shit they pulled bothered us. If they thought it wasn't going to bother us, they WOULDNT have done it. Period. I never appreciated wastin my gas on them (just like [Tiffany] didn't wanna take [Ivyana] to the airport)...I never appreciated using my meal plan on them...I have ADD...I never appreciated being forced to sit in a room 5 nights out of 7 and be expected to be able to study WHILE being harassed...who says that I COULD study after being put through all of that? Who says that I COULD study when I was nervous/scared that they could show up at any moment...u dont see how they're trying to turn this back on us? THEY don't trust us?...WE don't trust THEM with our lives! Did anyone mention that to them? ....I don't feel as if I should have to live in fear of the next phone call, the next knock on the door, scared that if I turn the corner I'm going to run into one of them. That's CRAZY! If ur going to be my sister then BE one. ...Don't treat me like shit and then when I cross u hug me and pat me on the back (I'd prolly duck actually)..but naw boo boo that's not how I operate...and I sure hope that's not how Y'ALL operate. I don't feel as if i should have to be terrified of my sisters. What kinda friendship/sisterhood is it when I do all the work and you sit back and chill while making ur next list of things for me to do. that's SLAVERY...not SISTERHOOD. Honestly y'all...I think they don't know the definition of respect. Their brains are warped or something to believe that for us to give THEM respect, we have to do as they say WHENEVER they say. In order to be respected, you have to give it. They think that Respect is a one way street. They treat us like fuckin toilets and shit on us all day and night and the thing is...they REALLY expect us to be okay with it. THEY really think its okay. They think its what they're supposed to do. That's the REAL PROBLEM...they REALLY REALLY REALLY REALLY think thats part of a process. But honestly, I also believe that deep down they all know its wrong and they're just fuckin evil and just doing it just for shits and fuckin giggles lol (well some of them...like [Ivyana])....If any of you remember, I was her FREE RIDE to the airport when [Tiffany] refused because of gas.....shits fucked up! I shouldn't have to hide out at work or pretend like I'm doing something so i don't have to do something that I don't want to do. I should be able to say HELL NAW BITCH...but I couldn't!...and don't say that I could've [because we] were all in positions where we were too scared to actually say no to them...And that's why [Epsilon] is fucked up now. <-Wow sorry I vented for a while on this paragraph

Someone PLEASE explain to me how the following are part of a process: picking [Ivyana] up from the airport and cleaning her house BEFORE we're even pre-pledging and BEFORE we've even gotten picked, [Tiffany] pushing me into a wall at a [Nu Pi] party back in January JUST BECAUSE she THOUGHT I was about to get a drink, a few of the TETs gangin up on [Amber] in a room and grabbin at her clothes and pullin her hair and shit, paying for their meals when we go out to lunches with them (y'all know half the time they only agreed to eat lunch with us [was because] they were hungry)...<--FYI that is ALLLL BEFORE PRE--PLEDGING STARTED so that just goes to show how fucked up this has really been and I can almost GUARANTEE that everyone can add to this. NOW I'll move onto the pre-pledging part: taking [Sasha] food everyday...spending our own money on their food...spending our own meal plans on them (which is blatant disrespect to our parents whose hardworking money paid for those)...cleaning people's houses, being forced to go hang out with them but doing house work instead. being forced to go study with them, being called in the middle of the night to bring someone their keys or to call safe rider for them when they know they could call for themselves...being made to drive people all over Pittsburgh and sometimes out of it (for example: TO THEIR [PARENT'S] HOUSE SO THEY CAN GET MONEY CUZ THEY DONT HAVE ANY...how the fuck do you have no money?! WE buy everything for [U!]...YOU HAVE A JOB!!! but you don't go! WHY? cuz she wanted to be delivered food all day and "cuddle" with people...ur BROKE [SASHA]...DO SOMETHING ABOUT IT)...and also being forced to drive them PERIOD...being forced to go buy/replace broken dishes that they prolly broke themselves because they were UNDERAGE drinking lmao, being told to go to someones house just to check if the heater is working, being told that if u wanna graduate with good grades then leave,..and y'all know there is so much more to add to this (but for the sake of time and energy..and my poor fingers..I'll stop there) THEY...ARE...RECKLESS and they don't feel bad about anything, they're just SCARED. They don't care about us right now, they're just nervous that we're fed up and they know that we don't know them like that nor care about them like that to take a hit for them or go down for them in the end. Maybe if they REALLY HAD taken the time to get to know us and [showed] us that they really [cared], we wouldn't be in the situation that we're in now (and I'm talking about a few things right now)....

They claim that all of those things were part of a process...but in actuality..that stuff is just to prove to everyone that is watching that we are whipped and will do whatever they say...it's all for show (for example: [Ivyana] calling me at 2 or 3 am to bring her her keys to the auditorium in front of [a Nu Pi]....or [Sasha] and a few others making someone go get McDonalds for her and NON-[EPSILON]-MEMBERS...or having u running from one side of campus to another cuz u gotta get somethin to somebody in a certain amount of time<--trust me, the people who know what to look for KNOW EXACTLY what we're doing...especially when there's taco bell or some other type of food in our hand...)...Another example of them just wanting to have us whipped is [Julia]: Her infamous "We have something that y'all want"...This clearly translates to, whatever I say goes because I'm [a TET]...and you ALL know this...Moreover, them always threatening to drop us to make us do whatever they say is another example of them USING us and trying to CONTROL us...this is REALLY in all of our hearts and we would do alot to get it and we definitely did...but according to them...THIS IS NOTHING!....also, whatever happened to being humble? [...] some of these people weren't shit before they became [TETs] so what's this now all of a sudden? They supposedly had to do it during THEIR process...what happened from the time between their process to now...o, i know...NOTHING...except for the fact that they are [TETs]...it defines them. They don't do community service, they don't have good grades...what do they have to show for themselves? ...(someone can TRY to fill that in)...I know personally that I would never let an organization define me...I want to be someone who plays a role in defining the organization and giving something back to it. I think their main goal is for us to not actually realize what they're doing to us...they want us to continue to believe that this is how it's supposed to be...and I'm almost certain that they're scared that we've realized it (well some of us)...so they're SHAKIN in their BOOTTTSSSSS!! lol...but they're so caught up in what everyone else thinks of them. They didn't want to be the ones to challenge anything for fear of people calling them paper. [Sasha] will always be the first one to jump up and tell you that she was ALWAYS runnin to the cut to take wood for someone else..I have never too much cared what people thought of me and I'm damn sure not going to start now...they are all so insecure and I'm not sure if they were like that before or if the process fucked them up that badly...if we need to make a change to better the organization as a whole then I say we do it...but if nothing's going to change BEFORE fall 08's process begins (IF it begins lol)...y'all can seriously count me out. Cuz I know what I believe and I know what I stand for and I refuse to let a group of nothings control my mind, my body, and my spirit.

Sorry this was so long everyone. But that's how I feel and I had to get it all out. Feel free to comment...luv y'all but I really need to do the right thing and honestly, if [TET] is in yall's hearts too then you wouldn't do anything to jeopardize it..([Teresa])

XXIII. Taken Aback

A few days after Teresa posted her response on the account, I noticed that things were missing. The set pictures of Ivyana, the "info on them" document, the Epsilon lineage, and the poems and notes we had stolen from the mind books were all deleted. In that moment, something told me to immediately save all of the emails that were on the SH account. I forwarded them to myself and called as many SHs as I could to ask about the missing documents. I didn't reach everyone, but when I mentioned it to the few that I called, they were dumbfounded.

No interpersonal issues were solved that week. They became worse. Jamie and Amber were mad at each other, Shelby still didn't trust Vanessa, Brooke and Eva were upset about the missing documents, Candace was confused, Mya was "accidentally" answering her phone for the TETs, Teresa was livid, and I was wishing that certain people would grow a backbone and stick to the plan.

In one last attempt for unity, we decided to have a group chat via instant messenger on July 2, 2008. We tried to fix all of the issues that had been plaguing us: the fact that Vanessa lived with Kamille, the fact that the TETs found out about Amber's mom without Amber telling them anything, and the fact that things were missing from the document. After about four hours of chatting, it became apparent that we were too split and there would be no unity. We blamed Vanessa for telling the TETs about Amber's mom. Although Jamie admitted to being the one who removed the missing things from the document, Vanessa and Mya had known about it. Shelby and Amber continuously attacked Vanessa, and after awhile, the chat became pointless.

It felt like we had become divided. It hurt, but I didn't see a point in trying to mend things so soon. I focused on myself and took time to think about what I wanted to do about TET.

We were told that we could only call Tiffany and Sasha for the rest of the summer, and in the fall we would see the flyers for rush and be brought in as paper.

I called a few SHs to see where they stood on everything that had happened. I called Eva first.

"Hey Eva, how are you?" I asked.

"I'm fine. This stuff is all so crazy. I never got a chance to write on the document, but I think that the chat was enough."

"Yea, everything completely fell apart."

"I just don't understand. When I told y'all interesting facts about myself and hung out with you, it wasn't just so you could have an interesting fact to give the TETs. It was because we were supposed to be getting to know each other and becoming friends. When Mya immediately sent out a text about how she took Amber off her mass text list because Amber was done, that showed me something."

"I really don't get it. Everybody wavers. The TETs even said that they wavered when they were on line and they were on line for what, eight weeks? How long have we been pre-pledging? Way longer than that. I don't see how someone couldn't waver after going through all that."

"True. Let's just see what happens in the fall, Whit. I'm sure we'll have to talk to them then."

When I got off the phone with her, I called Teresa. "Hey Teresa, what's up? How do you feel about everything?"

"I feel like people don't listen to me," she sighed. "I feel like what I said on the chat was right. Mya, Vanessa, and Jamie are in it for themselves. I don't know why the rest of y'all can't see that."

"Teresa, I really don't—"

"Explain something to me Whitney. Tell me why the TETs *magically* knew about Amber's mom when none of us were talking to them. I didn't say anything, you didn't say anything, Eva and Brooke hadn't called in forever, Candace was out of the country, Shelby didn't call, and Amber didn't call for herself. That leaves *three* people, the same three people who knew about the documents being taken off the account."

"Yea, but—"

"You don't have to believe me. I know that they told. It's the three of them versus the seven of us. I guarantee it. And you wanna know something else?"

"What?"

"I find it quite funny that all of sudden the three of them think that they're so close with the TETs. I think they forgot what happened last semester. If they really want to be a part of a sisterhood that bad, then shouldn't they be looking out for us? Shouldn't they be trying to understand where we're coming from and not be running to the other side?"

"I don't know."

"You *do* know. You just don't want to accept the truth."

I was mad at myself for compromising so many of my morals, and I couldn't believe that I had been passive about losing Renee as a friend.

I called her one afternoon and talked to her about pre-pledging. I told her that things had fallen apart and that I wanted her to be my friend. I told her that TET was just a club and that all the work we did wouldn't mean anything when fall came around. She and I talked for hours, and when I hung up the phone, I realized that she wasn't the only person I needed to address.

From: Whitney Williams <whitney██████████@gmail.com>
Date: Tue, Jul 8, 2008 at 9:26 PM
Subject: A letter
To: < [Sasha]>

Dear [Sasha],

With the recent events that have surfaced amongst the girls from the study group, I wanted to write you a letter about an issue that I've had on my chest for quite some time. I know that I could've easily pulled you to the side last semester to speak about this matter, but I needed time to recuperate my emotions and say everything I wanted to say. Since you asked two people of the group what their grievances were here's one of mine:

On March 18, 2008 after study session, between the hours of 10pm and 12 [am], I was pulled to the side by four members of the sorority ([Tiffany Stringer], [Latoya Riley], [Nicole Ballard], and [Sasha Irons]) to discuss my "attitude". Another study group member was present and can witness to the events that unfolded:

I apologized for coming off as a person having an "attitude," but I explained that my experiences in the past (like everyone else's on this planet) shaped me and affect how I react to certain things, and my "attitude" isn't directed towards anything or anybody. I explained that I had been working on it. I attempted to be vulnerable and open up for the first time about past struggles in my life: welfare, homelessness, etc. I also said that that particular day was not the best time to talk to me because I was having an emotional/ bad week because it was a year ago that same week that my father was murdered (March 20, 2007).However, in the midst of my explanation, a member of the sorority interrupted and said,

"Whitney, you are not the only one that has ever struggled!! My boyfriend died when I was seventeen! I had to watch them pull him out of the car because the accident was so bad! I loved him! I told him everything! I still cry about him! Do you know what that's like? I grew up in the hood too! I went to twelve funerals when I was seventeen! When I was on line my mother had cancer and I still had to go to set!! People are not going to care about your struggles when they're busy "making" you...." This member also told me that I needed counseling, and when I told her that I was already having counseling she insisted that it wasn't working. She said that I was so stuck in my ways that I would never grow through the [Epsilon] process if I kept holding on to sob stories/stuff from my past and acting like I've had the most hard times. She told me that I was not humble, not "hungry," and that I used my past "as a crutch."

Seriously, how dare you [Sasha]? How dare you compare the death of a father to a boyfriend you had? (Was your boyfriend's name on your birth certificate?) Don't you think I loved my father too? Don't you think I told him everything too? Don't you think I still cry when I think about how he'll never get to see me graduate from college, how he missed nine years of my life but will never be able to reconcile with me and answer my questions? How dare you bring up your parent who's still alive and survived cancer to mine who is six feet under the ground and will never recover? How dare any sister (or human being for that matter) do that? You wouldn't say that to [Regina] or [Cari], so why would you say something like that to me? I don't share sob stories about my past because I choose not to, and I don't need people to compare their past to mine because I don't know what they've been through, and they really don't know what I've been through.

You didn't know I had ever been homeless or on welfare or struggled at all until that night, so please consider that logic useless and feel free to consider how someone can use their past as a crutch when they never use it as an excuse, let alone bring it up.

Please believe the only reason I made that comment about how "I brought you burger king every Monday Wednesday and Friday when I had pneumonia " (that you've repeated in disdain these past few months because you think I "was out of line" and because when you were on line you "had bronchitis and pneumonia and didn't let that stop [you] because [you] had to get stuff done") was to prevent myself from becoming too heated. Whether you made those comments inadvertently or consciously, I felt that you were wrong. I have yet to receive an apology or a simple, "I didn't mean it that way," comment. [Tiffany] called me once to attempt to correct things but her phone cut off and I did not choose to call her later or to bring up the matter again. I called [Julia] crying the very next day and she suggested that I speak to you on several occasions but I couldn't because I was hurt. I was hurt, I was angry, and I was disturbed. But I'm not hurt, angry, or disturbed anymore.

I've had a lot of time to think about it and I've realized that perhaps you were trying to connect with me on a more personal level. Perhaps you didn't realize that you said what you said and were more concerned with the surliness of the "burger king" comment. Perhaps you were so distressed with your own past problems, that you couldn't understand how anyone else could possibly be as hurt as you ever were. Either way, I want you to know that there is a line, and you crossed it.

I needed to write this for closure,
W.G.W.

From: Whitney Williams <whitney█████████@gmail.com>
Date: Tue, Jul 29, 2008 at 8:12 PM
Subject: convo with [sasha]
To: studybuddies040507@gmail.com

So, today I called [Sasha] to discuss the email i sent [because] she expressed to [Candace] that she wanted to talk to me (and Im guessing she thought I wouldn't pick up if she called me? lol) I had [Candace] on 3-way (on mute of course) and this is pretty much what was said

1.) She apologized (A LOT) for coming off the way [that she did]. She didn't mean to seem heartless or cruel. She said she was "touched" that i felt that way about her and that she didn't want anyone to hate her. She said that she was trying to let me know that things happen in life that you can't control and you can't let them rule your life after they've happened. You kind of have to accept them and move on the best way you can. She said that she was emotional that night as well, but that was no excuse for what she said to me. She said that she was hurt by the email, and that she talked to [Tiffany] about it and really wanted to call me but [Tiffany] said, "do you really think she wants to listen to you right now?"

She said that she feels like I put up a wall and doesn't feel like that's the best way to deal with things. I told her that I tried to be open and vulnerable that night but I got shut down, and it's hard to open up to ppl after they've shut you down that way she did. She said that she can understand that and she really didn't mean to hurt my feelings and she regrets doing that---she apologized.

2.) Her grandmother raised her for most of her life and her grandmother passed [a couple of years ago]. She said that it really hurt her and she couldn't get over it--she took time off from school but it turned into a complete year and she regrets that, but she now knows that she won't let tragic things affect her that bad anymore.

3.) Attitudes. She said that she sees a lot of herself in me ([Candace] shed a tear lmao jk jk)--she said that she would've done the same thing (email) and that she realizes that half the time I' m not trying to have an attitude and she doesn't try to have an attitude either (dnt know about that one...but hey). She said that it was never her intention to come off as "better than anybody else because I'm not. I'm human, and I make mistakes...I apologize." She says that I come off like I don't care sometimes (I agreed) but she realized that I'm not consciously trying to do that

4.) I expressed the fact that I didn't learn anything last semester by buying food and other items for them and since those acts are part of the pledging process that's a likely reason why some ppl decided not to continue bc they (and myself) realized that it really served no purpose. I brought up the fact that sp 07 attempted to convince [Jamie] and [Vanessa] that we didn't use our time to run errands effectively and could've got to know them during the errand. I said, " I just don't see how I was supposed to connect with [Ivyana] when I was running from melwood to chesterfield to bring her a shirt on Easter Sunday, and I'm pretty sure that sometimes when y'all asked us to run an errand you were just trying to get the errand done, not get to know us."

5.) I told her that last semester I felt that I didn't really connect with a lot of them bc they either a) didn't pickup or b) would call back five minutes later and make me run an errand. I said that I could ask you a million questions but I still don't know you any better.

6.) She asked about [Shelby]--I said that "[Shelby] is going to be very busy next semester and you should probably talk to her but, her decision was based on what she wanted to get done next semester."

7.) In regards to buying them stuff/running errands/lost connections she asked, "Well...if none of these issues have vanished...like...are you...how can i put this..ummm.. still tryna do it?" I said "I mean.... yea but I won't have money next semester to be buying stuff for y'all. I'm broke." and then she said, "well y'all won't have to worry about any of that stuff i mean...idk....i really don't know what to tell you Whitney...like, I'm not tryna blow you off, i promise i'm not--i just honestly don't know what's going to happen." She said, "I'm honestly just a neo myself" (LOL—a [damn near] two year neo ahahahahaha)

8.) I told her that the sequence of events were really messy and there was a lot going on as to why I didn't call them. I asked her how they found out about [Amber] not wanting to do it anymore. I said, "I know that we all were supposed to call you one night and tell you why we wanted to be a part of your org and two ppl didn't call and one of those ppl was studying abroad. I know she didn't turn in her assignment, but was that how you all came to that conclusion?" She said, "Well yea!" and laughed.

9.) I started saying something about next semester but then she said she would call me back in 20...definitely didn't lol Oh well ☺ Whit'

From <[Mya]>
Date: Tue, Jul 29, 2008 at 8:27 PM
Subject Re: convo with [sasha]
To: Whitney Williams whitney█████████@gmail.com

all in all.. I think it went well, and better than expected. She acknowledged that she was in the wrong and apologized, and did it all without yelling or hanging up.
P.S. I love how [Can*] was on 3-way :)
*[Mya]

From: <[Candace]>
Date: Wed, Jul 30, 2008 at 3:30 PM
Subject: Re: convo with [sasha]
To: Whitney Williams <whitney███████@gmail.com>

lmao yea...and even worse my phone cut off so i called whit back in the middle of their convo and she still linked the call!
im sure 3-way is always done to us (like im pretty sure [Tiffany] was on the phone when [sasha] called me back). i was just there to remind her of points she wanted to bring up or tell whit if she started getting too much of an attitude...but it wasn't necessary b/c i think the convo went pretty well like you said =)

From: <[Amber]>
Date: Mon, Aug 4, 2008 at 5:26 PM
Subject: Re: convo with [sasha]
To :Whitney Williams <whitney███████@gmail.com>

That's great. i hope [Sasha] grows as a person from this conversation. i am still shocked that she actually apologized. i never thought i would hear that from her lol... i am also impressed with you, whitney, for expressing so many important things. you didn't hold anything back. you just spoke your mind and you weren't worried if there were gonna be any later consequences. that's why i love talking to you about this bull shit. i hope everything works out for the better once school starts... only 3 weeks away! we'll see... but i'm still gonna be wearing [violet] on the first day of classes like i told you... haha
Ttys [Amber]

For the remaining weeks of the summer, I helped my little sister prepare for her freshman year of college, went over interior designs for my apartment, and traveled with friends. I knew the TETs were going to ask me how I felt about everything when I returned to school, so I only left a voicemail for Julia in August to wish her a happy birthday.

XXIV. Clean Slate

When I returned to Pittsburgh, I was elated. I was excited about my classes, my new apartment, and becoming a TET.

During orientation weekend, with the exception of Vanessa and Jamie, we held a surprise party for Brooke. We spent time reminiscing about the spring and wondering when we would get a phone call to discuss where we stood in our interests. I called Deborah and Julia to ask, but neither answered.

Mya called me one afternoon and said that she had spoken to Sasha. She said that we needed to have a meeting to go over what was going to happen to us. Shelby didn't show up to the meeting, and after waiting for Eva and Brooke for half an hour, we decided to begin without them.

ME: So, what's the news?

MYA: Well, I talked to Sasha last week and she said that we have to start over. She said that when she talked to Whitney this summer it seemed like Whitney was under the impression that they owed us something and they don't. She and Tiffany said that the study group doesn't exist anymore. I think it's because of trust issues.

CANDACE: When she said, "start over" did she mean going back to being a regular interest again or "start over" as in we never knew them?

MYA: I think she means being a new interest again.

ME: Okay, someone please steal the magic wand that Tiffany is using so I too can erase last semester and still have eight hundred dollars in my pocket. Get real. I am NOT starting over. They're just going to have to take a split line if they don't trust all of us.

MYA: We can't just go to them and say, "We want a split line!" That's mad disrespectful!

ME: They really don't have a choice.

JAMIE: It's not really *all* of us. It's mostly Amber. Like, if Amber called Sasha right now, I swear we would all get calls to be at the basement at some time next week and that would be the happiest day of my life.

ME: Are you *serious*?

TERESA: That's…Anyway it's not that easy.

AMBER: No, it's really not.

VANESSA: All you have to do is call and say, "I made a mistake."
AMBER: I didn't make a *mistake*. I don't want to get beat, I don't want to spend any more of my money, and I don't want to be told what to do by any of them anymore. I've done enough and way more than I should have. They can make me paper.
JAMIE: You could at least try to pledge. You used to want to.
AMBER: This summer changed all of that.
TERESA: Yea, it changed things for me too. I'll pledge, but I'm not doing any of the stupid shit.
JAMIE: Like what?
TERESA: Like getting—
JAMIE: Hold up, hold up. I'm letting you know now, that if we ever get the chance to go on line and you don't take wood, I'm not fuckin' wit you. It wouldn't be fair. Like, Whit if you saw me gettin' my ass beat you wouldn't jump in the kut for me?
ME: (sighing) I would.
AMBER: I wouldn't. That's your *choice*. And taking wood shouldn't determine if can fuck with me.
ME: I'm just not buying them anything. I can't—unless they explain to me that what I'm buying is making me a better person or teaching me a valuable life lesson.
JAMIE: Whatever. As long as we go on line I won't care. I just want to be a TET.
AMBER: Me too. I still want to be friends with everyone though. I'm willing to look past all the summer drama, Jamie. Do you want to try to mend things between us?
JAMIE: No. I don't.
AMBER: Well, okay then.
JAMIE: I just don't understand why you did some of the things you did. And now you're talking about how you won't even try to call Sasha for the benefit of everyone else. We all might end up being paper because of you and your name will be *tarnished* in the Greek community.
TERESA: I don't think it's that deep.
JAMIE: It is that deep! The funny thing is, they may have been extra reckless with some of the stuff that went on last semester, and they might have taken things too far, but they liked us! (laughing) They really liked us!

Silence.

ME: I just don't see why we have to start over completely. That's crazy!

VANESSA: It's because we all stopped calling in the summer. I shot myself in the foot too. I was calling at first, but then I stopped calling like everyone else. I guess they feel that we all have to suffer together.

TERESA: We only had a month and a half of summer left!

MYA: That's too long to go without calling them.

ME: Are you okay, Vanessa?

VANESSA: No. I don't understand anymore. Last semester, I joked about not taking wood and not running errands and y'all got mad at me and kind of turned against me. Now, y'all are dead ass serious about not taking wood and stuff and I'm supposed to be okay with that? I don't have a choice, but I just find that point very interesting and a bit unfair.

Vanessa picked up her bag and stood up. She muttered goodbye, and she, Mya, and Jamie walked out of our apartment.

CANDACE: I see where Vanessa was coming from.

TERESA: Yea, but back then we were all brainwashed so that doesn't apply now just because she, Jamie, and Mya still are.

ME: I don't think Mya's brainwashed.

TERESA: I *know* she's brainwashed and I don't trust her.

ME: Mya? I can somewhat understand you not trusting Vanessa and Jamie, but Mya too?

TERESA: Think what you want, but I'm telling you that she's on the TETs' side. I've been saying this for the longest but no one wants to listen to me. It's been the three of them versus the other seven since the summer, believe it or not.

ME: Here we go again.

CANDACE: Anyway, are y'all going to start over like Sasha said?

AMBER: Nope.

ME: Hell no.

TERESA: No, that's definitely not happening. We're juniors! Why would we waste another year being interests when we were supposed to be on line this fall? Of course *Jamie* wouldn't mind starting over. She never had to *start* to begin with! She missed all the stuff we had to do during the fall of our sophomore year because she was partying it up with the freshmen!

ME: True.

AMBER: And I like how she said that my name would be *tarnished* in the Greek community. I don't care. Who are they to me? There are only like fifty of them. They're not that active on campus, and I won't see any of them in two years so it doesn't even matter. She's so caught up in popularity and what people think.

ME: I can't get over the fact that Sasha really thinks that I'm going to start over. They've got two weeks to call me and tell me something. If not—

TERESA: If not, what?

CANDACE: Yea. If not, what?

ME: I don't know. I really don't. I think they'll call all of us though. They're not stupid.

A rumor began to swirl around. It was spreading like wildfire, burning itself into every eardrum saying, "Half of the girls who pre-pledged TET in the spring would be allowed to pledge in the fall. The other half would be made paper in the spring." When it came to me, I called all the SHs. I didn't want to believe it was true. I didn't believe it was true. We decided that we should call the TETs to ask what was going on.

We called. We called every day. We called for a week. Not a single TET answered. They all hit ignore and they didn't call back.

On September 3, 2008, while I was sitting in the living room, Candace received a phone call from Deborah. I heard her say, "Okay, I'll be right there." She went to her room to get dressed, and when she came back into the living room she looked at me and said, "I'm going to meet with Deborah. Please don't say anything to anyone."

"I won't," I said, and as the door closed behind her I felt my heart speed up. I wanted to know why Deborah called her and not me. I wanted to know what was going on.

Forty minutes later, Candace came back. Instead of saying anything to me, she put her things into her room and walked towards the door.

"I can't talk to you about it right now," she said. "I need to talk to my mom. I'll be back."

When she returned, I decided that I wouldn't ask her anything. I would just lighten the mood by telling her what I heard earlier. I said, "You don't have to tell me what happened, but I heard this rumor earlier today about what's going to happen with fall 08."

"What is it?" she asked.

"I heard that they were going to keep half of us, replace the rest, and have a fall 08 line. Then, whoever got replaced would be made paper in the spring," I started laughing. "Isn't that crazy? They're not that *dumb*! That doesn't make any sense whatsoever! Why aren't you laughing?"

"Because that's almost true."

"What! Which part?"

She sighed. "Deborah called me to a room similar to where we all had our first interviews. All of them were there, and they made me sit kind of next to them and were like, 'So, what's the plan?' They said that they're not taking any of my roommates for membership. The study group never existed to them. They told me that if I wanted to be a TET I would have to move out...They wanted me to choose between my friends and TET. So there," her voice started wavering. "I'm not going to be an interest anymore."

"They told you to move out and it never crossed their minds that your roommates would ask why the hell you're moving out when we just got here?"

"I guess not."

"And they really expect you to find somewhere else to live that quickly after you've already paid to live here for the whole semester?"

"Yea. I can't choose between my friends and TET. That's not fair. Me, you, Amber, and Teresa all knew each other before any of this TET stuff so I can't imagine doing it without you all."

"They can't be that *dumb*. They can't be that dumb to think that they can actually get away with this. What are they thinking?"

"They just feel that their chapter is at risk and if they take y'all, y'all might take them down."

"And the solution is to pick brand new people that they don't even know? If Amber's mom was going to tell on them she would have told on them a long time ago. She definitely wanted to, but Amber begged her not to."

"True, but they think that taking her might give her leverage on them."

"I can't understand their logic. We didn't say anything last semester because we assumed that we were going to be TETs. But now that we're not, what's holding us back from saying anything? Better yet, they don't trust us enough to put us in the basement, but they trust us enough to think that we'll keep our mouths shut if they cross a new line?"

"I guess. I don't know. I can't believe that I'm not an interest anymore."

"This is bullshit."

"I have to call her by Friday and tell her my decision."

"Tell her that I'm not going to let them get away with this bullshit while you're at it."

"What do you mean?"

"I don't know. I don't know right now. I think they still need to talk to all ten of us before they make any decisions."

"They probably won't. I think their minds are made up."

"It doesn't make sense. How did they even decide who would get picked and who wouldn't?"

"I don't know, Whitney. I really don't. I'm telling you what they told me. They told me I have until Friday to give them my decision, and it's going to be a no. I don't know how true the replacement stuff is. I'm just thinking about how my life is going to be without TET. I'm really not going to be a TET this semester."

"Are you going to be okay with that?"

"I'm probably going to be real sad for the next few days, but I think I'll get over it eventually. It's just so unfair. I did all of that stuff last semester to end up choosing between my friends and TET? I can't even think right now. I'm going to talk to you tomorrow."

I was furious. I couldn't believe that the TETs weren't even going to consider how I felt or hear what I had to say. I wanted to tell someone about their plans in asking Candace to move out, but I promised her that I wouldn't tell a soul. Instead, I continued calling the TETs and encouraged the other SHs to send the TETs short, discreet emails requesting to speak with them. Only Amber and Teresa complied.

Subject:	Hi!
From:	wgw███████.edu
Date:	Fri, September 5, 2008 7:20 pm
To:	███████.edu (more)
Priority:	Normal
Options:	View Full Header	View Printable Version

Hi,
    I hope that your semesters are off to a great start and that you're enjoying another year in Pittsburgh. The weather has been wonderful so far, and I hope that it remains that way for a few more weeks. We haven't spoken in a while due to varying degrees of miscommunication, but I feel that it is imperative that we speak soon.

Enjoy another beautiful day!
WGW

There was no response, but I couldn't stop trying. I refused to give up on being heard. I continued to call them and a few days later, I poured all of my feelings into a four page letter and emailed it to all of the TETs.

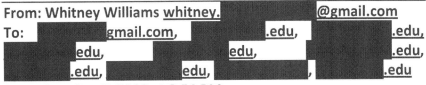

From: Whitney Williams whitney.███████@gmail.com
To: ███████gmail.com, ███████.edu, ███████edu, ███████edu, ███████.edu, ███████.edu, ███████edu, ███████edu, ███████, ███████.edu
Date: Sun, Sep 7, 2008 at 8:54 PM
Subject: A letter

Dear [Sasha],

I'm writing this letter to let you know that I am still interested in becoming a member of the Epsilon Chapter of Theta Eta Theta sorority, Incorporated. I feel that there has been a lot of miscommunication on both parties' behalf, and since I have not been able to communicate with anyone, I'm going to take a risk and explain everything to you, since we've somewhat spoken before.

*I'm going to refer to the group as "study group" when I'm speaking about them collectively in this letter. Also if there's an asterisk at the end of the sentence, that sentence is addressed at the end of the letter.

1.) To say that "a lot of stuff went down this summer," is a complete understatement, especially since you didn't see what was happening behind the scenes and could only assume what was going on. On June 20, 2008 we had an assignment due. However, a few nights before the due date each of us was to call you ([Sasha]) and let you know "why we still wanted to be a member of your sorority." You received 7 calls instead of ten. The missing calls were [Candace Blake] (who was in Costa Rica), [Shelby Stone], and [Amber Jackson]. When the assignment was due, Julia received nine projects, missing one from [Amber Jackson.]

All of a sudden, everyone in the study group was receiving calls left and right from you all, wanting to know what was going on. But we didn't pick up because we didn't know what to say. A few people picked up and let you know that [Amber] and [Shelby] were "done." However, others continued not to pick up phones because 1) we didn't want to speak for them so soon and 2) we didn't think that it was our place to speak on either of their behalves at the time.

Then, our study group started to fall apart at the seams. People realized that they somewhat agreed with the reasons behind the departures and others felt that the departures came at the wrong time. In addition to this, people had extreme personal issues between each other, and we decided that we should all talk with each other to attempt to get on one accord. But we couldn't and we figured, "how can we talk to them if we have no idea what to say and some of us disagree with what has happened/potentially could happen in the future?" So, needless to say, we continued to not pick up our phones, and said that we would discuss/attempt to fix our inner relationships for one week, and then call [Britney Lynn] afterwards to tell her everything.

2.) On June 22, 2008, [Tiffany Stringer], [Kamille Jackson], [Britney Lynn] and you sat down with Vanessa and Jamie and spoke to them about your concerns with the study group: You were concerned and hurt that if questions and reservations arose about you and the process that we didn't ask. The grades situation was brought up, and [Kamille] apparently said that you all understood that our grades are important to us. You said that a lot of us were in study sessions and didn't take advantage of our time, and as a result some of our grades suffered. You said that you KNOW that parts of your process hurt you all and those may not be included in the next one.

By picking us for study sessions...you liked us, and clearly wanted us for your organization. And clearly...you trusted us with the future and continuity of your chapter. But when we don't pick up and ignore you, to the point that you don't know what is going on with your organization, you become upset and don't trust us anymore.

You said that by separating ourselves, it seems as if we WISHED to be paper. You said that we are trying to CREATE our own process without having experienced one. You ([Sasha]) said that if we really and truly want to be a part of this chapter/organization it's okay to quit when it's TOO MUCH, but not when it's just hard.

When we heard everything that you all said in that conversation, we understood where you were coming from, but it seemed as if you were only concerned with what was currently going on, and not our feelings. We felt that (collectively) everything you said was only in your best interest, and not in ours.

At some point (I honestly have no idea when) you all found out that someone had told someone close to them who was also a member of the organization "everything."* I think that's the reason you all blocked us on Face book (I think...). And because of that, a few of us interpreted that as you all saying, "We don't know the study group anymore, don't call us, don't talk to us anymore," and the plan to call [Britney Lynn] fell through. We were told that [Tiffany] said that we were only allowed to call her and you ([Sasha]). (We were also told that fall 04 and fall 05 didn't even want to know us/deal with us anymore.) But some of us felt closer to others and since we weren't allowed to call them, we didn't call at all.

On July 2, 2008, the study group made another effort to attempt to reunite and come up with some sort of way to agree on who wanted to continue and who didn't. However, (and this is complete honesty) it was a disaster. People didn't agree on the simplest of ideas, people who still hadn't resolved personal private issues brought those into the light and didn't want to discuss anything else, people felt betrayed and felt that they were being attacked, people still wanted to pledge but were catching flack for wanting to, people were name calling, and people just weren't agreeing on much of anything. So, as a result we sort of fell apart---it became a divide between the "people who wanted to pledge," "people who wanted to pledge but wanted explanations," and "people who hadn't made up their minds."

Now personally, I never wished to be paper, but when people voiced their concerns about the "process" and asked "well, whit, what was the point of doing xyz?" and I didn't have a legitimate answer or a logical reason, I had to take a step back. I realized that my motto for pledging was, "as long as you don't kill me, I don't care." That was a problem. (Seriously lol) So, I decided to just not talk to anyone—study group or your group for a few days. I realized that I was still angry at you ([Sasha]) for what had happened in March, that I wanted to ask about some instances from last semester, and that I was seriously confused.

After I took a break, I realized that I still didn't want to be paper: I decided that it would be best if I wrote you ([Sasha]) a letter (that was officially emailed on July 8, 2008), explaining how I felt. I felt relieved after I sent the letter, and hoped that I would speak to you about it and possibly everything else soon.

On July 23, 2008 [Candace] spoke to you on the phone and you dispelled the word that we could only call you and [Tiffany]. You said, "What? You can call whoever you want to call." You asked who was done out of the study group and she said that she believed that "[Amber] and [Shelby] were kind of done" You asked, "Well, what about Whitney?"

[Candace]: I'm sure Whitney's not done

You: Even though she sent that angry email?

[Candace]: Yea, I'm pretty sure she's not done, and I don't think she meant for it to come off as angry...I feel like you all should talk, but I think she tried to call [Tiffany] to talk about it

You: So, she called [Tiffany] to talk about what was going on between us?

[Candace]: Yea...it would probably be better if she called you to talk about it

You: Yeaaaaaa...ya think?

On July 29, 2008 I called you to speak about the email. You apologized for coming off the way you did and that you didn't mean to seem heartless or cruel. You said that you were "touched" that I felt that way about you and you didn't want anyone to hate you. (For the record, I don't, and never did). After about twenty minutes our conversation ended and I thought it had gone well. I told you that the sequence of events was really messy and there was a lot going on as to why I didn't call people in your group. I asked her how you found out about [Amber] not wanting to do it anymore. I said, "I know that we all were supposed to call you one night and tell you why we wanted to be a part of your organization and a few people didn't call and one of those people was studying abroad. I know she didn't turn in her assignment, but was that how you all came to that conclusion?"

You said, "Well yea!" I do recall telling you a few of my grievances and you responding, "Well...if none of these issues have vanished...or going to go away....are you still tryna' do it?" I responded, "Yea, but I'm broke, so I probably won't have money to spend on people like last semester." You said, "hmm, well y'all don't have to worry about that...like, I don't know what to tell you Whitney, I honestly don't...."

Although [Candace] informed us all that we could call everyone again, so much time had already gone by that we didn't know where to start or who to call. So, for the remaining few weeks of the summer we hardly called. When I got back to school, [Mya] informed me that she had spoken to you and that you said that the study group didn't exist anymore. She said that we all had to start over as new interests, because based on the conversation you had with me weeks prior, you felt that "we thought that we were entitled to something."

I had no idea what she was talking about, and she said that according to you, I had made some comment about how I said that in the fall I wasn't going to do anything. I don't recall ever saying that, and I find it quite hard to believe that I said that at the same time when I was attempting to have a "heart to heart" with you. What I said was that, "I'm broke, so I probably won't have money to spend on people like last semester." Yes, I did earn money this summer, but in June I learned that my friend was not going to be able to afford to take the necessary credits to finish her stay at community college. I had saved up $1700, so I gave her $650 and never thought twice about the consequences that might occur. Although I did question the meaning behind buying things for you all, I never said that I wouldn't try my best to do whatever [else] it takes to make it. I was, and still am, a bit hurt that my words were completely taken out of context.

Recently, I heard a rumor that you all had picked new girls to go through the process, and were just going to let us alone. Regardless of whether I believed it or not, there are no words to express the mix of emotions I've been feeling for the past few days. Before I had even heard the rumor, I had attempted to call both Julia and Deborah to tell them everything that is currently being said in this letter, a week before, but to no avail.

I told all of the girls in the study group the rumor that I heard and we all met up to talk about it. People were emotionally distraught, disgruntled, and didn't understand. We came to the conclusion that we should each attempt to speak to your group, but few of us have had luck in that endeavor, which is the reason I am writing you now.

For the record, everyone in the study group is down to do whatever it takes to become a part of your chapter. We realize that not calling you towards the end of this summer wasn't the best move, but we were blinded by the interpersonal issues that were going on between us and couldn't see what was more important. Everyone in the group is willing to speak with you and the other members of your group because we are all very much interested in becoming a part of your organization.

*In regards to the person who spoke about what was going on to her relative, she is extremely willing to speak to you all about it.

I really hope that we all get a chance to speak with the members of your group in the near future.

Sincerely,

WGW

That same night, at an SH get-together, we wondered if any of the TETs would respond to my letter. When we got tired of talking about that, we reminisced about errands, imitated the TETs, and dissected what we thought had gone wrong in the summer. When things fell quiet, Teresa stood up. "Hey, I was just wondering, do you guys remember how we used to have access to their email accounts during study sessions? How we used to have their passwords?"

"Yea. I remember that," Amber said.

"I wonder if the passwords are still the same. Let's go check."

We followed Teresa into my room, and after trying to remember what the exact order of the letters was, we found ourselves logged into Ivyana's email account.

"Let's go to their chats. No wait, let's just go back to June when all this mess started and see why they're acting so stupid right now. Okay, I found June. I'll just read it out loud because there are way too many of us in here," she laughed.

"Just type our names in the search box," Amber sighed. "I don't want to know about any of the other stuff."

"Okay, good point. I'll type you in first. You're in a couple emails. Whoa, your name is in the subject of this one, let me read this."

From: [Sasha Irons] <███████@tmail.com>
Date: Sun, Jun 22, 2008 at 5:00 PM
Subject: Amber Jackson
To: Ivyana <████████1908@gmail.com>

Ivyana,
Amber Jackson dropped. She sent an email to all the other girls telling them how she hates the Epsilon chapter and how she thinks that all of them are brainwashed. I spoke to my prophytes and my line sisters about this issue and they think that if we're going to put someone in her place we should move now and that we should all agree on the decision. I'm going to send an email to everyone about this now so we can decide what to do.

From: <[Sasha]>
To: <[Epsilon chapter account]>
Sent: Thurs, July 3, 2008
Subject: issue

Vanessa spoke to Amber Jackson a moment ago and she said that Amber is trying to get back on the line. This is SUS! We cannot take her at all. Shelby is still done and Whitney is uncertain because she doesn't care for me. Teresa claims that she doesn't have money, but she is still on, so they say.
So, here's the game plan: answer their phone calls if you please, but do not talk about anything TET related. They have been told that they can continue to call if they want, but it is no longer required. They were also told that they will be notified when it is

time for rush because we will let them know when we put up the flyers. If we have to, we will have to take a split line. They have way too much power right now and are too floppy. We just need to see who truly wants the Epsilon process. We can analyze this issue again later, but for now, and my dean agrees, we have to bring them in as paper.

AMBER: I never sent any of you a letter this summer. As a matter of fact, I never wrote an email saying *anything* about y'all being brainwashed. I only said that to people over the phone.

EVA: Yea, I only remember actual letters from Whitney, Teresa, and Shelby. What's the date on that email Teresa?

TERESA: Sunday, June 22nd.

ME: Wasn't that the week we all agreed that we weren't going to call them?

TERESA: Yea, I think so....Let me read these other ones.

AMBER: Before you even finish reading the other emails, did I *ever* say that I wanted to get back on board this summer?

BROOKE: I don't remember that.

TERESA: Me either.

EVA: Unless it was that time when we were on the chat and you said, "What if someone changes their mind?"

AMBER: But I wasn't referring to myself back then. I was just saying that in a general way.

TERESA: Okay, I'm just going to go back through June and July and read all these other ones. They're out of order though.

From: <[Tanya]>
Date: Fri, July 4, 2008
Subject: Re:
To: <[Epsilon Chapter account]>

SORORS....These girls clearly have no idea that the Epsilon process needs to be treated like the privilege that it is!!!! They want to complain about pledging, quit, and try to get back on??!!!

We should think about letting the girls feel what it's like to be paper on the yard.... let the girls who really want it...know it's everyone or no one...and have them take on the responsibility of getting the MAJORITY if not ALL the girls back on the line...

Epsilon history has shown us that split lines are not a good thing to have in the chapter:

1. There is an inevitable strain between the made sorors and the paper sorors.

2. There is not a high level of sisterly relations because there is always a struggle between the two sides.

3. The ability to take in a complete made line after the split line is IMPOSSIBLE

4. The mentality of "all for one and one for all" disappears and this enables insider snitching....my prophytes...my line sisters...... ALL OF US...worked TOO FUCKIN HARD to bring Epsilon back to what it is now...way too hard for some stupid bitches to think that this is a GAME!... A process in this day and age is not a promise... it is a treat, a luxury, and an HONOR that must be WORKED FOR!!!

From: <[Raven]>
Date: Fri, July 4, 2008
Subject: Re:
To: <[Epsilon Chapter account]>

Good Morning Sorors,

I'm just now seeing these e-mails. ALL contact with these girls should STOP! This is complete and utter chaos!

From: <[Julia]>
To: < [Epsilon chapter account]>
Sent: Fri, July 4, 2008
Subject: Re:

I see all sides and I concur that they have left us with no choice as to bring them in paper and make them work for the process....and with any luck they will. I think the major problem that we face as a chapter that wants to make MADE sorors is that girls are coming into college knowing that they don't have to do anything to become a members because of legacy status. They probably felt that way throughout the entire process. It is dreadful and astonishing that we don't have the six women from Fall 04 who went several times to get that Epsilon process or the seven from Fall 05 who realized there was more to be done for sisterhood despite what others may feel or the nine from Spring 07 who saw no other way to the road to Epsilon. The values that were in all of our minds from these last three lines are unfortunately not in theirs.

I think we should gather our data and see who calls the most and I think we should interview new girls.

From: <[Tanya]>
Date: Sat, Jul 5, 2008
Subject: Telling the prophytes...
To: <[Epsilon Chapter account]>

So...here is what I know...I wasn't around much last semester but this is what I have been told:
1. A legacy named Amber Jackson (who is also the current girlfriend of Ivyana's Ex-Nu Pi boyfriend) has said that Epsilon is corrupt and that we are not "ladies of high standards." She claims that Sasha and Tiffany beat her up in a corner at a party. NOTHING ABOUT HER CLAIM IS TRUE!!
Said that she was sick of running herself "ragged" for the last year and wasn't going to continue to do it any longer. She told her mother (her mother pledged fyi and is the president of a grad chapter in New Jersey) about everything that happened during pre-pledging. She was trying to get the other girls to stick together and not be a part of our chapter or start "changing" things.
2. Amber's Mom thinks that she "pledged and Amber shouldn't have to" and has said that since she is a delegate in the sorority that she thinks that it is her job to turn in any illegal activity. She asked Amber for our grad advisor's name.
3. Other study session girls have been very hesitant about their dedication and plans for chapter memberships (latest # was 5 of the 10)

4. THIS IS THE PROBLEM: Because of our own lack of care EPSILON is in a severe situation in terms of being able to deny things. There's the undeniable document trail:

EMAILS: Misc. emails to Ivyana. Bio/Resume emails, Transcript emails, Summer Assignment emails, etc.

PHONE REPORTS: Numerous Texts & Incoming calls from sorors at all hours of the day and night

PRE PLEDGE ACTIVITIES: spanning 2 semesters: Fall'07-→ Amber Jackson cleaned Ivyana's place in September……. Spring'08-→ Interviews; Private/Remote Group Study Sessions; Various errand running…summer'08→ Summer Assignments; the 10 girls formed a Gmail group. Is there anything else I need to know?

From: <[Persephone]>
Subject: Re: Telling the prophytes...
Date: Sat Jul 5, 2008
To: <[Epsilon Chapter account]>

Thank you, Tanya and Tiffany for telling me everything. Are you telling me that you all were making these girls run errands when they weren't even on line?

If you're going to pre-pledge people, pre- pledge people by having them get to know you. You also had them attending that many study sessions when they weren't on line yet? I really really really hope that you all were not pledging, screaming, intimidating, or threatening those girls. The goal should be for the girls to know you and trust you, not for you to haze them.

Learn from fall 94 and fall 95, you need to have the girls' trust first. Hazing them does not help with that. When it comes to pledging, if you are going to pledge girls, you need to have them get to know you first and get to know them as well. That way, when they're on line and you have to be "mean" they'll know that you're not just doing it to be evil. If they trust you, they'll know that you have their best interests at heart.

From: <[Sasha]>
Date: Sat, July 5, 2008
Subject: Re:

To: <[Ivyana]>

Hey, we still have a few girls that haven't been hesitant at all. Let's throw a few new girls in there and forget the hesitant ones because they are giving warnings, saying that they don't wanna be EPSILON sorors (LOL at these bitches). Some of them are saying that "they have to take us, because we pre pledged" I talked with a few of my LSs last night and this what we're thinking....Do you think we could completely smirk Teresa and Brooke [because they're the tallest and the shortest and they won't be mad and tell on us] and worst case take Amber and Whitney, because of their moms and not make those two....Then we could add maybe 4 new girls and pledge 9 of them and just have two be skaters... We could put AJ and Whitney as #'s 1 and 2 and start the line off at 3, that way they can still wear their numbers and there won't be any discomfort. Amber and Whit are both short and they could go in front. Is this too much to even consider? Or should we just let these girls be paper and let them see how that feels and have them post pledge in the spring? Message me back.

BROOKE: WOW! So, they're just going to SMIRK me and you Teresa?

TERESA: They think I won't be angry? They clearly didn't get to know me well enough last semester.

ME: Wow.

AMBER: My mother is *not* president of a graduate chapter in New Jersey. Where did they get that?

ME: I had reservations because I didn't like Sasha? That wasn't why I had reservations. And why are there exact quotes from Amber's mom?

BROOKE: Why are there exact quotes from anyone at all? I thought part of our agreement this summer was not to tell them anything.

TERESA: I thought Vanessa said that she stopped calling them. Sasha's email is dated for July 3rd. When was our IM chat? I feel like it was *on* or *after* July 2nd.

BROOKE: What does that matter?

TERESA: Vanessa and Amber weren't exactly on the best of terms before the IM convo, and they definitely weren't on good terms after. Amber couldn't have told Vanessa that she was trying to get back on board that day.

AMBER: I *didn't* tell her that I wanted to get back on board.

ME: Is that why Jamie and Vanessa didn't come to Brooke's party? You think the TETs told them to distance themselves from us? I know Mya's sick, but do you think that's why they didn't come tonight?

EVA: I don't know. Wait, go back to our study buddies account so we can compare the dates and stuff.

TERESA: Okay hold on…All the emails are deleted.

AMBER: WHAT?

TERESA: They're deleted. All the ones from the summer are gone. A couple irrelevant ones are still on here though. Let me go back to Ivyana's account. I'll just skim through this next one. It's a new response from today. It's about the letter you sent them, Whitney. Deborah's LS says, "Whitney seems unstable. Maybe someone should talk to her. Actually someone should talk to all of those girls and apologize on behalf of the chapter and let them know that y'all are not in a position to take them right now, and assess the damage from there." Okay, so maybe we're gonna at least get an apology. Oh wait, we're not. A few lines later, Deborah says, "We don't owe these girls anything! We don't need to apologize to them! We need to move on with the few that we have and the new girls. We can't afford to talk to them. It's too much of a risk."

For the rest of the night we read through the emails and it became clear that the rumors were true. They had no remorse about anything I mentioned in my letter or anyone else who pre-pledged. As we continued to read, we realized that Vanessa, Jamie, and Mya had been in contact with the TETs over the past few weeks. Teresa had been right.

I became angry. The emotions that came over me couldn't be expressed by words. I felt betrayed by Vanessa, Jamie, and Mya. I hated the TETs. I wanted to hurt them like they had hurt me. I wanted to beat them up. I wanted them to feel what it felt like to have something in hand and have it ripped away with no explanation. But I couldn't do anything. All I could do was cry. I immediately called my mom. There was no point in being discreet for the Epsilon chapter anymore.

"I'm not going to be a TET, Mommy," I heard myself say after telling her everything over the course of two hours. "I just wanted to say this right now so you won't be waiting for me to call you with the date of the probate or anything."

"I really can't believe that Whit. Those young ladies are *not* my sorors. What's the grad advisor's name?"

"Why?"

"I want to talk to her."

"No."

"Why not?"

"Because it's not necessary. And I don't want you to."

"What are you going to do?"

"I don't know Ma, I don't know."

"What you need to do is email all of them and the grad advisor your interest letter and ask when the rush is."

"That's not going to do anything."

"How do you—"

"I've emailed them already! I've called all of them already! They don't care! They're just going to keep screwing people over because they're going to keep getting away with it."

"Well, I'm sorry," my mom sighed. "Whit, I really—"

"Its nationals' fault, they're so stupid. Did they really think that banning pledging in 1990 was going to work? Did they really think the class of '89 was gonna be like 'Okay, well we can't pledge anybody else because it's illegal now?' Yeah, right. I just…When those girls drowned they should have seen the glitch in the system! They should have done something. They should have stepped back and came up with a new system because they know this three-day process is bull. I can't completely blame Epsilon, but how can they be so *dumb*? I don't get it! What they *heard* about what we were thinking shouldn't matter! How can you replace *seven* people? *Dummmmbbbbbbb*!"

"Calm down, Whit. Calm down."

"I can't! This is unfair! I HATE them!"

"Whit, calm down. Stop getting so riled up. Why don't you try calling them a few more times?"

"And say what?"

"Say how you feel about everything. Maybe they'll reconsider."

"They only care about their chapter. They could care less about how I *feel* right now."

"You never know Whit, try it. Don't do anything irrational or anything out of anger though."

I tried to calm down. I tried not to be mad. I tried to get over it. I told my roommates that I was done being an interest, but I couldn't sleep. I sent the dean an anonymous email from a fake account.

From: <████████gmail.com>
Date: Mon, Sep 8, 2008 at 6:17 AM
Subject: HAZING
To:████████.edu

Dear Dean [Smith]

I am writing this letter to ask you a question. I was formerly interested in joining a sorority at the university [...], and I thought that the rules clearly stated that hazing would not go on. However, I was hazed [...] and I have nothing to show for it--I never got into the organization because I realized how naive and foolish I had been throughout the process, and I voiced my concern to the members of the sorority. They shunned me and refused to accept me for national intake. Although these girls treated me in a horrible manner I do not wish to get them expelled or suspended. If I revealed my identity and brought to the light the concrete evidence that the hazing activities were going on for months, would my academic stay be in jeopardy as well?

Anonymous

From: ████████.edu
Date: Mon, Sep 8, 2008 at 9:00 AM
Subject:RE:HAZING
To: <████████gmail.com>

The dean emailed me her telephone number but I didn't call. I didn't want to talk to her. I didn't want to get them in trouble. Instead, I told myself that I would just have to let go.

I saw Julia and Nicole in the computer lab and they acted as if I didn't exist. I saw Tiffany and Britney in a lecture hall. They both turned away from me. I saw Deborah by the union and she looked straight through me.

I wore violet, green, burgundy, and every color that I could find. I went out to parties. I applied for an overnight position at Rite-Aid and started working within the same week. Yet, every night when I went to sleep, I woke up crying. On the nights that I was at work I was at peace, but when I returned home—home to the place where three SHs lived—I couldn't help but to think about Theta Eta Theta.

A couple of weeks into September, Teresa called me into her room and read out other emails that the TETs sent. I told myself before she read them that I wouldn't get upset. I told myself that I wouldn't react.

First I really really miss you!! I hope you all are doing great! I can't wait to see you all at our 90 year reunion in October! Now I'm probably the last person that you'd expect a long message from but this is really bothering me and I feel really bad... I really wanted to have a fall 08 line but with all that went down this summer, it seems too risky. I have a list of why we should not do this...please read.

1. The Assistance. Although our prophytes have said that they will back us up in whatever we decide to do, they have pretty much stepped away from guiding and providing input due to all the implications and drama attached to the situation thanks to Ms. Amber Jackson. This is a MAJOR issue. I know that we think we can pull in a line by ourselves, but WE CAN'T. Are any of you wondering why they have completely stepped back?! That's scary, ladies...I think there's a reason why they've done so!

2. The interests. So I'm under the impression that in addition to Shelby and Amber not being included, a lot of the other girls are not being considered for intake. I concur that they should not be considered at all, but I feel that by not taking them it will draw major attention to us and what we are doing. If we start the process with new girls I feel that a lot of ppl will be asking questions because LOTS of ppl know who was pre-pledging...This is going to lead to a lot of talking and questions and if the wrong person finds out (i.e. Dean Smith) she might take EPSILON away. (Y'all know that she is already anti- pledging) If we were just not taking ONE girl, this scenario would be feasible. But (minus Amber and Shelby) 3 or 4 more of those jokers!! Amber Jackson's mom knows everything and now that Amber is trying to get back on the line you don't think she's going to get mad and tell on us if we don't take her? In addition to her you have Whitney who also has TETs in her family! You don't think they're gonna get mad?

3. The Process. The most important aspect of the process is timing. If we decide to have a process this fall, we will have exactly eight weeks to get them through. THAT's CRAZY! We

won't have any time for them to be dropped, they won't be ready for preparing their ivies, they won't have much of a hell week, and they'll probably be getting done right before Christmas break! We won't have the cushion time we need for when they get injured and hurt. And we won't have that extra time for if we need to stop if stuff starts getting crazy and people start watching.

This situation is really hurting me ladies. I really think we should bring a line in paper and allow them to post pledge in the spring. We don't have to do intake this fall; sure people are going to ask questions, but I feel like if we start intake now, something bad could happen. ...Epsilon is all that matters so please keep this in mind and weigh all your options before making any drastic decisions.

I couldn't let it go. It was personal.

I started calling the TETs again, hoping that one of them would pick up, just once. They didn't. When I asked Candace what Deborah had said, after she told her that I wasn't going to let them get away with replacing anyone, she informed me that Deborah brushed it off as if it didn't matter.

Fury locked itself around me.

I went through Ivyana's email account one last time. I searched for every email that dealt with fall 2008 and forwarded each one to my old email account. I called nine of the TETs two times each. None of them answered.

I waited for two hours. I had to think through everything one more time.

For almost an entire semester and half of the summer I had spent my time, energy, and money on the Epsilon chapter. I fell back in the summer due to an awakening, never thinking that I would get replaced. I'd been betrayed by people whom I had trusted greatly at one point, and if I stood back in the shadows, not only would Epsilon get over on me, but no more than three SHs and a group of girls who had no idea what they were getting themselves into would become TETs in a matter of weeks.

I had emailed them and I had called them. I had expressed my feelings, exposed my soul, and they had refused to respond. I read through every email again. I called Julia and Deborah one last time. When they didn't answer, I blocked my number and called the dean.

"Hello?"

"Hello, may I speak to Dean Smith please?"

"This is she. May I ask who is calling?"

"I'm the one who sent you the email pertaining to the sorority," I said.

"Oh. Hi, how are you?"

"I'm alright."

"I wanted you to call me because I wanted to make sure I understood where you were coming from. I take it you're remaining anonymous?"

"Yes."

"Okay, that's fine. Could you tell me about your experience with this organization? You don't have to tell me what the sorority's name is at this point. I just want to know what happened."

"Well, I was an interest in the fall of 2007. I basically had to call the members to get to know them, and eat lunch with them every now and then. In the spring semester, I got a call to be at a study session in February and that's when pre-pledging began. For the rest of the semester me and nine other girls spent four to five days a week in study sessions and were pretty much their personal assistants. We bought them food, did their errands, cleaned their rooms and houses, and did whatever else they told us to do. Then, in the summer we had to do assignments and continue calling them at a consistent rate. But after a while, a few other people and I realized that what we were doing was pointless and wrong, and we kind of woke up and didn't want to put up with them for a while. When I got back this fall, I still wanted to be a member, but I found out that I was getting replaced."

"Have you tried contacting any of the members of this sorority?"

"Several times, but none of them have responded."

"To be honest, my job as the dean is to ensure that other young women at the university don't have the same experience that you have had. I know that you might be worried about your reputation, but the only way to—"

"I don't want my name attached to this."

"I understand, but unless there's significant proof that they hazed you and those other girls then there's not much I can do."

"Well, I had access to their email accounts while we were in study session and the password is still the same so I can prove that they knew what they were doing."

"Hmm, I'm not sure about that. I would have to see them first to see if they could be used as evidence."

"Okay. Is there a way I could drop them off sometime this week?"

"Sure, I'll transfer you over to my secretary and she'll give you a time slot okay?"

"Okay, thank you."

The secretary gave me an appointment and took down my fake alias. I went to the computer lab and printed out the emails. I placed them all into a blue folder and tucked it into my purse. I handed that folder to the dean two days later and said, "I really don't want anyone to get suspended or expelled. I really don't."

She promised me that no one would get expelled, but she couldn't promise that the chapter wouldn't receive some type of punishment. When I walked out of her office, I felt lighter.

I didn't tell my roommates. I didn't tell my mother. I acted as if everything was normal and pretended to seem content about not becoming a TET.

Candace, Amber, and I were in the living room going over decoration ideas one afternoon when Teresa called out, "Guys! Guys! Guys! Come in here! I want you to read this email before I send it."

"What email?" I asked.

"I'm sending an email to the dean. It's anonymous though. I just—I don't want to get the chapter snatched or anything, but I want them to know that we're not going to be passive about this situation."

"Okay. I'll read it out loud," Amber sat down in front of Teresa's computer. *"Hello Dean Smith, I am writing this email as a former interest of the Epsilon chapter of Theta Eta Theta Sorority, Incorporated. Before I begin to explain why I am sending you this email, I would like to let you know that TET has always had a major influence on my life and at one point I had hoped that I would be able to impart that influence on someone else.*

Nonetheless, I will not have the opportunity to join the organization at this university. For almost a year I ran errands for members of the sorority—driving them places, cleaning their houses, buying them food, etc.—and it was recently made clear that despite my efforts, I would not be chosen to become a member. Despite all the money I spent, all the hours I spent in numerous study sessions, and all the weeks spent under the mandate of 'social probation', I will be receiving nothing in compensation.

I am writing this email to let you know that I was wronged, and so were countless other females who did the same, less, and in some cases more than I did. I have no desire to get anyone in serious trouble, but I would like to let the members of the sorority know that what they did was wrong. Is there any way I could speak with you privately regarding this matter?

Have a nice day,

Anonymous"

After Amber finished reading the email, I pretended to be genuinely shocked.

"Wow, I can't believe that you actually sent the dean an email! Do you think you'll end up telling on them?" I asked.

"Ummm I don't know. I don't want it to go that far. I just want certain people to get in trouble. But, if it comes down to it, I definitely will."

She, Amber, and Candace continued to discuss the email. I pressed my back against the wall, refusing to mention the fact that I had already met with the dean, that I had already shown her the emails, and that despite the nonchalant demeanor I had exuded for the past few days, I was breaking down inside.

Days later, I went to the dean's office again. The receptionist told me to wait inside a small side room, and the dean came in and closed the door.

"I read all of the emails that you gave to me," she said. "But they can't be used. As a matter of fact, I can't do anything about them."

"Why not?"

"Because, although they're incriminating evidence, the way you obtained them was unethical. I know that they gave you the password, but they gave you that password for a *specific* purpose, and you used it for another purpose. So, legally you have nothing. And since I'm the dean for *all* students, it would be very unfair for me to suppress any student's legal rights, especially since the emails were from their *personal* email accounts."

"Well—"

"The only way that you can get justice is if you come forward, and if you get someone else to come forward with you. I'm telling you now that coming forward alone would be very difficult, because if there were ten girls and only one came forward, it would look a bit unbelievable. However, if you had two or more, and you all had the same story then it would be more plausible. Think about it though. I know you don't want to get anyone in trouble, but consider everything you went through, and what you got in return. I'll be in my office until the evening for most of this week, so if you want to come back and talk to me feel free, okay?"

"Okay."

"I have to go to a meeting now. I'll talk to you later."

She left, and I stayed in the room for what felt like an hour. I didn't want to come forward. I didn't even want to think about coming forward. I was scared of what people would think of me if I went against Epsilon. I feared being socially out-casted. I thought that no one would talk to me ever again and that my last years of college would be miserable.

Later that night I went to Tiara's apartment to contemplate things. I asked, "If you were me, what would you do?"

"Well, I never would have done all of that in the first place," she said. "So, I really don't know. I will say that what they're planning to do is evil—to just erase y'all is ridiculous. But in the end, everything is up to you. It's *your* decision."

I started crying. "I'm so tired of thinking about this stuff. I thought that if I started getting involved in other stuff TET would just slip my mind, but it won't. I think about it even more. I can't imagine going to a fall 08' TET probate that's not mine. That wouldn't be fair. And I tried talking to them. I even broke down and called four of them today, *twice*! And there was still no answer."

"Have you weighed the pros and cons of both sides? Like the benefits of not telling on them versus the benefits of telling on them?"

"Yea."

"And?"

"There's more of a reason to tell on them," I dried my eyes.

"What are the reasons?"

"Well, for one, if I let them get away with something so reckless, that would solidify their belief that they're invincible. Two, I never said, 'I'm not interested anymore.' Other people were running back to them telling them how they thought I felt. And even after I sent all of the TETs a long email in my own words, they wouldn't even give me a chance. Third, I spent a lot of time, energy, and money on them thinking that I would be a TET at the end of the fall. I was discreet, I completed errands, and they were supposed to make me a TET—paper, made, plastic, whatever. But now that they're not, I have no reason to hold up my end of the deal. The answer's clear, I'm just—"

"Scared?"

"Yea."

"I feel you son, but I don't think you're really scared of telling on them. I think you would do that in a heartbeat. I think you're more scared of what people would think."

"I think that's it too."

"Well, who cares what people think? They didn't go through what you went through and I can guarantee you that if they did, they would be having this same conversation with one of their best friends. People's thoughts aren't going to affect you getting a degree or being successful. They're just going to talk about you behind closed doors. That's it. That's all they're going to do, because they're way too scared to say what they're thinking to your face."

"I guess I—"

"Seriously, Whitney, you've got to stop caring about people who don't care about you. If people get mad and act funny towards you if you tell on the TETs then they weren't your real friends in the first place and you don't need them in your life. If you do it, I'll be there afterwards, Alexis will be there afterwards, Renee and Candace will be there, and so will everybody else that knows the real you."

"You're right. I just have to think about it some more."

I needed a second opinion. I needed to talk to my mother. When I did, she expressed similar sentiments to what Tiara had said.

"Well, I never thought that you would take action so fast. I just wish there was a way to salvage the chapter," she sighed. "And I still think that I should have ten new sorors this fall. Are you sure that you don't want to talk to the grad advisor instead of going through the school?"

"I don't trust their grad advisor. She probably knows what goes on. She would just try to cover it up."

"You sure? Maybe I could—"

"Ma, please don't try to get in contact with her. I really don't want you to do that. Please don't."

"Okay, I won't."

"The dean wants to speak to you though. Would you be willing to speak with her?"

"Sure, have her call me on one of my off days. One thing though, if you came forward against the chapter would you be the only one?"

"I don't know. The dean told me that it would be better if I had more people with me."

"Yes, that would be very smart. She still doesn't know your real name right?"

"Right."

"And if you came forward, could you still be a TET?"

"I don't know."

"Well, when I speak to her I'll be sure to ask about that. I am so sorry all this stuff happened. I was really looking forward to you becoming my little soror."

When my mom spoke to the dean, it was over a forty minute conference call with me. The dean explained that she had no control over TET intake procedures. She felt that the ten SHs should be initiated, but she could only control whether or not the chapter was active on campus. She asked my mom questions about her undergrad experience with TET and was stunned that my mom's process was so different. There was more that was said between my mom and the dean, but all I could hear was a small voice in my head saying, "You're going to have to go forward to make this right."

I read over my journal entries. I wrote down list after list of pros and cons. I dreamt scenario after scenario about "what if I told," and "what if I didn't tell." I called Tiara and Alexis five to six times a day proposing hypothetical situations. Yet, at the end of every conversation, at the end of every list, and at the end of every dream, the solution was the same.

I decided that I would go forward, but I would need help.

One afternoon, I asked Amber to walk with me to a lecture building. I told her that I had something to get off my chest. After twenty minutes of small talk, I broke down. I told her everything. I told her that I hadn't been able to get TET off my mind. I told her that I had been crying for days, that I couldn't let the Epsilon chapter get away with what they did, and that I had gone to the dean and shown her the emails.

She sighed. "Wow. I agree with your decision. Like, we're not dispensable, and we all proved our loyalty last semester by doing all of those errands. They could have at least made us paper, which is what I want anyway."

"Really?"

"Yes. I'm so far removed from hazing now. The Epsilon chapter is so backwards, and I'm mad that it took me so long to realize it. Why would I join an organization that emphasizes scholarship and service, but when I go on line I risk losing my scholarship? And when I get in, the chapter doesn't do any community service? Why? So I can walk around feeling like I accomplished something by getting beat? Or so I can get respect from people I don't even know or care about? I respect myself already. I don't need validation from anyone else."

"I feel you. I'm just hurt that they wouldn't even hear us out. Where is the *logic*? On top of that, I just don't understand how someone can be that wrapped up in the process. That's all they talked about, that's all they were. And if someone goes through months of pre-pledging and has a change of heart, you can't just act like those months never happened, and you definitely can't listen to assumptions. You should *ask* all of the people who pre-pledged how they feel."

"Yea. When I look back and think about it, I realize that I never got the chance to tell them on my own. It was done for me by someone else and most of the things that were said about me weren't even true. What happens when you come forward?"

"Well, I told you everything because I was hoping that you would come forward with me. The dean said that if it was just one person all the sorority has to do is deny it, because it'll seem like I'm just quoting hearsay. But if there are two or more people, it'll be more believable, and it'll be harder for them to deny anything."

"I'll have to think about this. I'm on your side though. Just let me talk to my dad about it first."

The next morning, Amber came into my room and said, "I'll come forward with you, but my dad told me not to give my real name until I'm completely sure about what could possibly happen."

"Okay cool. Do you think we should ask Teresa?" I asked.

"Yea, I think she would come forward with us. What about Candace?"

"She's not going to come forward."

"You don't think so?"

"I *know* so. That's just not her. I think we could talk to the dean and gage what we want to do, but not say anything until something is set in stone you know?"

"Okay. That makes sense."

She and I explained everything to Teresa later that afternoon. When we were done telling the story, we settled on the upcoming Wednesday to meet with the dean. We spent the rest of the night wondering what would happen.

Wednesday, September 24, 2008, the three of us found ourselves in the student judicial affairs conference room. There were two other people in the room, a man and a woman, and we filled the gaps of silence with football talk until the dean entered the room.

DEAN: (shutting the door) Just so you all know, hazing is a crime. It is illegal in the state of Pennsylvania, and depending on the severity, the criminals can be sent to jail or fined. This is serious and we're going to take *serious* action. Do you want to get the police involved?

ME: No.

AMBER: No that's okay.

TERESA: No.

DEAN: Well, just in case you didn't know the other two people in the room, the woman sitting in front of the coffee table is the conduct officer, Ms. Jones, and the gentleman at the end of the table is the director of Greek Affairs, Kenneth Ferguson.

It felt surreal. I couldn't believe I was sitting across from the dean, about to possibly expose the sorority, about to give up my chances of ever becoming a TET in college. I tried not to think about the consequences. I tried to focus on telling the truth.

MS. JONES: (tapping her legal pad with her pen) Okay ladies, what are your names?

AMBER: We don't want to give our real names yet. We want to go through everything first and make sure we're doing the right thing. I'm Debbie for now.

TERESA: I'm Bobby.

ME: Elaine.

MS. JONES: Alright.

DEAN: I've somewhat spoken to Elaine before, but I want to get the story straight. What happened?

AMBER: Well, I personally have been doing things for members of the sorority since the end of my freshman year. I had to clean one member's house, buy her coffee, and take her out to lunch on several occasions. For other members I took them out to lunch a lot.

DEAN: When you say, "take them out" what do you mean?

AMBER: Well, I had to pay for it most of the time unless they had a meal plan.

DEAN: Oh, okay.

AMBER: I did that for a while, and then one day I got an interview, and a few days later I got a call to be at a study session on the weekend.

MR. FERGUSON: Study session?

AMBER: Yea, it meant that for the rest of the semester me and nine other girls had to be in a room for hours and get yelled at when they chose to show up, and during the day we would run errands whenever they called us.

MR. FERGUSON: Where were these study sessions?

AMBER: On some days they were in the nursing hall and on some days they were in one of the engineering halls.

MR. FERGUSON: *Set* on school property?

DEAN: What's "set"?

MR. FERGUSON: Back in my day, "set" and "study session" were the same thing. It's pretty much a hazing session where you get beat.

AMBER: They never beat us in study session though. They just yelled.

TERESA: And threw stuff occasionally.

DEAN: Alright, go on.

AMBER: Well, we were in study sessions ever since February of last semester up until the weekend before finals week, but we were still running errands after that. This summer we still had to call the members and turn in summer assignments, but in the middle of the summer I realized that everything didn't make sense and things kind of fell apart from there. They didn't pick us to do intake this fall.

DEAN: But how do you know they didn't accept you for intake? Did you go to rush and get rejected?

TERESA: Nope, we never went to rush. Even if there was a rush, the Epsilon chapter only makes it known to the people that they want to know about it. We had access to their emails and saw that out of the ten people that pre-pledged last semester, they were only going to take three.

MR. FERGUSON: Wow, so wait. How much, like a general idea, how much money do you each think you spent on them?

ME: About eight hundred dollars.

AMBER: Well, including everything since the end of my freshman year, including dining dollars and real money I'd say at least a thousand.

TERESA: Yea, I was doing stuff before pre-pledging too so at least a thousand, and most of it was on gas.

DEAN: Gas for what?

TERESA: I drove the TETs around, and when our group had to go buy stuff to make gifts for them or go to a specific store or restaurant, I would use my car.

DEAN: That's wild, I can't imagine. One thing I can't understand is why they would only pick three people out of ten after they've hazed and abused you all for that long. That doesn't make any sense.

TERESA: It doesn't at all, but a few other girls from our study group had been going back and telling them how we each felt about the process so I guess they felt that they couldn't trust us. I don't care about that. I just think it's stupid that they wouldn't even hear what we had to say because it's not like we didn't try to contact them for almost a month to talk about things.

DEAN: That process or pledging stuff doesn't make any sense to me. Why does someone have to beat and tear you down to be your sister? When I was in school, pledging was out in the open and girls were getting thrown down the steps and getting cursed out on the yard, just out in the open for everyone to see. I liked the sisterhood part and the community service aspects, but I could never convince myself to pay, first of all, to give someone hundreds of dollars of *my* money, so they could put their hands on me and make me feel like I was their sister. No ma'am. Did any of them ever put their hands on you three?

AMBER: Yes. There was one time that I was at a Nu Alpha Pi party with my boyfriend who is a member of that fraternity, and two members, Sasha Irons and Tiffany Stringer, pulled me into a corner and pulled my hair, grabbed at my face, and talked down to me.

TERESA: For me, at that same party, Tiffany pushed me into the wall when she was drunk because she thought I was about to get a drink from the bar. Then another time at study session, this member named Deborah threw stuff at me.

ME: They never touched me.

MS. JONES: Could you ladies give me the names of all the sorority members?

AMBER: Which ones?

MS. JONES: All the ones you ever had contact with.

TERESA: So Spring '07, Fall '05, and Fall '04?

MS. JONES: (clicked her pen) Sure.

TERESA: Okay. Spring '07.

ME, AMBER, TERESA: *Kamille Jackson, Sasha Irons, Latoya Riley, Julia Benson, Cari Jones, Britney Lynn, Nicole Ballard, Regina Addison and Tiffany Stringer.*

TERESA: Fall '05.

ME, AMBER, TERESA: *Riana Lewis, Arizona Hilton, Felicia Cross, Deborah Parsons, Mila Thomas, Ivyana Tate, and Amara Van.*

TERESA: Fall '04.

ME, AMBER, TERESA: *Tanya Gaines, Tamera Clarke, Selena Lewis, Raven Black, Cassandra Turner, and Hannah York.*

DEAN: Why do you know all of that?

TERESA: Because we had to memorize it. If you're interested in knowing their parents' names, birthdays, or very interesting facts about each of them, we can give you those too.

MR. FERGUSON: (laughing) Are y'all sure y'all weren't pledging?

DEAN: (laughing) No, you don't have to give us all of that.

MS. JONES: Okay. Now that I have all of their names, I need to know which ones had direct contact with you. I need to know the ones that were present at the study sessions. I'm assuming all of Spring 07?

AMBER: Yes.

MS. JONES: Are all of them currently enrolled?

AMBER: No. Sasha Irons isn't and Latoya graduated.

MS. JONES: What about the others?

AMBER: Well it was just Ivyana, Deborah, and Felicia.

MS. JONES: Is that it?

AMBER: Yes.

TERESA: Are they getting punished individually?

DEAN: No. We are going to pursue the chapter as a whole, but for the people who aren't currently enrolled we are going to PNG them.

TERESA: Um, PNG?

DEAN: It means persona non gratis, and it means that they are no longer welcome on our campus or in any of our facilities. If they're seen on our campus, all you have to do is call the campus police and they will be arrested and charged with trespassing.

TERESA: Oh okay, sounds fair.

DEAN: Back to this issue of pre-pledging though. I want to make sure I was hearing this right. Since February of 2008, you all spent money and time on these young ladies and in the summer, which was *months* later, certain people saw the light so to speak, and because you did, or because they *heard* that you did, they decided not to take seven out of the ten of y'all?

TERESA: Yea, that's it. It sounds crazier and crazier every time I hear it.

MS. JONES: It's up to you ladies if you want to come forward on this situation or not, but we can only go through the judicial process if you give your real names.

TERESA: Can I say something real quick?

DEAN: Go ahead.

TERESA: Wait, I forgot. Come back to me.

DEAN: Well—

TERESA: Wait, I remember now. To be honest, if I come forward I want something to happen. I don't need them to be running around campus throwing up their middle fingers at us (alternating her pumping fists into the air) like "nana—nana—na!"

Silence.

DEAN: Okay...Based on what I'm hearing the ladies of this chapter think you're expendable. I find it hard to believe that they were going to take all ten of you ladies anyway because that would mean that there would be a lot of TETs on campus. They like *small* groups, they like feeling elite. I might be wrong, but I doubt that all ten of you were going to make the final cut anyway.

AMBER: I never thought about that. What would happen if we were to come forward with our real names?

MS. JONES: Well first, we would notify the sorority that charges have been brought against them for violating university policy. Then I'll set up a meeting with them and go over the charges. They'll have the option of admitting to the charges and accepting punishment or going to a hearing.

DEAN: And in most cases, people opt to go to the hearing.

MS. JONES: Exactly. At that point, you and the sorority will be assigned separate advocates, who are like lawyers, and you will meet to decide how you will present your case. Then, there will be a hearing and a jury panel will listen and decide which side wins.

ME: When would they find out who brought the charges against them?

MS. JONES: If you came forward and they opted to go to a hearing, they would find out your names whenever they met with their advocate. The sorority would then be on temporary interim suspension, which means that they will have to cancel all events until the verdict of the hearing.

ME: Wait. When you say "temporary suspension" does that go for canceling their reunion too?

MS. JONES: Yes.

ME: But what happens if they just admit to the charges and bypass the hearing?

DEAN: In situations like this, I'm telling you that they are definitely going to go to a hearing. They're not going to say "Yea, we did it, we're guilty." They're going to have a defense.

ME: But what if a few people were a bit more extreme than the others? There's no way that they could be tried individually and not as a chapter?

MS. JONES: I'm afraid not.

TERESA: They were all knowingly present as far as I'm concerned.

DEAN: That's how I see it. Personally, if it was me, and I did all the things that you all did, I would come forward. I know you have the rest of your college careers to think about but let me put this in perspective for you. The black community here is relatively small. If the entire black community out casted you, which I *severely* doubt, there would still be twenty thousand students here that you could network with. Let's just be honest for a few seconds. There aren't that many black Greeks here. What are there, forty? Fifty? They raise a few thousand dollars here or there, they walk around in their small, elite circles and they do the minimum. White Greeks? It's a completely different story. They're raising tens of thousands of dollars, and while black Greeks are throwing mixers and get-togethers, white Greeks are hosting *cotillions*! While the Greek systems are completely different, that just goes to show you where the importance is placed.

TERESA: We understand. Could the three of us talk about our decision alone for a moment?

DEAN: That's fine. We'll be in my office. Come and get us when you make your decision.

The dean, Mr. Ferguson, and Ms. Jones left the room.

TERESA: Okay. Now that they're gone, how do y'all feel about everything? I wanted them to leave so this can be *our* decision and they're not in our ears pushin' us to do this. Do y'all want to come forward?

ME: I mean, I do and I don't. It's just that Regina, Cari, Kamille, Nicole, Britney, and even Latoya weren't as bad as everyone else. They asked us to do stuff here or there, but they were never as *extra* as Ivyana and Sasha, the two people who aren't even *active*.

TERESA: They were all *knowingly present* though—they're just as guilty as Sasha, Ivyana, Julia, Deborah, and Tiffany.

ME: I know that. I'm just saying—

TERESA: No, I'm just saying. I didn't do all of that stuff for *nothing*! Well, clearly I did, but that's not that point! The point is, they knew that what everyone else was doing was wrong. And then, they *all* voted to *not* put us on line. They're not thinking about you right now, so why are you thinking about them? On top of that, they *all* got your long email and they *all* decided not to respond.

AMBER: It's just not right what they did. They really think they're invincible. Plus, they were too proud to give us a simple apology.

They couldn't even *apologize* because they don't think they did anything wrong.

ME: I know all that, and I completely agree. It's their chapter's ninety year reunion though. That's huge. *Ninety* years.

TERESA: So! That aint got shit to do with any of us, and if they really cared about their reunion *or* their chapter they would have talked to us. We sent them emails, we called, we did everything and they didn't even *respond*!

ME: I really don't understand why they didn't pick up at least one of our calls. They were really going to pledge new people, have a probate, and act like we never existed.

AMBER: Exactly! Who does that? I could see if we hadn't spent any money and were just *studying* in study sessions. Then we wouldn't have the grounds to say much of anything. But pre-pledging for months without being given the chance to get in? That's unacceptable.

TERESA: My thing is, if I put my name out there something *better* happen y'all. This is not a game. If we go to this school trial and lose, I'm taking them to real court. I have lawyers in my family, who happen to be TETs as well, and I'm sure they'd be happy to help me out.

ME: Really though? If we go to trial here, they're definitely going to lose. You wouldn't need to take them to real court.

AMBER: You don't know that. They've got Ivyana on their side and you know she can come up with some pretty exaggerated stories. Remember how she got Deborah to make use of that pee cup for her drug test?

ME: (sighing) True. I just don't want them to have to cancel their ninety year reunion or get the people who really didn't do anything in trouble. But then again, y'all are right about the knowingly present stuff and the fact that they *all* don't care.

TERESA: Okay, good. I just don't want any of the other Greeks to get in trouble or be under scrutiny because of this.

AMBER: The other Greeks here would never pull this. I don't think they have anything to worry about. I'm down.

ME: Me too.

TERESA: Alright. I'm gonna get the dean.

Teresa left the room. Amber and I sat in silence. I couldn't believe that I was sitting in a conference room about to give my name and appear in a hearing against the Epsilon chapter. I wanted to cry, but I kept my composure. I kept thinking, "I did all I could do to prevent this. I did all I could do."
The dean and Ms. Jones came into the room and sat down. Teresa shut the door.

MS. JONES: So, what have you ladies decided to do?

AMBER: (looking at Teresa and me) I'll come forward, but I'm not coming forward alone.

TERESA: I'm Teresa Lane.

AMBER: I'm Amber Jackson.

ME: I'm Whitney Gracia Williams.

Ms. Jones wrote down our names and repeated what would happen if Epsilon opted to go to a hearing. The dean assured us that we were doing the right thing and that our futures wouldn't be determined by whether we joined a sorority or not.

Days later, I sat in Candace's room and told her what the three of us had done. After I finished explaining, she sighed. "I tell you everything and you waited a week to tell me this?"

"It happened four days ago, and I didn't know *how* to tell you. I figured you wouldn't come forward I—"

"You were right, but you still could have told me."

"I'm sorry."

"So, when I came in the apartment the other day and you three were sitting in the living room and I said, 'Aww I missed family time' y'all were talking about the trial and stuff?"

"Yea."

"That hurts Whitney. I'm not gonna lie. I see where y'all are coming from, I honestly do. I just wish that of all people *you* would have told me."

"Well, I apologize again, but I did what I thought was best at the time."

Amber overheard us talking from the hallway and walked into Candace's room. "I thought we were all going to tell her together?"

"I just had to...I'm sorry I couldn't wait," I looked down at the floor.

Amber and Candace became upset with me. I became frustrated.

Candace left the apartment for a while and I sat in my room writing in my journal. The trial hadn't even begun and I felt as if I was already being tried.

Subject:	Hearing
From:	"[Ms. Jones]" <████████████.edu>
Date:	Wed, October 1, 2008 4:00 pm
To:	"[Teresa]" <███████.edu> (more)
Priority:	Normal
Options:	View Full Header	View Printable Version

```
Hello Ladies,

Just   an   update.   The   hearing   is   tentatively
scheduled for Friday, October 17 at 1:00. Sometime
next week, an Advocate from my office will contact
you to discuss the information you forwarded and
answer any questions you may have.

Best regards,
[Ms. Jones]

Assistant to the Dean
Division of Student Affairs
```

Subject:	Judicial Affairs--Important
From:	"[Reed]" <███████.edu>
Date:	Thu, October 2, 2008 4:31 pm
To:	"Williams, Whitney G" <wgw█████.edu>
Priority:	Normal
Options:	View Full Header	View Printable Version

Whitney,
I will be representing the University in the
upcoming hearing against [TET] sorority on 10/17/08
at 1:30 PM.
    Thank you for coming forward with your complaint
and for your willingness to cooperate. It is my job
to make sure your complaints are properly heard and
that the University is adequately represented.
    I am not a lawyer, but function like one in the
hearings. I need to meet with you as soon as
possible to discuss this case. Please call our
office manager at ███████████ to schedule a
meeting with me.
    If you have any questions for me, feel free to
reply to this email, but please do
not discuss any facts of the case in email form.

Thank you.
[Reed]
Advocate
Office of Judicial Affairs

Subject:	RE: Judicial Affairs--Important
From:	"[Reed]" <███████████.edu>
Date:	Mon, October 6, 2008 11:15 am
To:	"Williams, Whitney G" <wgw█████.edu>
Priority:	Normal
Options:	View Full Header	View Printable Version

Hi Whitney,

I talked to [the secretary] and know that we have a
meeting planned next week. In the meantime, would
it be possible for you to write out a description
of the events in your own words and get that to me
this week?

I'd prefer that you do it on paper, and not email,
as the email could get misdirected. Thanks.

[Reed]
Judicial Affairs Advocate.

Amber, Teresa, and I met with Reed and he suggested that we print
our phone records, text message records, emails, and anything else
that would prove our story was true.

It was real. There was no turning back. I really wasn't going to be a TET in undergrad. My opportunity would be gone forever as soon as I took the stand in a couple of weeks.

The TETs had yet to meet with their advocate and had no idea who filed the complaint. Rumors around campus were all pointing to Amber Jackson.

One night, I was studying in a small room in one of the lecture halls. It was a room tucked away in a corner and hidden behind two pillars. I had been studying for a few hours when the door opened and Mya walked in.

ME: Hi Mya.

MYA: Hi Whitney. How are you?

ME: I'm alright. How are you?

MYA: I'm…okay.

ME: Do you have a test soon?

MYA: Yea, something like that. I have to finish reading this book by the end of the night so—I didn't know you were in here. I'll go to another room.

ME: Wait. Do you have a few minutes?

MYA: Sure.

ME: Well, it'll actually take more than a few minutes. I have something to tell you.

She took a seat across the table. I sighed and closed my folder. I told her how I felt about everything that happened in the summer, how I found out that I was getting replaced, and how everything led up to Teresa, Amber, and I deciding to go forward. When I got done telling the story, her face turned red.

MYA: I—I don't even know what to say. What y'all did was not cool, Whitney.

ME: I—

MYA: I don't even know what to say. How could y'all? How could *you*? Why didn't you tell me earlier?

ME: I tried telling you before, but you ignored me at the last peer leader session so I didn't see a point in reaching out to you then.

MYA: I did speak to you!

ME: Mya, no you didn't. You may have thought you did, but you didn't. That's neither here nor there though. Now you know.

MYA: I just…Were you that angry?

ME: Damn real, I was ANGRY! What did you EXPECT? You wanted me to just let it go? I can't! I couldn't! I wanted it just as bad as you did!

MYA: So you take it away from *everyone*?

ME: No. You, Vanessa, and Jamie took it away by telling them what we were saying behind our backs this summer.

MYA: They asked! What were we supposed to do? They thought y'all we're done!

ME: You should've asked ME what to tell them or said, "I don't know," instead of selling me out when you weren't even sure what I was thinking—and I'm talking about *Vanessa* and Jamie more so than you.

MYA: Don't say Vanessa's name like that please.

ME: I'll say her name how I want. She sold me and everyone else out!

MYA: We all went through last semester *together*—

ME: Exactly! So why is it okay for just *three* people to continue?

MYA: There was just no communication between us. All of a sudden I hear that they're suspended? Why didn't y'all tell us?

ME: First off, they're only temporarily suspended. We haven't gone to trial yet. Second off, why didn't you tell us that we were getting replaced? You really thought we wouldn't care?

MYA: I didn't know that I had been picked!

ME: I just find that hard to believe. All three of y'all gradually stopped talking to us.

MYA: I really didn't know! They didn't tell me anything!

ME: Okay, fine but that doesn't change anything—and I'm sorry, but I just can't believe that you knew nothing. If *you* didn't, Vanessa and Jamie had some kind of idea.

MYA: Whitney, what are you getting out of this? Did you think about anyone else?

ME: Did you think about me?

MYA: I never thought that—

ME: You never thought what? It makes no sense, Mya! Replacing seven people? *Seven* people! And besides that, three of the people that they treated the *worst* are getting replaced? You didn't think we would get mad? You honestly thought we were going to show up to a TET probate that wasn't ours?

MYA: That's not the issue. All of a sudden book-club is canceled and the TETs don't know who to trust! Julia wouldn't even look me in the eye yesterday! This is all because of y'all and because y'all didn't get picked!

ME: No offense Mya, but the only reason you feel the way you do right now is because you're going to possibly feel what it's like to not get something you worked hard for, which is the exact same feeling I've had for the past month.

MYA: I'm not trying to be dramatic or anything, but I feel like…I feel like you stole my dream.

ME: Well then, Vanessa stole my dream.

MYA: I just don't understand. *Why?*

ME: I'm still willing to talk to them. I'll drop the charges if they just talk to me. I don't know about the other two. Regardless of what happened this summer, we still put in work and we should still be compensated at the end of the day. They could have at least made us paper.

MYA: There were trust issues! I didn't make the decision not to pick y'all! This isn't my—

ME: Trust issues? Okay Mya. I work at Rite Aid. If my manager comes to me at the end of my shift and says, "I don't trust you working on the cash register anymore," does that mean that I'm not gonna get a check for those hours I just worked?

MYA: I have to go.

She gathered her things and went to the door. She opened it and looked back at me. "If I see you out on the street and I don't look happy to see you—"

"If you don't want to be my friend that's fine, Mya."

XXV. Forward

It was October 17, 2008, and it was the second time that the day after my birthday revolved around TET. A year ago to that day, I was meeting with Deborah, apologizing for sending her the wrong text, and expressing my interest in Theta Eta Theta.

I was groggy and drained. I had slept for three hours the night before, tossing and turning, thinking about what was going to unfold. I took my time getting ready and tried my best to hold it all together. I flipped to the page in my journal where I had written down my reasons for going forward and read them over and over.

I arrived to the hearing late. When I stepped off the elevator, a group of Chi Beta Omicrons were sitting in chairs. They stared at me for a few seconds, and instead of rolling my eyes, I murmured "Hey," and made my way to Reed's office. Teresa, Amber and her parents, and Reed were standing around the desk.

"You're late. Ms. Jones thought you were backing out," Amber said.

I ignored her comment and smiled. I greeted her parents and took a seat while Reed closed the door.

"Now that you're all here I just want to go through this again. I'm going to call you in individually and ask questions. Then, Michelle is going to cross-examine you. If the jury panel has questions they'll be able to ask you afterwards. Are you all okay? You ready?"

I probably said, "Yes, I am," but I remember thinking, "I just want to go home."

"Well, I think you're ready," Reed took a swig of water. "Let's all go in for the briefing."

The hearing room was small. There was a long rectangular table towards the front and two smaller tables towards the back of the room: one for the TET's advocate and representative, and one for Reed and Amber's mom. Ms. Jones was sitting at the end of the long table and three panel members sat to her right, facing us.

The TETs were dressed in black suits with varying green and violet button up shirts. Their advisor stood alongside them, seeming calm and unworried.

"We are here today for the case of the University versus the Epsilon chapter of Theta Eta Theta Sorority, Incorporated on the count of violating the student code of conduct," Ms. Jones announced. "The witnesses will be questioned separately and the defending advocate will be able to cross-examine each of the testimonies. Each question is to be answered verbally and as truthfully as possible to ensure a fair verdict. The three panel judges sitting before you are members of the university's faculty with the exception of one student who is a student conduct officer. Does anyone in the room have a problem or feel that there is a conflict of interest with any of the members who are currently sitting on the panel?"

There was silence. Ms. Jones continued, "The time is 1:20 and this will be noted in the records. Is the representative for the complainant ready to begin?"

"Yes, I am," Reed said.

"Is the representative for the accused ready to begin?"

"Yes, I am," Michelle answered.

"I am going to ask that every person minus the panel judges and myself excuse themselves from the room. You will be called back in shortly."

We returned to our separate rooms and waited. Amber left the room to testify first.

"We better win this trial," Teresa said to Mr. Jackson.

"I'm sure you ladies will. They're handling of the situation was just wrong," he said.

"I don't understand their *brains*. We tried calling them. We even tried emailing them, but since they were too big to apologize or talk to anybody we had to come here and do this."

"Yea, it's really sad."

I eventually joined their conversation and we discussed our future plans and what we wanted to do for a living after college. After an hour passed, Amber walked into the office smiling.

"Reed was a beast," she said. "He asked really good questions."

"What about their lawyer?" her dad asked.

"She asked good questions too, but since they lied to her in the first place, she didn't really have anything to go off of."

"What do you mean?"

"Well, Reed brought up the phone records and started asking me about them and Michelle really couldn't find anything to say. She was swole!" she laughed.

"What else did he ask?"

"He asked about everything. He asked me what my GPA was before study sessions began, which showed that I was smart to begin with and didn't need any type of tutoring. And then he went into how long I had been an interest, which was a crazy explanation in itself."

While Teresa was testifying, I went to the post office to pick up a package my mother had sent me for my birthday. I considered walking around the park, not returning to the hearing, but there was no point in backing out.

When I returned, Teresa, Amber, and Amber's dad were sitting in Reed's office.

"I want their letters taken," Teresa said.

"Me too," Amber sighed. "They don't deserve them."

"I think we're doing enough already. I don't think we need to do that," said Amber's dad.

"I agree," I nodded my head. "I think this is enough."

"Whitney, we're ready," Reed popped in and motioned for me to follow him. I took my seat at the front of the hearing room, and Reed closed the door and sat down.

"State your name and classification for the record please," Ms. Jones announced.

"Whitney Williams. Junior."

"Thank you, questioning may begin."

Reed stood up. "Ms. Williams, when did you first begin to show interest in the Epsilon chapter of Theta Eta Theta?"

"The spring of 2006."

Tiffany let out an exasperated sigh.

"Excuse me, I meant the spring of 2007."

"How did you show your interest in the spring?" he asked.

"I just went to a few of their events."

"Did you have to call anyone or buy anything for anyone?"

"Not at that point, no."

"Did you continue to show interest in the fall of 2007?"

"Yes."

"And how did you show your interest then?"

"I went to their events, signed their attendance book, went out with them to lunch, and called them on the phone."

"Why did you call them?"

"To get to know them better."

"I see. Were their phone numbers listed publicly in the student directory?"

"No."

"Did you get them off of Face book?"

"No."

"MySpace?"

"No."

"Then, how did you get their numbers? Did they just give them to you when you came to their events?"

"No. If I saw them out on the street, I would ask them, but I had to stalk a couple of them to get their numbers."

"I see. What did you talk to them about?"

"General stuff like majors, our hobbies, and what I knew about the pledge process."

"How did you transition from being someone who called all the time to ending up here today?"

"Well, I got a call in February for an interview. The next day I got a call to be at a study session on February 3rd, 2008, and that's when pre-pledging started."

"Study session? Pre-pledging? Permission to approach the witness?"

Ms. Jones nodded her head, and Reed walked towards me and handed me a sheet of paper.

"Could you read the yellow highlighted section of this document?"

"Candidates that are interested in Theta Eta Theta Sorority should not partake in any activities that are not outlined in the official initiation process. This conduct includes, but is not limited to study sessions or any form of illegal pledging."

"Did the sorority members ever share these rules with you at the rush ceremony?"

"I never attended a rush ceremony."

"You never signed anything at an official sorority sponsored rush saying that you were aware and would follow these rules?"

"No."

"Thank you," he took the paper from me and took a few steps back. "What was your GPA before these study sessions began?"

"A 3.0."

"Did you ever receive any academic help from the sorority members during these *study sessions*?"

"No."

"None of them helped you with your schoolwork?"

"No."

"What actually went on during these study sessions?"

"Well, it depended. Sometimes they would come in and yell at us, quiz us on information, and then sometimes they didn't and we would study."

"How often were these study sessions and what time did they begin and end?"

"At first it was four times a week, but eventually it was increased to five. They started at nine and on the weekdays we could leave at midnight, but on the weekends we weren't allowed to leave until they gave us permission."

"Are these study sessions the only thing that went on during the spring semester?"

"No. During the day we had to run errands."

"What kind of errands?"

"Like buying them food, buying gifts here or there, cleaning their houses, printing off their papers, cooking things, using safe rider passes on them, things like that."

"How much money would you say you spent last semester?"

"About $800."

"$800? Are you sure?"

"Yes, I kept most of the receipts. About $400-500 was from my meal plan, for takeout food for them and anytime we ate in market central I used eleven dollars because the meal plan system was different back then and I couldn't use swipes on guests."

"And the remaining $400 was for what?"

"That was money I used on small gifts, another girl in the study group's gas money, food that didn't come from the campus dining places, and paying for small items here or there. But I mostly used it for other girls in the group who didn't have big meal plans and whenever I didn't have my meal plan card on me."

"Did you ever consider not showing up to a study session?"

"No, not unless I was too sick."

"At the end of the semester, you didn't have to do anything else for members of the sorority anymore?"

"No. During the summer I still had to call them and complete certain assignments."

"Wait a minute, excuse me. I want to make sure I'm hearing this correctly. You previously said that this all began on February 3, 2008. This went on until the summer?"

"Yes."

"How long into the summer?"

"Mid-June."

"I see. So is it safe to say that you did all of those things— the study sessions, the food runs, the errands, and the gifts for approximately five months, which is about twenty weeks, because you thought you would be initiated into the sorority?"

"Yes."

"So, what happened between the time that you ran the last errand or had the last phone conversation with a sorority member and this afternoon?"

"This summer a few people in the study group realized that we didn't learn anything from pre-pledging. We attempted to express our concern, but we weren't heard out. When we got back, out of the ten of us, they had planned to replace seven, myself included. We attempted to call them, email them, you know try to talk to them, but..."

I became more nervous. My heart started racing—I felt the same fear I had felt during the spring semester.

"I see. No further questions."

"You're free to cross examine," Ms. Jones motioned to Michelle.

Michelle stood up and looked at me. "Miss Williams, you stated that you were not able to sign any of the official documents regarding the rules because you and the other girls were never invited to a formal rush, correct?"

"Correct."

"Permission to approach the witness?"

Ms. Jones gave a slight nod.

"Please read the section that I have underlined here."

"Any candidate who knowingly participates in illegal hazing activities will not be awarded membership into Theta Eta Theta Sorority, Incorporated. Hazing consists of, but is not limited to physical hazing, financial hazing, shameful and demeaning acts, study sessions, et cetera," I handed her the sheet of paper.

"So you had no idea that these were the rules although they are accessible to the public on the organization's website?"

"I knew what the rules said, but the Epsilon chapter had their own rules, so I had to follow *their* rules if I wanted to get into *their* chapter."

"You mentioned that you spent about $800 on members of the sorority last spring. How much do you normally spend on your own food?"

"I probably spend about five to seven dollars a day if I don't have groceries."

"So, when you gave the figure of $800 are you taking into account the money that you spent on your own food?"

"No."

"Are you saying that you didn't eat at all during the spring?"

"I ate during the spring, but I usually used my other friends' meal plans so I could have money to spend on the TETs. I did spend my own money on myself, but eventually most of my money went towards them."

"Is it true you were aware that you would possibly be hazed before pre-pledging began?"

"Yes."

"Well, why didn't you say anything last semester when you were actually being hazed?"

"Because I thought I would be made into a TET this fall."

"No further questions."

Ms. Jones turned toward the panel. "Does the panel have any questions for this witness?"

"I do," the woman to my right looked at me. "You said that in the summer you all wised up about the process you went through. But when you got back, why did you still want to continue?"

"Because I still wanted to be a TET. I thought that they were still going to offer it to us, sit us down and talk about it, or make us paper."

"Okay and how did you feel when you found out that you had been replaced?"

I turned away from her and looked at Tiffany. "I was angry at first...But I was more hurt than anything."

"Okay, thank you. That's all."

"Thank you, Miss Williams." Ms. Jones stated.

I went back into Reed's office and slumped in a chair.

"How'd you do?" Teresa asked.

"I think I did well. I'm so tired now."

"Did you cry at all?"

"I wanted to, but I didn't."

"I couldn't help it. I can't believe it's almost over."

"Yea...over."

Moments later, Reed came into the room. He told us the panel decided that the TETs were guilty and they were deliberating on what punishment they would give. I sighed and walked towards the window. I looked down at Schenley Park and cringed. Everything looked different, bleaker.

Reed walked us into the hearing room. The TETs stood adjacent to us, and I couldn't help but to think that months ago the TETS and us had been in study session rooms together. We had once been in the same room without other people forcing us to look at each other.

Ms. Jones asked, "Has the panel reached a decision?"

"Excuse me Ms. Jones," Reed interjected and looked back and forth between the TETs and us. "Before we go into the proceedings, may I say that regardless of the decision will both sides agree not to make an emotional outburst?"

One of the panel judges stood up to read the verdict. "In the hearing of the university versus the Epsilon chapter of Theta Eta Theta Sorority, Incorporated, let the record show that the panel suggests a two year suspension for the Epsilon chapter and $100 in restitution for each complainant."

"They're not getting any of our money. We don't have any to give to them," Tiffany hissed under her breath.

"Thank you," Ms Jones stood up. "The decision will not be final until after it has been reviewed by the dean of students. At that time, if either side feels the need to appeal the decision, you may file the necessary paperwork. The defendants and the panel may now be excused from the room."

The TETs filed out quietly, and when the last TET left the room, Ms. Jones shut the door. "I would like to apologize for my agitated demeanor today. Today was just not a good day. There were Chi Beta Omicrons sitting by the elevators in support of the TETs I guess, but we don't allow other students near this floor during a hearing. I had to ask them to leave several times and that annoyed me. My integrity and fairness were put into question because certain people felt that I would be biased, but the verdict is never my decision. We always find a panel of people who have limited or no prior knowledge of whatever the situation might be. I don't say anything to them prior to the hearing except for the reading of their responsibilities and conduct. Anyway, how are you three? Are you okay?"

We murmured "Yes" and "Yea," and Ms. Jones took a seat. MS. JONES: Ms. Jackson, Amber's mom, do you feel that the proceedings were fair?
AMBER'S MOM: Yes, I feel that they were. You ladies did the right thing.
ME: Did they admit to anything?
AMBER'S MOM: No. As a matter of fact, they said that they never knew any of you.
ME, AMBER, TERESA: What!
AMBER'S MOM: Well, Tiffany was the only one who testified. She said that she never knew you Whitney. She said that the only

interaction she had with you was after Christmas break when you came up to her and said, "Look at my bangs, I got them cut just like yours!"

ME: That's the best defense that they could come up with?

AMBER'S MOM: She said that she would never ask Teresa to drive her anywhere because she has a car of her own, and that Amber was just one of the many groupies who was attracted to all the fame her line gained when they crossed.

TERESA: Are you for real?

MS. JONES: Unfortunately so. She denied everything even when the phone records and evidence were presented. You know, if she would have just admitted to something, the punishment probably would have been different.

TERESA: How is the restitution money going to work out?

MS. JONES: Well, they'll pay the amount to us and we'll deposit it into each of your school accounts.

TERESA: And if they don't?

MS. JONES: They'll have holds on their accounts and won't be able to register for their spring classes.

AMBER: Wow.

MS. JONES: Well, I have to go speak to the other young ladies. Excuse me please.

We sat in the room asking Amber's mom more questions about what had happened.

When we neared the elevator to leave, the TETs were sitting in the hallway chairs. They laughed. As soon as the elevator doors closed, Teresa fumed. "See? That's why we need to take their letters. They think this is a *joke*."

"Teresa," I sighed.

"Whatever Whitney," she rolled her eyes.

We got off the elevator and stood in the lobby, debating on what we wanted to do for the rest of the day. As we were talking, Mya walked by and looked away. I could tell that she was hurt but I didn't care.

Amber's parents treated Candace and us to dinner on the waterfront and we spent the night reliving moments of the trial.

I wish I could write, "After the trial, everyone on campus agreed with our decision, understood why we did what we did, and our lives moved on peacefully," but I can't because that's not true.

XXVI. Port of Call

To say that people were "mad" would be an insult to the word "understatement." The black Greeks went up in arms, most refusing to believe that the Epsilon chapter had actually done something to deserve a suspension. They changed their Face book statuses, posted cruel remarks on the campus gossip site, and rolled their eyes or ignored me whenever I came into their presence.

At first, none of this bothered me. At first, I was fine. But after a while I was hurt that no one, with the exception of a few close friends, understood. I was disheartened that people were buying into the rumors without knowing the entire story. I spent my time wondering what people thought of the situation and what people thought of me.

The first probate of the semester was held by the Chi Beta Omicrons. As Amber and I looked on, we could see Sasha and Tiffany glaring at us.

"Sasha isn't supposed to be on campus!" Amber walked away from the crowd.

"Where are you going?" I followed her outside.

"I'm calling the campus police…Hello? Hi, I'm calling because someone who is supposed to be on the PNG list is on campus…Sasha Irons…Oh. Oh okay," she hung up her phone.

"What did they say?"

"They said she wasn't on the PNG list."

"What? What do they mean she wasn't on the list?"

"It means Ms. Jones never sent out those PNG letters."

My friend Chris crossed Theta Phi Theta weeks later and I knew that he would want me to tell him the whole story. I sat in his room and told him everything. When I got done he sighed.

"I can honestly see why you did what you did," he said. "I really can. I just don't see why you had to go through with it."

"What do you mean why I had to go through with it?"

"It's their chapter Whit. Y'all took away their *chapter*."

"They took away my dream."

"They crossed in what, Spring 07? They didn't even get a chance to fully enjoy being neos."

"Am I supposed to feel sorry for them?"

"You could have done something else."

"Like what? Fight them?"

"You're going to be known as the girl who snitched on the TETs."

"I used to really care about that, but that doesn't matter anymore. None of my friends will know me as that so whatever."

"Are you happy?"

"No, I'm not. But I will be once I get my feelings out."

"How are you gonna do that?"

"I started writing. I think it's gonna turn into a book."

"Whit…"

"What?"

"You're gonna publish it?"

"Um yea, what's the point in writing a book and not publishing it?"

"If you're writing it for your own feelings, wouldn't you be satisfied just getting your feelings out when you finished? Wouldn't you be satisfied just having it to yourself? "

"What's the point in graduating from college? Why don't we just stay here forever enjoying each other's company and be satisfied not getting degrees?"

He laughed. "Ah Whit, you've got balls. I'll give you that. But you took their whole chapter. Can't you see their point of view?"

"Yea."

"Really? Do you understand why they thought that they couldn't take y'all?"

"I can see why they *thought* that, but replacing us was stupid. I can honestly see why they thought the way they did. We stopped calling, they thought they had the inside scoop from Vanessa and Jamie, and they really thought that we wouldn't tell on them."

"Most people wouldn't. That's just—"

"That's just what? Because they're *Greek* they're supposed to be held to a different standard? They're normal people. If it was any other situation, it would be okay for me to tell. But because they're Greek and everyone thinks that Greeks are the shit, I'm supposed to keep my mouth shut when *they* did *me* wrong? Please."

"I get what you're saying Whit, it's just that—"

"It was their chapter."

"Exactly."

He and I debated for the entire night, and although we never came to an agreement, I was glad that he could at least see things from my point of view.

In November, at a Nu Alpha Pi probate, Amber and I cheered to support the new initiates of fall 2008. As the Nu Pis twirled their canes, recited history, and sang greetings, I couldn't help but want to cry. It was supposed to be me. I was supposed to be probating, I was supposed to be crossing, and I was supposed to be done.

Their show came to an end, and after congratulating the new members that I knew, I left. I walked around campus for a while in the cold before returning home. When I came into the apartment, Teresa was sitting in her room.

"Well, that was fun right?" I asked.

"What?"

"The probate? At the club? Did you have fun?"

"You don't know what happened do you?"

"No. Something happened?"

"Yea," she sighed. "Sasha threw a drink on Amber."

"What?"

"Yea, Amber's on her way home now. This was exactly what I was talking about. They're *reckless*!"

Amber came home later, sporting a massive red stain on her white dress, crying tears of anger.

"I can't believe this!" she cried.

"Are you okay?" I asked. "What happened?"

"No, I'm not okay. I'm so angry right now! I was sitting at the bar with my friend Aaliyah. Sasha was sitting in the chair right next to me. One of the Nu Pi's sisters, who is a TET, was doing little mirror poses and strutting in front of us and we were cheering her on and laughing. All of a sudden, out of the corner of my eye I see Sasha throw her drink on me, and some of it got on Aaliyah. Look at my dress! It looks pink! I can't even tell that it was white! Even after she threw the drink on me I tried to stay calm. I got up and went to the bartender and asked him where the security guard was. I told security what happened and asked if they could remove her from the club, but he said that he couldn't throw anybody out unless the person in charge of the party said it was okay. So, I went around the club searching for the Nu Pi president, and when I finally found him he had all of the TETs thrown out of the club. Then I found out that Ivyana had pushed Aaliyah onto floor because Aaliyah was under the impression that Ivyana had thrown the drink."

"Did you leave then?"

"No. I stayed at the party for another hour and a half. I saw a few of the TETs sneak back in, but they didn't bother me so I didn't say anything," she paused. "When I left, a bunch of them were sitting outside in a car with the windows down. I feel like they were waiting for me to come out so they could jump me. If I hadn't been with Mike they probably would have."

"They sat in the car for an hour and a half waiting for you to come out?"

"Yea, this is getting ridiculous. I'm done. They really think that they can just keep messing with us and that we're not going to do anything about it? I'm calling the *real* police."

A city policeman was in my room within an hour, explaining the steps that Amber needed to take to file a harassment claim. She took down his name and number and vowed that she would call if she had any more questions.

The next morning we went to Ms. Jones office and explained what happened. She took down our information once again and swore that she would send out the PNG letters as soon as possible.

A few days later, Amber and Sasha's city court date was set for January 7, 2009.

Subject:	Meeting with [TET] Nationals
From:	<████████.edu>
Date:	Wed, November 26, 2008 11:10 am

Good morning ladies,
The [TET] Nationals are flying in for 1 day on Tuesday, December 2, 2008 to conduct an investigation. [Ms. Jones] asked that I contact you to see if you can come in to meet with them at 8:30am on Tuesday. If 8:30am [is] not possible, please let me know what time would be good for you. I am not sure how long the meeting will be.

Thanks ladies. Have a good Thanksgiving break.
Office of Student Affairs

I didn't want to meet with Nationals, but I forced myself to. Since we were to meet with them individually, I decided to meet with them in the afternoon.

AMBER: She didn't look like she believed anything I said. She wouldn't even look at the photo of Aaliyah's bruise on my phone! She made it seem like I concocted the story because she repeated the fact that we all live together.

TERESA: I've told the story so many times that I left so much out!

When it was my turn, I found myself in the same room where the hearing had taken place.

"Hi Whitney," a woman said as she shut the door. "I'm Georgia Johnson from the Heritage committee and on the phone is another member of the committee, Juliana Stone. Do you know why we're here today?"

"To know why the Epsilon chapter is suspended from the university?"

"Well, not really. We're here to conduct an investigation and we'd like to know which members were acting against our code of conduct."

"Oh."

"Can you tell me what happened?"

"Starting from pre-pledging or just from me being an interest?"

"Wherever you want."

"Okay. I was an interest in the fall so I had to call—"

"Who told you that you had to call?"

"Those are the rules."

"Says who?"

"Says any of the TETs."

"None of them told you that you *had* to call?"

"They said that I needed to get to know them if I wanted to get into their chapter."

"But they didn't say that you had to *call*?"

"Those are the rules."

"Okay, go on."

"Well, for a semester I kept calling and going out with them to lunch and when we went out to lunch they would ask me questions about the pledge process and they wouldn't deny anything. They would tell me that they weren't a paper chapter and that all of them were *made*. Then—"

"So they *trusted* you?"

I wanted to get up and leave. She wasn't trying to believe anything that I had to say. I thought back to the times that the TETs had told me personal things, to the emails I'd read that held personal information, and I realized that they did trust me.

I continued to tell her the story, leaving out the fact that we all had an email account, leaving out the fact that some people were more reckless than others. When she asked me to give names, I left out more than half of the chapter.

She thanked me for coming. I smiled and left.

We received letters from the university, letters that said that the TETs were on "no contact" orders with us and that the chapter would not be able to apply for reinstatement until May 2010. Although we got justice, something still didn't feel right. I was still hurt.

Time wasn't helping the pain to go away. Every day I was plagued with the questions, "Did I do the right thing?" "What if I hadn't told?" "What would have happened if I had waited?" and

"Was it meant to happen anyway?" Over Christmas break, I spent every waking moment typing my feelings onto my laptop's screen.

All of my anger, all of my pain, and all of my frustration came out effortlessly. It was pure memory.

The day before I returned to Pittsburgh, Candace texted me, "Sasha's mom died." My heart stopped. I didn't know what to say. All of a sudden, Sasha became more than the mean-spirited soul who had treated me horribly. She became human.

I wanted to call her and tell her that I was sorry for her loss. I wanted to say that everything was going to be alright, but it wasn't time.

The first week of classes, Sasha called Amber and Teresa, apologizing to them for everything she'd ever done. She told Amber that she would be unable to make it to their court date, but she would pay the necessary costs to replace the white dress. She called me around midnight and I didn't pick up. I called her back at four in the morning. When I told her it was me on the other end of the line she said, "Hi, Whitney. I got your number from Teresa but...Never mind." I said, "Alright, bye" and turned my phone off. Her intentions were understood and I took time to reflect on mine.

I immediately realized that I had wasted so much time asking, "What does he think about it?" or "What does she think about it?" that I nearly forgot how *I* felt about it.

It matters not how strait the gate,
How charged with punishments the scroll,
I am the master of my fate:
I am the captain of my soul.

XXVII. Disembark

If I wasn't in class, at work, or hanging out with my friends, I was writing about my experience with Theta Eta Theta, wondering where it all went wrong and trying to make sure that my decision was just and fair.

After writing and re-writing, reading and re-reading, editing and re-editing, I've realized that all of events and the sequence in which they took place happened as they were meant to happen.

If the TETs had tried to form bonds with us instead of making us run a myriad of errands, we would have never felt as if it were "us against them" and half of the summer emails would have never been sent. If Amber hadn't dropped, maybe Shelby wouldn't have dropped, and perhaps Jamie, Mya, and Vanessa wouldn't have told the TETs anything about what was going on in our group. If Vanessa hadn't lived with Kamille, if Candace had been in the country, or if we had all not answered our phones for that one week, I would have written a different book. I would have written about how great black Greek life was, how *thorough* I was, how I sincerely believed that the pre-pledge process (and the pledge process if I'd made it) taught me how to be a better human being and instilled humility, selflessness, and sisterhood.

But I didn't write that book. I couldn't. Aside from learning how to effectively lie, cheat, and steal with a group of nine other girls, I didn't learn anything. I didn't learn anything about what Theta Eta Theta truly stood for.

It wasn't about sisterhood. It wasn't about scholarship. It wasn't about service. It was about the process.

If it was about sisterhood, the TETs would have spent more time getting to know us instead of asking us to run errands. They would have never considered replacing their future little sisters. If it was about scholarship, they would have allowed our "study sessions" to be used for studying only. If it was about service, they would have spent more of their time encouraging us to volunteer in the community, and less time harassing us.

I do believe that at one point the TETs liked me, but they didn't like me for who I was. They liked me because they thought that I would make it through the process. They liked me because they thought that they could mold me into what they were: insecure and misguided.

They allowed the fact that they pledged to define them. They preached being "women of substance" when they themselves were empty. They fed into the stereotypical image of TET and started to believe that being part of an organization, a social *club*, made them who they were. They forgot that they had identities before they crossed. They forgot the previous nineteen or twenty years that were void of TET ever happened.

Even though it's easy to attack Spring 07 and a few others for everything that they did, I realize that their behavior was learned. They didn't decide to have study sessions and haze us out of their own volitions. The prophytes of Fall 04 and Fall 05 tortured Spring 07. They taught them that the way to properly "make" people is to treat them horribly. They taught them that the process itself was more important than the sisterly bond.

The demise of the chapter can be attributed to each SH, each TET, and fate. Although not every TET hazed me, several of them knew what was going on and as a result, they were all at fault.

I'm sure that many arguments will be made against my actions, but I don't regret a single thing I did and I wouldn't take it back if I could. Through my experience, I learned a lot about myself and what I believe. I don't believe that getting beat makes someone a better person. If this was the case, abused children would never make the morning headlines. I don't believe that there is such a thing as "pledging the old school way," with cell-phones and email accounts. I don't believe that the process should be the focal point of one's undergraduate experience in a fraternity or a sorority—it should be what that person achieves *after* he or she gets into the organization. I don't believe that going against an organization's rules to illegally pledge deserves any admiration. In saying this, I'll never look down or criticize any one for going through a "process," but I won't give him or her any extra respect.

I believe that there should be a process, but I don't think it should physically or mentally harm the participant. I believe that instead of forcing people to sit in study sessions for hours at a time, harassing them for months, and making them run errands incessantly, you should teach them how the chapter operates; make them participate in community service for weeks at a time, have them learn to appreciate the history of the organization without being condescending and belittling; spend time with them and truly get to know them so they can see that you're trying to be more than their friend—so they can see that you're trying to be their *sister*.

I can't change how people feel about this subject, and I won't attempt to. I know how *I* feel, and that's all that matters. I can't worry about what other people think of me or spend too much time being concerned with who doesn't like me because I can't control that. I can only control my own thoughts, and through this experience I've realized that I'm not "the girl who snitched on the TETs." I'm the girl who published a memoir in undergrad. I'm the girl who stood up for herself and realized what was more important. I'm the girl who learned that she doesn't need three letters or artificial respect from insecure Greeks to make her feel like she's worth more of a person.

I'm the girl who gets to choose who is in my life and who isn't. I choose who gets playing time, and who gets to watch from the sidelines. I decide what choices I make, what path I follow, and what crossroad I choose to take. I determine the steps to my destiny and I, and no one else, am in control.

I am the master of my fate. I am the captain of my soul.

Whitney Gracia Williams is a graduate of the University of Pittsburgh (A&S '10). She received degrees in English Writing, Communications Rhetoric, & Honors Philosophy.

13661705R00210

Made in the USA
Lexington, KY
12 February 2012